Reflective Teaching of History 11–18

Also available from Continuum:

Reflective Teaching of History 11–18

Continuum Studies in Reflective Practice and Theory

Robert Phillips

continuum
LONDON • NEW YORK

CONTINUUM

The Tower Building, 11 York Road, London SE1 7NX
15 East 26th Street, New York, NY 10010
www.continuumbooks.com

First published 2002
Reprinted 2005

British Library Cataloguing-in-Publication Data
A catalogue record for this book is available from the British Library.

   ISBN 0-8264-5274-4 (paperback)
   ISBN 0-8264-6043-7 (hardback)

Typeset by SetSystems Ltd, Saffron Walden, Essex
Printed and bound in Great Britain by
CPI Bath

CONTENTS

ACKNOWLEDGEMENTS

This book is the product of nearly twenty years' teaching and lecturing experience. During that time, I have either worked with or been influenced by a wide array of talented, creative professionals. I would like to thank a number of individuals who either directly or indirectly should take responsibility for some of the strengths of this book, but certainly not its weaknesses.

Anthony Haynes at Continuum continues to be a brilliant editor. At Swansea, my colleague on the history PGCE course for many years, Wendy Cunnah, has been highly influential in shaping my views and has been a great friend and colleague, particularly during difficult times. Others at Swansea who need special thanks include Sue Sanders, for constantly shrewd advice, John Plessis, John Parkinson and Mike Rowe. Madeline Rogerson and the rest of the library staff, secretaries like Anne Fisher, Anne Seagrove and Jackie Curry have given me continual practical support.

Many mentors and former students have been instrumental in forging a genuine partnership between Swansea and schools. Mentors who need special mention here include Dave Thomas, Ian Kilcoyne, Paul Thomas, Martin Williams, Paul Rogers, Dave Eynon, Maria Edwards, Ian Davies, Lana Picton, Sam Evans, Margaret Simpkins, Kevin Hewitt, Angela Williams, Kirsty Rogers, Liz Thomas, Amanada White, Mark Williams and Carol Turley (especially for her help on Chapter 10). I have taught, worked with and learned from so many former students that it would be unfair to mention any individuals by name but I hope they know how much I appreciate the two-way dialogues we have had about history teaching over the years.

In the advisory service, Alan Kelly, Dave Maddox and Stuart Broomfield have been great fun to work with and I would particularly like to thank Alun Morgan from the Office for Her Majesty's Chief Inspectorate, Wales (OHMCI) for his support, friendship and humanity; he has been particularly supportive in terms of encouraging a creative, research-based approach to history teaching.

Colleagues in the history education world like Chris Culpin, Mike Riley, Dale Banham and Ian Dawson have been excellent for sharing ideas with. Christine Counsell needs special mention here: we met many years ago as teachers and it was clear then that we shared very similar philosophies on history teaching. Unsurprisingly, she has done wonders with the journal *Teaching History*, which provides such a vibrant support to history teachers. Academics within the University of Wales like Richard Daugherty and John Furlong have been good colleagues and co-editors. Former teacher colleagues like Mike (Chalky) White, Steve Tibbs and Steve Morrell remain great friends and despite all the insanity of the last twenty years of education reform, maintain their sense of humour. Last, but not least, to Dennis Chainey for his intellectual inspiration.

This book is dedicated to all teachers who are struggling to inspire pupils, often in almost impossible circumstances, when their work seems to be constantly called into question by those outside the profession who have absolutely no idea whatsoever about how demanding and complex that work is.

BIBLIOGRAPHICAL NOTE

Robert Phillips is Senior Lecturer in Education at the University of Wales Swansea. He is an experienced teacher and lecturer and has written extensively on history teaching, education policy and nationhood. His book *History Teaching, Nationhood and the State* (Continuum) won the Standing Conference for Studies in Education (SCSE) prize for the most outstanding scholarly work on education in 1998. Other recent works include *Issues in History Teaching* (co-edited with James Arthur, 2000) and *Education, Reform and the State* (co-edited with John Furlong, 2001). He is also Director of the *British Island Stories: History, Identity and Nationhood* (BRISHIN) project, funded by the Economic and Social Research Council, which explores the interrelationship between history and national identity.

ABBREVIATIONS

The following abbreviations are used in the book:

ACAC	Curriculum and Assessment Authority of Wales (later renamed Qualifications, Curriculum and Assessment Authority of Wales: ACCAC)
AV	Audio Visual
A/S	A level/Subsidiary
CCW	Curriculum Council for Wales
CHATA	Concepts of History and Teaching Approaches 7–14
CSE	Certificate of Secondary Education
DES	Department of Education and Science
DFE	Department for Education
DfEE	Department for Education and Employment
DfES	Department for Education and Science
ERA	Education Reform Act, 1988
GCSE	General Certificate of Secondary Education
ESTYN	Inspectorate in Wales
'E & R'	Effective and Reflective
HEI	Higher Education Institution
HMI	Her Majesty's Inspectorate
HWG	(National Curriculum) History Working Group
ICT	Information and Communications Technology
INSET	In-Service Education and Training
ILEA	Inner London Education Authority
ISM	Initial Stimulus Material
ITT	Initial Teacher Training
KS	Key Stage
OFSTED	Office for Standards in Education
OHMCI	Office for Her Majesty's Chief Inspectorate (Wales)
OHP	Overhead Projector
PGCE	Postgraduate Certificate of Education
QCA	Qualifications and Curriculum Authority (England)
QTS	Qualified Teacher Status
SCAA	School Curriculum and Assessment Authority

SCHP	Schools' Council History Project (later renamed Schools' History Project: SHP)
SEN	Special Educational Needs
SENCO	Special Educational Needs Co-ordinator
SPEAR	Social, Political, Economic, Artistic/Cultural, Religious
TGAT	Task Group on Assessment and Testing
TTA	Teacher Training Agency

CHAPTER 1

History teaching, standards and research: bridging the theory/practice divide

Give a man a fish and feed him for a day; teach a man how to fish and feed him for life

(Confucius)

There is nothing more practical than a good theory . . .

(Christine Counsell)

Introduction

This chapter orientates the reader towards the central theme of the book, namely the relationship between research and history teaching. It considers the ways in which different types of research can be used to promote effective teaching and, in the process, it helps meet the requirements set down by the government for the regulation of Initial Teacher Training (ITT) (www.canteach.gov.uk). The 'Standards' set down by the government, and monitored by the Teacher Training Agency (TTA) and the inspectorate (OFSTED in England, ESTYN in Wales) govern the orientation of teacher training courses in England and Wales. The chapter begins by considering the evolution of the Standards and their implications for the ways in which teacher-training – or teacher education – courses are planned, constructed and managed. Although providing a framework for effective teaching, these Standards provide only a particular model and are not entirely beyond critique. The chapter considers the ways in which research can be used, not only to meet the requirements of the Standards but in the process produce effective, reflective history teachers.

The 'Great Debate', teacher education reform and partnership

In the last two decades of the twentieth century, all aspects of social policy in England and Wales underwent transformation. Few spheres of policy received more public and political attention than education, reflected in a vast number of education-related reforms passed by successive governments, both Tory and Labour (Phillips and Furlong, 2001). The so-called 'Great Debate' over education was initiated by a famous speech delivered by a Labour Prime Minister – James Callaghan – at Ruskin College, Oxford on 18 October, 1976. Many of the themes raised in the speech were to dominate debates over education for the next twenty-five years (Phillips, 2001a). Callaghan argued that the central state had a fundamental right to involve itself more directly in schools, which had been relatively autonomous, particularly with regard to curriculum decision-making, since the 1944 Education Act. The Prime Minister said that not only government, but also parents and industry, should have a greater say in debates over education policy and practice.

References to teacher autonomy may seem alien to student teachers embarking upon teacher training in the early twenty-first century. After all, teacher education (I prefer this term to 'teacher training' for the reasons I articulate below) is now heavily regulated. In many ways, the Standards represent a culmination of the Callaghan desire to improve standards by ensuring that government plays a more proactive role in influencing the ways in which teachers are trained. The reform of teacher education led to a reconstitution of teacher professionalism (McCulloch, 2001). At the heart of the reform process was a desire to make teachers and education more accountable.

Although professionals at the time criticized particular aspects of the reforms, research suggests that the reforms to teacher education have been, for the most part, essentially beneficial (Furlong, 2001). One of the central features of the legislation was to increase the role of schools in teacher training. Thus, on Postgraduate Certificate in Education (PGCE) courses, for example, trainee students now spend two-thirds of their time in schools, and the rest of the time in Higher Education Institutions (HEIs). Central to the new system was the establishment of the concept of teacher education *partnership* between schools and HEIs (Booth *et al.*, 1990). Thus, whereas prior to the reforms, progress of teacher trainees was almost exclusively the preserve of HEIs, schools now play a central role in the observation, training and evaluation of student teachers. The vast majority of courses are now carefully planned, organized and structured.

Essentially, partnership involves the following features:

- Student teachers work closely with experienced teachers in schools, and work particularly closely with mentors who have responsibility for their school-based progress.
- Student teachers are not 'thrown in at the deep end' as they very often used to be on teacher training courses; after a short time in the university, student teachers are encouraged to observe experienced teachers 'in action' before embarking upon teaching themselves.
- Student teachers are then given feedback on their progress by school mentors and HEI tutors who visit them in schools.
- Student teachers are encouraged to evaluate their own progress, which is done in the university and in school.

Thus HEIs, in partnership with schools, determine whether students reach what is termed Qualified Teacher Status (QTS). In order to achieve QTS, students have to demonstrate to the partnership that they have reached a level of competence in the Standards (see the *Teaching History*, 1998, November, p. 37 for a summary).

Training for competence or education for reflection? The professional craft knowledge of the history teacher

Clearly, the present system has considerable advantages for students, schools and HEIs. Prior to partnership, many student teachers complained about what was termed the 'theory/practice' divide, where much of the work done in the HEI was irrelevant to the practical context of the school. Teachers played little part in the training process, and for many students the courses on offer provided inadequate preparation for full-time teaching. By contrast, partnership can provide a very effective means by which student teachers can learn the complex craft of teaching, with the professional experience gained in school being enhanced by the analytical environment of the HEI. Both are seen as essential in the partnership.

Many partnership courses are actually based upon a 'reflective practitioner' model of teacher education (Schon, 1983; Edwards and Brunton, 1993). Reflective practice, as its name suggests, refers to the ways in which professionals 'make sense' of their own practice through evaluation, analysis and experience (Brown and McIntyre, 1993). Moon (1999, p. 4) defines it as a way of thinking 'that is applied to relatively complicated or unstructured ideas for which there is not an obvious solution'. Reflection provides a means for understanding teaching. An essential feature of this involves equipping the emerging teacher with the capacity to understand why certain practices are effective and others are not. For this to take place, a wide variety of professional knowledge is required, which is acquired through discussion, experience and sharing practice with others (see below). A fundamental principle behind the reflective practitioner model of teacher education is the belief that in order to progress as professionals, student teachers not only need to know *how to teach in certain ways* but also *why those methods are effective*. Thus, in order to make sense of professional practice, emerging teachers need to be able to *conceptualize* and this in itself involves a degree of theorizing, which explains the importance of the references to Confucius and Counsell above.

As I have argued elsewhere (Phillips and Cunnah, 2000), one of the most dangerous and pernicious aspects of late twentieth-century educational discourse was the view that teachers needed no theory at all. In some senses this was understandable, given the 'theory/practice' divide referred to above. But some critics of teacher education took this too far by claiming that teachers needed virtually no theory at all, only the competencies and skills required for the 'craft' of teaching. In many ways, the Standards reflect this 'competence' model of teacher education, which sees teaching as a process akin to jumping through hoops or driving a car.

This is too simplistic a view of teaching and the teacher education process. As Flores stresses:

> learning to teach entails a constellation of complex factors. It is a process that goes beyond the mere application of a set of acquired techniques and skills. Not only does it imply the mastery of practical and more technical issues, but it also encompasses the construction of knowledge and meaning in an ongoing and challenging dialogue with the practice.
>
> (Flores, 2001, p. 146)

This is confirmed in nearly all books that offer practical advice to student teachers in their training (see Capel *et al.* 1995, 1997; Baumann *et al.*, 1997; Dean, 1996; Dillon and Maguire, 1997; Hayes, 1997). Teacher education requires a carefully planned programme, rigorous training and a reflective environment to understand it.

The Standards provide a useful framework through which training for effectiveness can be developed. But there is a difference between training and teacher education in this respect. Whereas the former views the training course as preparing for a series of specific tasks, the latter takes a more holistic view and sees the teacher educative process as a means of preparing teachers to think critically about teaching. This is because all teachers need to think conceptually and reflectively about the teaching process in order to understand it properly and to become effective. These elements are vital also for the creation of what Ashcroft and James (1999) call 'the creative professional'.

A useful model for understanding the complexity of history teaching is provided by John (1991), who argues that history teachers – like all teachers – possess a particular 'craft knowledge', which is essential to understanding the teaching process. Drawing upon the work of Shulman (1986) and Schon (1983), John argues that the craft knowledge of the history teacher involves a combination of knowledge and ideology.

Knowledge

John argues that the knowledge base of the history teacher is complex and includes:

1. *Knowledge of history*: This is built up over a long period of time, from school to university and beyond. It includes knowledge of historical events, personalities, topics, concepts and so on. It informs the teacher's view of history teaching, particularly in terms of planning, expectations, resource construction, teaching strategies and perceptions of pupils' understanding of the subject.
2. *Knowledge of teaching history*: This is sub-divided into the following categories:
   (a) *Pedagogical content knowledge* is the fundamental aspect of the history teaching process; it includes knowledge of the organization, structure and procedure of history teaching. This includes knowledge of the various teaching strategies available to history teachers, and how they work, such as questioning technique, group work, conducting role-play, evidence work, storytelling and so on. This type of knowledge is fundamental to how a history teacher plans his or her teaching.
   (b) *Curriculum knowledge* includes knowledge of the texts available to teach the subject, including the most appropriate textbooks, evidence and other sources of information.
   (c) *Organizational knowledge* includes knowledge of how to organize pupils, groups and classes effectively, including the different strategies needed for mixed and streamed ability, and the advantages and disadvantages of group work. It also incoporates knowledge about effective control, such as the monitoring of activities and the importance of seating arrangements in classrooms. This knowledge will have been built up mainly over the first three years of teaching and relies very heavily upon an implicit, routinized understanding of the importance and use of rules, regulations and conventions, which ensure proper organization and management in the classroom.
3. *Knowledge of the institution*: This element of the craft knowledge relates to the contextual knowledge of the school. This is also built up over time and includes knowledge of classes, members of staff, the fabric of the school, including ethos, discipline and assessment policies and aims. Crucially, it also involves a knowledge of individual pupils in the school, based upon past experience, including a knowledge of their strengths, weaknesses, interests, likes and dislikes.
4. *Knowledge of education*: This includes the teacher's beliefs, ideas, theories, perspectives and values (see below) relating to education in general. It will have been built up through teacher training, classroom experience, In-Service Education and Training (INSET) courses, reading and learning from others.

5. *Knowledge of how children learn history*: This involves understanding what problems children face when learning the subject, the most appropriate teaching approaches to use to help overcome them and how learning can be assessed most effectively. This is particularly important.

Ideology

John argues that history teachers are not passive, neutral deliverers of knowledge; rather they possess ideology (expressed implicitly and/or explicitly) comprising:

1. *Beliefs*: These relate, for example, to the philosophy of history – its aims, purpose and objectives; these beliefs will have an important impact upon how the teacher plans his or her history teaching.
2. *Values*: These include the values that underpin the teacher's view of the aims and purposes of education and schooling. They may include, for example, a commitment to educational equality or a moral desire to undermine racism. Values also influence the history teacher's views on the nature of a teacher's authority, pupil–teacher relationships or preferred learning styles. Values clearly influence planning.
3. *Attitudes*: This is mainly related to the history teacher's attitude to history, and is particularly closely connected to his or her enjoyment of it, which will also have an important bearing, of course, on pupils' attitudes to the subject.

Overall, John (1991, p. 11) argues that history teaching is a 'multi-faceted, complex task. History teachers are not passive deliverers of knowledge, nor simply adept as classroom managers, they are highly skilled professionals with a complex knowledge base, which they draw upon to produce learning in their classes'. Often, this professional knowledge, or what Haydn (1993) calls the 'chemistry of history lessons'. is held implicitly by the teacher and this largely explains why some of the most talented history teachers occasionally find it difficult to articulate the secret of effective teaching to student teachers (Brown and McIntyre, 1993; Cooper and McIntyre, 1992). Moreover, appreciating and understanding the nature of the professional craft knowledge is the first step in the learning process of becoming reflective.

Research and effective history teaching

As we said earlier, educational research itself has been subject to much debate (Phillips and Cunnah, 2000). Critics have argued that educational research is too complex, lacks rigour and is often irrelevant to practice (see Tooley, 1998). In recent years, however, the government has realized that research is fundamental in the process of creating a forward-thinking, modernized teaching force. Thus, the TTA's (1997) document, *Teaching as a Research-Based Activity*, demonstrates the importance of research for promoting effective teaching and learning. My book is also stimulated by the view that a knowledge and understanding of research is essential in order to produce reflective practitioners who are able to develop the range of skills, traits and attributes (the professional craft knowledge) of the history teacher. Throughout the book, research is used selectively in order to demonstrate the ways in which the subject can be taught and learned more effectively. Research relating to history teaching can be categorized in the following ways:

1. *Research on the philosophy of history teaching* considers fundamental issues such as aims, purpose and justification.

2. *Research on 'issues' in history teaching* is concerned with evaluating the ways in which research can help us understand how to teach sensitive issues – for example citizenship or 'race' – in an effective way.
3. *Research on the politics of history teaching* analyses the ways in which history as a discipline and as a school subject has been politicized.
4. *Research on student teachers of history* explores the ways in which student teachers learn most effectively and its implications for the ways in which teacher education is conducted.
5. *Research on assessment in history teaching* considers a central element of the teacher's role – assessment – and has crucial implications for the ways in which history is taught and learned.
6. *Research on history teaching and learning* is a fundamentally important type of research, which encompasses work that considers the ways in which pupils learn history effectively and also helps us to evaluate the effectiveness of various teaching strategies.
7. *Generic research* is also significant in that much educational research draws upon generic ideas from other disciplines such as psychology, philosophy, political science and sociology, as well as research on child development, cognition and learning, educational assessment and so on.

As you read through the chapters in this book, you will see that I draw upon specific research on history teaching as well as generic research. I also offer a very broad definition of 'educational research', which in large part derives from my experience both as a teacher and as an academic. Research was once perceived to be the preserve of academics but is now conducted more widely by practising teachers themselves, sometimes referred to as 'action-research' (Altrichter *et al.*, 1993; Elliott, 1991; Kemmis and McTaggart, 1992; see also Baumann *et al.*, 1997, pp. 175–8). This is supported in some cases by small government-sponsored research grants. Indeed, this recent growth in practitioner research has, in part, been stimulated by the moves towards partnership, reflected, for example, in the pages of the journal *Teaching History* or the *Welsh Historian*, which are full of interesting ideas about teaching, based upon a wide range of innovative practice in schools.

Research, teacher education and student history teachers: towards becoming 'E & R'

In this section I want to focus upon the ways in which research on teacher education (both generic and subject specific) can be used to understand how student teachers can become 'E & R', that is, effective and reflective. In this sense, as with other issues described in this book, this section has as much relevance to mentors as student teachers.

As we saw above, John (1991) sees history teaching as a complex, multifaceted task. The important thing to emphasize about this craft knowledge, however, is that very often it is heavily tacit. In other words, history teachers' skills knowledge is embedded deeply in their day-to-day practices (Brown and McIntyre, 1993; Moon, 1999). Thus, experienced teachers find it difficult to talk about or explain why they do certain things in certain ways – 'it just comes natural'. This implicit knowledge can often prove problematic for student teachers. If teachers find it difficult to articulate their own effectiveness, how can student teachers be expected to learn from them? An important priority here, then, is to encourage experienced teachers to talk more explicitly about their own effectiveness. Research suggests that partnership itself helps in this process, by encouraging experienced teachers to think about not only the 'how' of teaching but also the 'why' of the teaching process (Cunnah *et al.*, 1997).

A starting point along the path towards effectiveness and reflection is for the emerging teacher to recognize the major features of his or her own development from student teacher to qualified teacher. Edwards and Healy (1994), in a useful introduction to teacher education, argue that student teachers go through the following phases, which are then reflected in the teacher education process:

- 'Induction'
- 'Teaching collaboratively'
- 'Flying solo'
- 'Bringing it all together'
- 'Moving on'.

Even more extensive research by my colleagues Furlong and Maynard (1995) on the development of professional knowledge shows that student teachers go through six stages on the way to becoming reflective. The description below is based upon their work, supplemented by my own experience of having observed, taught and worked with student teachers of history for over ten years (any errors in the following are thus my responsibility, not Furlong and Maynard's!).

Stage 1: Idealism
When students embark upon a course, they do so for a range of reasons, from genuinely wanting to work with pupils, to not knowing what else to do! Most, however, base their decision-making upon their experiences as pupils, particularly in relation to their teachers. Thus, some want to base themselves on a very good teacher they once had ('I want to be like Mrs X') or, alternatively, reject the practice of a teacher they thought was ineffective ('I don't want to be like Mr Y'). Moreover, younger student teachers in particular sometimes empathize with the pupils more than teachers and are often motivated by the desire for their pupils to like the subject ('I want the kids to like me and enjoy history').

Stage 2: Myth making
Early days on a PGCE course reveal that students also have certain fears about the prospect of teaching. But they also have the perception that particular aspects of teaching will be relatively straightforward. This is where their lack of 'contextual craft knowledge' is highly relevant. Thus, research shows that issues relating to class management ('how will I possibly be able to control my classes?') and a perceived lack of content knowledge ('what if they ask me something I don't know?') are all quite major concerns for student history teachers (see Kerry, 1982a). On the other hand, they do not realize the significance of other challenges – such as meeting the needs of a range of individual pupils, the importance of 'open' rather than 'closed' questions, the need for managing group work in certain ways, etc. – which turn out, through experience, to be very important indeed.

Stage 3: Reality
Students reading this book will also be relieved to know that the vast majority of schools (and history classrooms) are not the centres of mad, chaotic ill discipline that

the media like to portray them as, and in fact, most student teachers find class control easier to manage than first anticipated ('X wasn't such a problem after all'). They also find out that they know more about their subject than the pupils. On the other hand, many of those subtle elements of the 'craft knowledge' soon start to pose challenges: student teachers find that pupils do not seem to be answering their questions effectively (there are embarrassing silences in response to seemingly 'obvious' questions); some pupils do not appear to be able to do certain tasks set, whilst others race through them and finish early; and even the most apparently well-planned group work turns out to be an opportunity for idle chitchat and organized chaos! ('Y and Z were far more difficult than I thought'.) Student teachers' focus of empathy starts to shift away from the pupils, and more to their fellow teachers, as they confront the reality of the challenges facing them. They realize that they sometimes have to do things that may cause pupils to view them slightly differently. In effect, they become socialized into teaching and although student teachers rightly hold on to cherished principles ('I still want the kids to like me and enjoy history') they also realize that in order to ensure that pupils learn and respect them as teachers, they have to start acting and behaving rather differently.

Stage 4: Coping mechanisms

After a period of observation and discussion with teachers, student teachers start to teach for the first time and reality soon sets in. Furlong and Maynard (1995) argue that as they gain some experience, they start to use 'tried and tested' methods, which work for them. Thus, whole-class teaching with a high degree of teacher exposition is the favoured mode of organization in the classroom. Teaching strategies that involve the minimum of 'risk' are also favoured, such as asking individual pupils to read from a textbook and then answering a list of written (low-order) questions. Moreover student teachers at this stage frequently tend to 'teach to the class' and see little need to get to know their pupils as individuals, often not even perceiving the need to learn their pupils' names. Consequently, they tend to teach to the 'middle' ability range, with very little awareness of particular individual learning needs. They also tend to favour teacher 'folklore' or 'common sense' ('go in there hard' or 'don't smile before Christmas': see Russell, 2000). This is because the sheer complexity and difficulty of teaching, as well as their own limited skills, experience and knowledge in comparison, force them to rely upon 'coping strategies'. Crucially, *they are almost completely preoccupied with their own needs as learners.*

Stage 5: Basic competence ('the plateau')

Chillingly, some student teachers never progress beyond Stage 4 and ultimately fail teacher training by not reaching the required levels of competence. If they are lucky, good tutors and mentors will spot these weaknesses early enough and advise that the student teachers leave the course. However, you will be pleased to know that research shows that the vast majority of student teachers progress to a stage of basic competence. At this 'plateau' stage, student teachers realize that they have adequate subject knowledge to teach pupils fairly effectively. They plan lessons well, but often this is short- or at best medium-term planning and sometimes lacks clarity in relation to learning objectives. Student teachers have now mastered 'tried and tested' methods in the class and use these fairly regularly, but at the same time lessons lack variety and it gradually becomes clear that pupils get rather bored and restless with the repetition, which may have a knock-on effect in terms of classroom control. On the other hand, classroom control is generally satisfactory but certain individuals cause problems, which student teachers feel powerless, at times, to do anything about. They assess pupils fairly regularly (this was something they did not really do either in Stage 3 or even in Stage 4) but the formative comments they are able to offer pupils are limited, and therefore assessment bears little relationship to teaching and learning. Pupil learning undoubtedly takes place but is sometimes inconsistent: there is still a tendency to 'teach to the middle', with the less able not being consistently catered for and the more able not really stretched. There is some emphasis placed upon self-evaluation and reflection by the student teacher *but the main focus of the reflection is still primarily on him or herself, rather than the pupils.*

Stage 6: Reflective practice ('post-plateau')

Not all student teachers become reflective practitioners as defined here. At this stage, their subject knowledge is well advanced but in a manner that is 'applied' in different ways and in different contexts, according to the needs of pupils; these student teachers are able to 'package' the subject effectively. This is, in effect, the 'pedagogical subject knowledge' referred to above by John (1991). Reflective student teachers generally plan well in advance, taking into consideration short-, medium- and long-term factors, with clear objectives geared towards learning. They also have the capacity to change these plans according to developing learning needs. 'Tried and tested' methods are still used but these are employed alongside more innovative, creative and 'risk-orientated' teaching and learning activities, which are well planned and which create more variety in lessons to enhance learning. Class management is now based upon mutual respect between pupil and teacher. Assessment is used diagnostically to inform both teaching and learning. There is emphasis upon meeting the diverse learning needs of individual pupils (differentiation) and pupils are challenged appropriately (progression). The reflective practitioner puts great emphasis upon self-evaluation, but the focus of this reflection is very much on developing teaching strategies that enhance the quality of pupils' learning. *There is clearly a shift in focus away from 'me, the student teacher' to 'them, the learners'.*

In this final stage, reflective practitioners think more in terms of pedagogy (a concept) than teaching (a process). Elliott (1991, p. 16) defines pedagogy as 'the performance of teaching, together with the theories, beliefs, policies and controversies that inform and shape it'. This reflective pedagogy is also creative (Postlethwaite, 1999). Reflective practitioners are thoughtful, organized and evaluative, and this is reflected in their relationship with mentors and tutors. At the beginning of the course, the relationship between student teacher and mentor is very much based upon the pupil-teacher but by the reflective practitioner stage it is based upon a 'co-enquirer' model, with the tutor or mentor being perceived as a useful 'critical friend' (Capel *et al.*, 1995: see below for further discussion).

Before going on, I want to emphasize that the model above should not be perceived as a linear one: not all student teachers progress at the same rates, in the same ways and at the same times. One of the most interesting things about the model is that after reaching 'the plateau', say about two-thirds of the way through the course, not only do some teachers never progress to Stage 6, they sometimes actually regress in the latter part of the course, as 'tried and tested methods' and 'coping strategies' dominate. All student teachers bring strengths and weaknesses to a course and progress in different ways, but generally I have been surprised at how useful the Furlong/Maynard research model has been for informing my students and myself about the nature of teacher education.

The mechanics of student teacher development: learning by discussing, watching and doing

The discussion above will already have given some indication of the ways in which student teachers can learn about teaching. Dean (1996) identifies the following ways that student teachers can learn:

- Learning through discussion with teachers (taking advice from experienced teachers).
- Learning through observation of other teachers at work (including non-historians).
- Learning from other individuals and groups (including experienced teachers and student teachers).
- Learning through experience (hands-on teaching in the classroom).
- Learning from reading (hopefully, by reading books like this one!).

All the research suggests that learning from teaching in the classroom is the most useful way of learning to be a teacher, but in order to learn most effectively (and to become 'E & R') ALL modes are highly relevant and important.

Learning through discussion

Talking to history teachers provides the first step in building up much craft knowledge, as well as being introduced to ideological aspects. Thus, student teachers' 'first encounters' with history teachers, for example, during a pre-course visit to a school or during the early days of teaching practice, provide opportunities to explore and discuss general views and beliefs on history and history teaching, and on the planning process, such as aims and objectives, schemes of work, the most useful textbooks, the nature of classroom control and issues relating to the organization of the classroom. A little later, there may be opportunities to develop knowledge of the institution, not only from history teachers but from other members of staff such as headteachers, deputy head-teachers, pastoral heads and other subject teachers.

Learning through observation

Researchers and teacher educators recognize that observation is fundamental to the learning process in teaching (Croll, 1986; Tilstone, 1998). This is where all aspects of the professional craft knowledge can be observed at first hand, particularly the nature of 'routinization' of organizational knowledge, and it provides the first opportunities to evaluate how children learn history. However, a word of warning also: Shaw (1992) and others rightly argue that 'unfocused' observation can be boring and actually deconstructive, and that structured observation, with a particular focus, is vital for effective learning. Wragg and Wood (1984) suggest that during their 'first encounters' of classes through observation, student teachers usually find the following useful to focus upon:

- Rules and Regulations (e.g. entry and exit procedures; discipline: control and management)
- Classroom (physical appearance, layout, resources)
- Lesson beginnings (teaching methods, expectations, timing, response of pupils)
- Lesson organization (tasks, amount of teacher talk/pupil talk, balance between written/oral work)
- Lesson endings (conclusions and summaries, exit from classroom).

Notice how these relate mainly to 'organizational knowledge', which so pre-occupy student teachers in Furlong and Maynard's (1995) 'early stages'. Later, as student teachers become more experienced and aware, so the focus of attention can shift to other aspects of the 'craft knowledge', including technical and specific issues, which I like to call a 'progressive line'. These include:

- *Lesson beginnings*: How, precisely, does the teacher 'gain pupil interest' at the start of lessons? What techniques and resources are used? What types of questions are asked by the teacher? What is the optimum length for a lesson introduction? When and how are lesson aims and objectives communicated to the pupils? Do the pupils know what is expected of them?

- *Lesson organization*: How are transitions and tasks managed? How long should be spent on tasks? What does the teacher do to ensure that most pupils work 'on-task'? What kinds of instructions and explanations are provided? How are less able pupils supported and the more able challenged? How is feedback obtained from the pupils and what is done with it? How are aims and objectives assessed?

- *Lesson endings*: How, precisely, does the lesson end? How much time is allocated to the conclusion? Is there time allocated for assessing aims and objectives? And whether pupils have understood what they have been doing? What needs to be considered for the next lesson?

Not only does it help to adopt a specific focus and a 'progressive line' of observation but it may also be useful to use different ways of observing in order to promote reflection and evaluation. Capel *et al.* (1995, p. 258), for example, describe the advantages of paired observation (e.g. done with another student teacher or mentor), which involves three steps:

- **Step 1:** Agree on the focus of observation (e.g. questioning technique, task management, etc.)
- **Step 2:** You observe each other teach, concentrating upon the agreed area of focus
- **Step 3:** You give each other feedback on the area/issue chosen for the focus of observation.

Learning from other individuals and groups
Student teachers, then, need to learn from a range of individuals. Some PGCE courses adopt the policy of actually placing student teachers in pairs, so that they can learn from each other. At the University of Wales Swansea, we adopt this policy and we encourage a 'developmental' or 'phased' (see discussion on Edwards and Healy (1994) in the previous section) approach to student teacher learning as follows:

- **Phase 1:** *Observation* by student teachers of experienced teachers
- **Phase 2:** *Collaborative work* with mentor, with student teachers taking responsibility for a section of the lesson (e.g. management of group work, explaining a task, starting or ending the lesson)
- **Phase 3:** *Paired teaching*, whereby students plan, teach and evaluate lessons together, each taking responsibility for particular parts of lessons
- **Phase 4:** *Individual teaching*, with paired observation and continuation of some collaborative and paired work.

You will also find that your PGCE student teaching group at your HEI provides an abundant source of useful feedback and mutual support, so use it profitably and value the opportunities it provides for reflective analysis and sharing of ideas. Clearly, however, the mentor is a vitally important figure in teacher education and research confirms that the quality of mentoring has a vital impact upon the development of student teachers (Booth *et al.*, 1990; Wilkin, 1992). The nature of the student/mentor relationship needs to change as the training process proceeds. Capel *et al.*(1997, p. 33) provide an immensely useful list of words to describe the changing mentor/student relationship: note how some aspects of the role are more relevant at different stages or phases of the training process:

Colleague	Diagnoser
Protector	Facilitator
Consultant	Challenger
Helper	Appraiser
Reviewer	Teacher
Expert	Listener
Guide	Trusted guide
Motivator	Counsellor
Assessor	Critical friend

Thus, at the beginning of the training period, when the student teacher lacks the experience and skills of the craft knowledge, it is appropriate that the mentor takes on the role of 'diagnoser', 'teacher' and 'facilitator'; towards the end of the course, however, the focus shifts towards becoming 'assessor', 'challenger' and 'critical friend'.

Learning through experience

This last point reminds us of the ways in which student teachers can learn from experience, but unless that experience is organized in certain ways, learning can actually be inconsistent. Unless student teachers take the role of evaluation, diagnosis, analysis and reflection seriously they will not progress at the rate at which they want to. We saw earlier from the Furlong and Maynard (1995) model that the crucial developmental stages for student teachers are Stages 4–6. From my own experience, I have actually seen some students who were on the verge of reaching Stage 6 revert back to Stage 4, due to a combination of over-confidence, complacency and a lack of critical self-evaluation. I still find the early Spring Term on the Swansea PGCE course an interesting time in this respect. Some students return to the university believing that 'they know it all' in relation to teaching, after spending just over half a term in school! One of my biggest priorities at that point is to switch to 'challenger' or 'critical friend' mode, demanding that my students ask some fundamental reflective questions such as:

- Where am I now? (self-evaluation)
- Where do I want to be in a term's time? (action-planning)
- How am I going to achieve this? (objective-setting).

One of the things we give our students at this stage is the list in Figure 1.1. Read it within the context of the Furlong and Maynard (1995) model above, the definition of effective history teaching given in the next chapter and the list of Standards.

As a group, we have a frank discussion on many of the themes shown in Figure 1.1. In order to encourage the students to move away from 'us, the teachers' to 'them, the

---

Could you do better?
Do you want to do better?

Knowledge and application

- Your subject knowledge has improved but it could be packaged more effectively
- You have sound subject knowledge but you are aware of some of the gaps that need to be filled

Planning

- You can plan lessons adequately but sometimes they don't go to plan!
- You plan learning objectives but sometimes they need to be sharper and clearer
- You have used mainly departmental resources but you'd also now like to start developing some of your own

Teaching and learning techniques

- Your lesson introductions are OK but your lesson endings/conclusions are far from satisfactory
- Your questioning technique is satisfactory but you know you can improve in many ways
- You use the Overhead Projector (OHP) quite regularly but you'd now also like to start using Information and Communications Technology (ICT) and Audio Visual (A/V) more
- You've used mainly whole-class teaching but you want to try other teaching methods too
- You've used some group work but you weren't entirely satisfied with how it went; you want to develop more effective ways of organizing group work
- You've tried some empathetic/role-play exercises but again, outcomes could have been better
- You've used 'tried and tested' teaching methods but you – and more importantly your pupils – have become a bit bored with them. You want to develop a wider range of teaching and learning methods

Class management and control/relationships with pupils

- You can manage and organize classes well but sometimes class control can be challenging
- Your relationships with pupils are, on the whole, OK but you find some pupils difficult
- You tend to 'teach to the middle'; you now want to find effective ways of meeting the needs of less able pupils and challenging the more able

Assessment

- You've marked pupils' books but, if you are honest, you could have marked them more often
- You've given marks/grades and recorded them but you could have given more useful feedback

Effectiveness

- You've set appropriate tasks but you've also experienced 'dead-time' in some lessons
- You've ensured that most pupils learn something *BUT COULD THEY LEARN MORE?*

Figure 1.1 *Progression of craft knowledge in history teaching*

pupils' and really explore the interrelationship between teaching, learning and reflective practice, we ask our students to analyse their present situation and future development in terms of a number of key self-evaluative questions:

- How do pupils learn?
- What have my pupils learned?
- How can I help my pupils learn more?
- How can I challenge my pupils?

Thus, the challenge is to ensure that the above translate into the following key objectives, namely, to concentrate upon:

- Being aware of pupils' learning needs
- Using a range of teaching and learning strategies
- Developing effective monitoring, evaluative and assessment strategies
- Providing diagnostic evaluation and feedback to pupils
- Continually setting targets for future development.

Reflective practice will therefore involve:

- Revisiting knowledge and experience already gained
- Rethinking how subject knowledge is used and packaged
- Reshaping lesson planning
- Restructuring lessons
- Revisiting thoughts on how pupils learn history
- Rethinking how assessment can inform teaching and learning
- Reorientating the focus of attention from the teacher to the learning needs of pupils.

Learning through reading

Hopefully, you will already have learned something about history teaching! This is a good opportunity to discuss how to use this book to help you make progress towards becoming 'E & R'. By making reference to effective pedagogical techniques through research evidence, I hope this book will take on something of the role of both 'helper' and 'challenger'. You should already have gathered that history teaching is an extraordinarily challenging task, one which you simply cannot grasp in its entirety straightaway. Many of you who have succeeded as an undergraduate will, in the early stages, find learning to teach rather frustrating. Learning to teach requires patience, an open mind and determination.

The book has been designed to meet your needs at various stages of development. I hope it will help you become a reflective practitioner and, in the process, make it possible for you to experience, like I do, the genuine excitement of being a history teacher.

CHAPTER 2

History teaching in a historical context: towards a definition of historical knowledge and understanding

> If history teachers do not analyse the history of their own subject, why should they expect their students to think historically?
>
> (Phillips, 2000a)

Introduction

Following Aldrich (1984, 1990) and Aldrich and Dean (1991), I argue in this chapter that only by analysing the debates over the teaching of the subject in the past can we really understand what history teaching is, as well as understanding how the subject is taught most effectively. Also in this chapter, I attempt to clarify a few misunderstandings about history teaching. As we shall see, history in schools became a source of profound controversy during what became known as the 'Great History Debate' over the teaching of the subject within the National Curriculum. In the process, history as a school subject began to be misunderstood. By discussing what history *is* (as well as what it isn't) the chapter offers a definition of history teaching at the beginning of the twenty-first century.

History teaching in a historical context

In my book *History Teaching, Nationhood and the State* (Phillips, 1998a), I argued that in the early part of the twentieth century, history teaching was not particularly controversial, because it reflected an essentially homogenous, patriarchal and stratified society. The chief diet of British (or English) political history, concentrating upon the 'grand narratives' of the British past, was unquestioned by a predominantly white, hierarchical society. This was referred to by Slater (1989) as the 'consensus' over history teaching and by Sylvester (1994) as the 'great tradition'. Even in Wales (and to a lesser extent in Scotland), pupils were taught mainly English political history.

Although the main mode of teaching involved 'transmission' methods, there were some innovative thinkers and writers on history teaching throughout the twentieth century, who attempted to develop new ideas about how to connect teaching more effectively with pupils' learning needs in order to improve effectiveness. Keatinge's (1910) book is rather extraordinary, for in it he articulated many ideas that were to form many of the key principles underpinning the 'new' history over sixty years later. Although more systematic research is needed to evaluate the extent to which these ideas permeated history teaching, it is likely that people like Keatinge were the exception, rather than the rule, as far as teaching methodology was concerned.

In fact, research in the 1960s showed that history was 'in danger' and was losing popularity in schools (Booth, 1969; Davies and Pritchard, 1975; Price, 1968). A number of factors account for this: British society was becoming more ethnically mixed and the radical nature of the 1960s meant that a range of groups began to challenge conventional hierarchies and traditional symbols of order. In particular, the retreat from Empire and what some analysts have called post-colonialism meant that a history curriculum that put only England at the centre of the historical record seemed out of date and irrelevant. History in universities also began to change: the growth of the history of women for example, as well as what historians like Raphael Samuel (1998) called 'history from below', challenged the traditional 'great men' view of history. Later, in the 1980s, the growth of demands for devolution in Wales and Scotland saw the emergence of distinctive history curricula in these countries, so that by the end of the century, Britain no longer had only one history curriculum – but four (see Phillips *et al.*, 1999).

The immediate response to the fact that history was seemingly 'in danger' in the early 1970s was to devise a radically new approach to the teaching of the subject, which came in the shape of the Schools' Council History Project, centred in Leeds. The SCHP (later renamed Schools' History Project: SHP) was to have an important influence on the philosophy of history teaching and the debates about the subject.

'New history' and the Schools' History Project

Of interest to us is that the SHP was very much influenced by research, particularly cognitive-related research on the ways in which pupils learn, as well as important work on the use of historical concepts developed by another project entitled Place, Time and Society 8–13 (see Blyth *et al.*, 1975). It was also influenced by work on educational objectives (Coltham and Fines, 1971). As we shall see, the SHP and what became known as the 'new' history was not without controversy. Indeed, Aldrich (1984) has argued that it was not 'new' at all, as Keatinge and others had been articulating similar ideas earlier in the century (see previous section).

Whatever the merits of this argument, it is clear that one of the major achievements of new history was that it provided a substantial critique to Piagetian ideas as applied in history. Piaget is, understandably, a well-known name in education and is discussed in detail in Chapter 3. His work on child development was immensely influential in the 1960s. But in many ways, Piaget's research represented something of a straitjacket to history and the social sciences because he argued that children go through a series of stages, from concrete to conceptual thinking (Cooper, 1994). If this was true, then this had serious, limiting effects upon the ways in which history could be taught. For if Piaget's ideas are taken to their ultimate conclusion, this could mean that pupils can only learn history at certain stages – or ages.

However, Piaget's ideas came under scrutiny from a range of educationalists, particularly those working in history education. Booth (1980) demonstrated, in fact, that pupils could grasp certain 'advanced' historical concepts such as change or causation much earlier than Piaget claimed. He argued that the crucial factor here related to the precise ways in which these conceptual ideas were taught. Booth and others had been influenced by another key thinker on education, namely Jerome Bruner (again, see Chapter 3). Bruner argued that although it may be the case that children go through certain stages of development, the crucial factor in the learning process was, in fact, the context of teaching and learning.

This gave the architects of the SCHP a useful, credible and essentially optimistic philosophy on which to base their project. If it was the case that the context of learning was crucial, then this provided a series of exciting opportunities to meet the needs of pupils. Indeed, to 'meet the needs of adolescents' was an explicit aim of the Project (SCHP, 1976). Aimed at pupils aged 13–16, the Project involved teaching alternative elements of history in new ways. The authors devised a series of activities – backed up with interesting, colourful resources – first of all aimed at pupils in Year 3 (now called Year 9) of the secondary school. This was known as 'What is History?' and involved the following structure:

Mark Pullen: Pupils were asked to use the clues to piece together the story of what had happened to a student called Mark Pullen. Pupils were asked to speculate about what transpired, based upon the evidence available to them. The objective here was to demonstrate to pupils that the judgements or conclusions that historians come to are necessarily contingent upon the evidence that they use.

Bodies in the bog and Sutton Hoo: Whereas the exercise above had been 'context free', pupils were next given a series of exercises that encouraged them to place what they had learned in a real historical context, namely by studying the famous Sutton Hoo discoveries and the exciting story of what had happened to the bodies found in the peat-bogs of Denmark.

History is about people: In order to discourage pupils from believing that history is only about processes, skills or concepts, a unit of the project encouraged pupils to see that history has as its core the multifaceted stories of people in a range of different contexts – social, political, religious, economic and so on.

Having provided pupils with a firm grounding in the skills, processes and substantive elements of what constitutes 'history', the SCHP designed an innovative examination course at 14+. This involved:

A study in development: The theme selected was the History of Medicine, which provided the opportunity to demonstrate both change and continuity in history. Thus, the history of medicine provided the opportunity to show the complex array of factors that had led to medical progress, but it also illustrated that in certain periods, medical knowledge did not advance and in some cases actually regressed.

A study in depth: As its name suggests, this unit provided the opportunity to study a historical topic in detail, using a combination of primary and secondary sources to do so. This also encouraged pupils to see people in the past from their own perspective – what became known as historical empathy.

A modern world study: In order to encourage pupils to see the importance and worth of history, the SCHP encouraged the study of an important event of contemporary resonance, such as Northern Ireland or the Arab–Israeli conflict. Starting with the analysis of contemporary newspaper or television accounts, pupils were then given the opportunity to analyse the historical roots or origins of such conflicts.

History around us: In contrast to the above, pupils were also encouraged to study an aspect of their locality, promoting the idea of the importance and relevance of history for understanding the world around them. A particularly innovative element of this unit, as well as the modern world study above, was that it could be assessed not by examination but through coursework.

Overall, therefore, the SCHP represented a break with the past as far as history teaching was concerned. By concentrating upon the processes of history, historical methodology and history's conceptual elements, as well as selecting new and varied historical content to teach, the SCHP offered an alternative to the 'great tradition'. This became known as the 'new' history.

New history and New Right

The influence of the SCHP and the new history in the 1970s and 1980s is subject to debate. The research of Patrick (1987, 1988a, 1988b) and Davies and Pritchard (1975) suggested that new history had relatively little influence. I have suggested elsewhere (Phillips, 1998a) that new history's real significance in the 1980s lies not in the sense of the actual uptake of the SCHP syllabuses at examination level but in terms of its influence over Her Majesty's Inspectorate (HMI), and for the ways in which its ideas, concepts and principles shaped the General Certificate of Secondary Education (GCSE), introduced in schools in 1985. Thus, the GCSE criteria (DES, 1985a) governing the new examination did not stipulate particular historical content: this was to be left to the different GCSE examination boards to decide through varied syllabuses. Instead, the GCSE criteria were general, stipulating that pupils would be expected to:

- Recall, evaluate and select knowledge relevant to the context and to deploy it in a clear and coherent form
- Make use of and understand the concepts of cause and consequence, continuity and change, similarity and difference
- Show an ability to look at events and issues from the perspective of people in the past (i.e. historical empathy)
- Show the necessary skills to study a wide variety of historical evidence

One can see clearly through the references to processes, methodology and historical concepts, the influence of the 'new' history permeating through. It also had a direct influence on HMI publications and guidance (see DES, 1985b).

It may seem rather odd that there was so much relative autonomy given to the SCHP, GCSE examination boards and schools themselves as far as curricular decision-making was concerned. This was what Lawton (1980) referred to as the 'golden era' of teacher autonomy, which was soon to be undermined in the subsequent decades. Even by the 1980s, the Secretary of State for Education, Keith Joseph, was reluctant to prescribe what was actually taught in schools, hence his agreement to the general criteria of the GCSE. Whilst Joseph himself argued that more British political history should be taught in schools, he also made it clear, in a speech to the Historical Association in 1984, that it should be schools themselves who are ultimately left to decide the details of what historical content should be taught (Joseph, 1984). Yet, within only four years of Joseph's speech, schools in England and Wales were to have prescribed and detailed history curricula, statutory from ages 5–16, via the Education Reform Act (ERA) of 1988. How did this situation come about?

The answer, rather unsurprisingly, lies in political factors, particularly the influence of the New Right, a political ideology that was a mixture of market liberalism and authoritarian conservatism. The New Right comprised politicians, pressure groups, academics, journalists and other influential people, who favoured radical reform of the welfare state. It became particularly influential after the Tory election victory of 1987, when Margaret Thatcher felt confident enough to embark upon a range of social reforms. This conservative strand of New Right thinking was very important as far as the history curriculum was concerned, for as prominent conservative thinkers argued, the nation state could only survive through a thorough knowledge of British history (Scruton, 1980). Moreover, the influence of these ideas coincided with the beginning of office of the new Secretary of State, Kenneth Baker, who believed that education reform could only be achieved through strong central initiatives from government.

The New Right launched an attack on history teaching in schools (Phillips, 1998a: ch. 3), what Ball (1990) has usefully called a 'discourse of derision'. A range of pamphlets appeared from New Right pressure groups such as the Hillgate Group or the Centre for Policy Studies (established by Thatcher and Joseph in 1974), attacking history in schools, particularly the new history and the GCSE (see Beattie, 1987; Deuchar, 1987, 1989; Hiskett, 1988; Kedourie, 1988; Lawlor, 1990; Partington, 1986). The 'discourse of derision' against history teaching centred upon four main issues:

1. *Process versus content*: The New Right argued that the skills and methodology of history had taken precedence over historical content, that the new history and the GCSE put so much emphasis upon the 'process' of the subject that it had relegated historical knowledge to secondary importance. This was not only misguided but also dangerous, according to the New Right, as pupils would grow up to be historically illiterate; moreover, the skills of the historian were far too difficult and demanding for pupils to understand, so it was misconceived to believe that pupils could think about history like historians in the ways advocated by new history.
2. *The 'flight from British history'*: Unsurprisingly, the New Right was appalled at the ways in which the new history and the GCSE had relegated the importance of British history. Furthermore, by concentrating on eclectic choices of historical content, school syllabuses were generating pupils who were also culturally illiterate. This, of course, revealed the New Right's distrust of multiculturalism and anti-racist approaches to history teaching.
3. *Empathy*: The New Right was highly critical of the teaching of empathy, as it believed that empathetic understanding was not only unattainable, but also nebulous in what it encouraged pupils to do, namely (according to the New Right) 'imagine' that they were a people in the past – which was impossible. Moreover, empathy was notoriously difficult to assess and encouraged misguided activities and exercises.
4. *Politicization*: At the centre of the New Right's discourse of derision was the belief that school history had been hijacked by the Left for political purposes. The emphasis upon social and economic history showed that teachers had become obsessed with class conflict, whilst world history merely encouraged multicultural-ism. It followed that teacher autonomy had to be curtailed, in order to prevent ideological indoctrination.

New history was particularly vulnerable to critique by the New Right because 'an emphasis on process and pedagogy could easily become perverted into an emphasis on skills and methods within a framework that was historical, but only in passing' (Brown, 1995, p. 3). Yet the New Right assault on history teaching in the 1980s has itself been the subject of critique (Crawford, 1995; Phillips, 1992a, 1996, 1997, 1998a). One of the characteristic features of the New Right's 'discourse of derision' was that by focusing upon a number of isolated examples, out of context, it often exaggerated problems. Moreover, by using the press to illustrate apparent inadequacies, the New Right made teachers feel threatened and defensive. Thus, potentially important issues, such as the claim that content had been relegated by skills, became unhelpfully polarized into 'an increasingly sterile divide' (Brown, 1995, p. 4), leading to what Counsell (2000a) rightly calls a 'distracting dichotomy'.

Similarly, the teaching and assessment of empathy was demanding and difficult and teachers faced many problems teaching it (see Chapter 4). However, to argue that history teachers should abandon historical empathy completely was equally unhelpful. Ironically, of course, by making these claims, the New Right was guilty of the very politicization that it accused teachers of being influenced by. As Stephen Ball (1993) has argued, the New Right had little understanding of the complexities and needs of the modern-day classroom; instead it seemed to be harking back nostalgically to the so-called 'good old days' of the past, which Ball rather cheekily calls 'the curriculum of the dead' (see Chapter 12). Finally, by stressing the ideological and cultural aspects of history teaching, the New Right's assault meant that 'the issue of managing and learning history had become confused with a predictable concern about a national history' (Brown, 1995, p. 5). School history would always be in the public and political spotlight from now on and, consequently, would never be the same again.

The 'Great History Debate' and the National Curriculum

The influence of the New Right was profound and the Hillgate Group in particular was very successful in influencing education policy. The Hillgate Group's so-called *Radical Manifesto* (Hillgate Group, 1986) advocated a whole series of policies – including the National Curriculum, a national testing policy, Grant Maintained Schools, increasing parental influence and so on – which would eventually find their way into legislation after the 1987 election, in the shape of the 1988 ERA. It seemed also that HMI were changing their views: the new inspector for history warned that the 'content question' could not be ignored (Hennessey, 1988) and in the same year, HMI published a document advocating a prescribed list of content centred around British history (DES, 1988a). Thus, after Kenneth Baker announced the National Curriculum in 1987, many teachers feared that the group charged with planning the history National Curriculum in England – the National Curriculum History Working Group (HWG) – would advocate a long list of prescribed historical content, dominated by British political history (Wales also had a history committee; see below for further discussion).

The omens were not great when Baker selected Commander Michael Saunders-Watson, a retired naval officer and castle-owner, to chair the HWG. Teachers feared that he had been a political appointment. Yet Saunders-Watson and his group were to earn a great deal of respect and praise from history teachers. Despite having to face a wide range of challenges (including massive press interest and alleged attempts by the Prime Minister herself to influence its work), the HWG went to great pains to listen to all parties, including teachers' groups and the New Right, in order to achieve a degree of consensus over the teaching of the history. The work of the HWG, including the political influences applied upon it, has been analysed in depth in *History Teaching, Nationhood and the State* (Phillips, 1998a) and I do not want to go over this ground again here. However, in summary, the HWG argued in its Final Report (DES, 1990) that history involved both the cultivation of historical skills and the accumulation of historical content, and there should be a balance of teaching between British, European and non-European (or world) history. It specified a number of aims of history teaching, which are still highly relevant today; the HWG said that the purposes of school history were:

- To help understand the present in the context of the past
- To arouse interest in the past
- To help give pupils a sense of identity
- To help give pupils an understanding of their own cultural roots and shared inheritances
- To contribute to pupils' knowledge and understanding of other countries and other cultures in the modern world
- To train the mind by means of disciplined study
- To introduce pupils to the distinctive methodology of historians
- To enrich other areas of the curriculum
- To prepare pupils for adult life.

The most sensitive (and most important) element of the Report, however, related to a detailed discussion of historical knowledge, which it defined as:

- Knowledge as 'information': the basic facts, such as events, places, dates and names
- Knowledge as 'understanding': the facts studied in relation to other facts and evidence about them, so that their significance can be perceived
- Knowledge as 'content': the subject matter of history, such as a theme or period.

In one of the most important statements in the Report, the HWG argued that:

> in order to know about, or understand, an historical event, we need to acquire historical information, but the constituents of that information – the names, dates and places – provide only the starting points for understanding. Without understanding, history is reduced to parrot learning and assessment to a parlour memory game.
>
> (DES, 1990, p. 7)

Thus it gave the example of the French Revolution; pupils may be able to remember the name of the King or the date of his execution but this 'information' is relatively useless to them unless they also know why the Revolution had occurred, its significance and long-term effects. This is because 'it is understanding which provides the frame of reference within which the items of information, the historical facts, find their place and meaning' (*ibid.*).

The HWG's Final Report won praise from a range of quarters, including the Historical Association, prompting the *Times Educational Supplement* (1 June, 1990) to declare that 'History report wins support from the ranks'. Unsurprisingly, however, the New Right was critical (Deuchar, 1992; Lawlor, 1990), citing familiar arguments that the Final Report placed too much emphasis upon skills, not enough upon the teaching or testing of historical knowledge and that it did not give enough precedence to British history. Margaret Thatcher demanded that the Final Report went out for further consultation and consequently, when the percentage of British history to be taught in school was increased, it seemed that the New Right had won its case. However, a careful analysis of the new proposals showed that the HWG's definition of historical knowledge-as-understanding had been retained.

Towards consensus in history teaching?

The National Curriculum was finally introduced in 1991 and mirrored the essential structure advocated by the HWG. However, the first version of the National Curriculum was a failure, as the curriculum in both primary and secondary schools was grossly overloaded. Originally, history was supposed to be a compulsory foundation subject for all pupils aged 5–16, but since this decision was overturned in 1991, history has been compulsory in schools in England and Wales only to the age of 14. Eventually, faced with massive teacher discontent, particularly over the testing regime at Key Stages 1 and 2, the government announced a review of the National Curriculum in 1993–94 under Sir Ron Dearing. The subsequent Dearing Review led to a scaled down version of the National Curriculum in 1995 and it was further scaled down as part of New Labour's 'Review 2000'.

An analysis of the current history programme of study within the National Curriculum in England (DfEE, 1999a) shows that it still largely follows the model originally proposed by the HWG in 1990. At the heart of each of the key stages is the combination of 'knowledge, skills and understanding', defined as:

- Chronological understanding
- Knowledge and understanding of events, people and changes in the past
- Historical interpretation
- Historical enquiry
- Organization and communication.

There is also the emphasis upon 'breadth of study' through a combination of British, European and world history. In Wales, which had its own History Committee for Wales (Welsh Office, 1990), the programme of study (ACCAC, 2000) is also organized around knowledge, skills and understanding. The main difference between England and Wales is that in Wales, pupils are taught about the history of 'Wales *and* Britain' (my emphasis) and are encouraged to consider the history of Wales within national, European and world contexts. (For a more detailed discussion of the history curriculum in Wales see Phillips, (1999); for Britain as a whole, see Phillips *et al.*, 1999).

Like the National Curriculum, the GCSE and A level/subsidiary (A/S) syllabuses were also subject to debate and reform. The mid-1990s saw attempts to reduce the perceived tendency in examination syllabuses and examinations to emphasize skills and concepts at the expense of contextual historical content (see Brown (1995) for a useful summary of this debate). More controversial was the attempt to increase the amount of British history being taught, not only at GCSE but also at A/S level. Thus, the GCSE criteria (www.qca.org.uk) require all syllabuses to 'build on the knowledge, understanding and skills established by the National Curriculum'; students must be given opportunities to:

- acquire knowledge and understanding of select periods and/or aspects of history, exploring the significance of historical events, people, changes and issues;
- use historical sources critically in their context, recording significant information and reaching conclusions;
- develop understanding of how the past has been represented and interpreted;
- organize and communicate their knowledge and understanding of history;

- draw conclusions and appreciate that historical judgements are liable to reassessment in the light of reinterpreted evidence.

Significantly, as well as ensuring that the selection of content is diverse, GCSE syllabuses must also contain 'an element of British history'. Likewise, the subject criteria for A/S level history (www.qca.org.uk) require that students 'study a substantial element of British history'; in addition, A/S and A level specifications require students to:

- demonstrate knowledge and understanding of the historical themes, topics and periods studied;
- assess the significance in their historical context of events, individuals, ideas, attitudes and beliefs and the ways in which they influenced behaviour and action;
- analyse historical interpretations of topics, individuals, issues or themes;
- analyse, evaluate and use historical sources in their historical context;
- demonstrate their understanding of key historical terms and concepts.

This chapter started with the premise that it was important to place history teaching in a historical context. In the next chapter, we consider the ways in which educational research has influenced its evolution.

CHAPTER 3

So how do pupils learn history? History teaching, pedagogy and research

> Children learn by the gradual accumulation of facts and ideas but perhaps more importantly they learn by seeing situations as a whole, by seeing a pattern of relationships that helps to build up a structure of understanding.
>
> (Fisher, 1990)

Introduction

This chapter goes to the very heart of what pedagogy should be about, namely the desire to connect teaching directly with learning (Fisher, 1995). It describes and evaluates four major types of research relating to learning, which all have profound relevance for the ways in which history teaching needs to be conducted, namely:

- Generic research produced by Piaget, Vygotsky and Bruner on how pupils learn
- The theory of multiple intelligences associated with the work of Howard Gardner
- Specific research, prior to 1988, on how children learn history
- Practitioner-orientated research on history teaching and learning since 1988.

The chapter aims to show the relevance of all four for understanding the context as well as the ways in which pupils learn history most effectively. It argues that in order to be effective, history teachers need to have a sound grasp of the important messages derived from these traditions of educational research.

Generic research on learning: the work of Piaget, Vygotsky and Bruner

A few decades ago, student teachers spent an enormous amount of time on teacher training courses analysing the implications of the research produced by these key figures. Today, some students complete their courses without having the faintest idea about what each of them said on the subject of learning, which, when we consider the importance of their theories they said, is rather alarming. This section of the chapter does not go into their work in any depth (see Cooper (1994) for a summary) but it does select the salient messages that are needed to inform practice. I hope that by summarizing their ideas around key phrases, words and concepts, you will see the direct relevance of their research for informing practice today.

The work of Jean Piaget had a profound impact on British education, particularly in the primary sector (Piaget, 1962; Donaldson, 1978). Piaget was a constructivist, that is 'he believed that children construct their own reality by means of experimenting on their environment and that this process follows a biologically predetermined sequence' (Baumann *et al.*, 1997, p. 43). Thus, the notion of *discovery learning* was born: the belief that teachers should act essentially as facilitators, by establishing learning situations where pupils could find things out for themselves. In this sense, Piaget's work was potentially very liberating, in that it was *child-centred* and this influenced the Plowden Report (1963), which itself had such a major impact upon establishing what became known as *progressive methods* of teaching in the primary sector.

However, as was mentioned briefly in the previous chapter, another important aspect of Piaget's work was potentially problematic for history teachers, namely his notion of *ages and stages*:

- **0–2 years** (*the sensory-motor period*): sees the growth of mental structure that starts to make sense of the world

- **2–7 years** (*the pre-operational period*): witnesses the crucial development of language and the growth in the ability to see the difference between past, present and future

- **7–11 years** (*period of concrete operations*): here, children can conceptualize but only in very concrete ways

- **11-adulthood** (*the period of formal operations*): witnesses the development of logical reasoning, hypothesizing, understanding causal links, as well as the ability to think conceptually without the provision of concrete examples.

Amongst many of the criticisms of Piaget's theory was that it was too formulaic, too structured, particularly in relation to the idea of the inevitability of cognitive and biological readiness. If pupils progressed in this structured way of thinking, did this mean that it was not worth attempting to challenge younger children to think more conceptually? And what was the role of the teacher in all of this? Piaget seemed to imply that the teacher did not matter.

Another criticism levelled at Piaget was that he failed to take into account the social context of learning, which, by contrast, went to the core of the work of L. S. Vygotsky. Working in the Communist Soviet Union, Vygotsky argued, in fact, that we only learn via interrelationships with others, including our peers, as well as teachers and other adults, such as parents. In marked contrast to Piaget, Vygotsky believed that children went through three stages of development: *instinct, training* and *intellectual functions*. Vygotsky (1978) argued that the key to development, or true understanding, was the relationship between pupil and others, particularly the teacher, and he termed this the 'zone of proximal development'. This encouraged the view that group work was sometimes more effective than individual work, the idea essentially being that two or more heads are better than one!

In order for the social/learning inter-action to be effective, however, children needed to be equipped to function within this situation effectively. Therefore, Vygotsky's work implied the need to help pupils develop the linguistic skills to be able to contribute to paired or group situations. A further implication is that pupils needed to be shown or taught how to work in collaboration with others, sometimes referred to as 'procedural habits'. Undirected, aimless or disorganized group work was as useless as unfettered 'experimental' learning (see Chapter 8). The importance of Vygotsky's work was clear, but his views were only really taken into account long after his death. Vygotsky argued that if the social context of pupils' learning is given greater consideration, pupils are capable of achieving more at earlier ages. He also placed the teacher at the centre of the learning process alongside the pupil.

The work of Jerome Bruner also challenges the basic idea of Piaget, and at the same time shares many of the ideas of Vygotsky, particularly in relation to the cultural and social aspect of teaching and learning. Like Vygotsky, Bruner believes in a more broadly based notion of development around three flexible and adaptive stages:

- *Enactive representation*: Bruner noticed that certain actions and functions that people perform in life, such as tying knots or riding a bike (or even teaching!), become internalized through actions and practice, what he called 'learning by doing'. Bruner therefore argued that in order to learn, pupils needed to be given 'doable' (or kinaesthetic) activities such as practical work, practice of skills, problem-solving via everyday or 'real-world' solutions and investigation.

- *Iconic representation*: Bruner believed in the importance of what he called connected images, that is spatial patterns, drawings, diagrams and colours to represent demanding conceptual ideas and knowledge.

- *Symbolic representation*: Bruner said this is the most advanced or sophisticated form of representation, whereby certain symbols, such as words, language and formulae represent meaning. Thus, we know, through a relatively sophisticated level of symbolic representation, what the word 'human' means; it does not look like a human – it merely stands for or represents it. The implication here, of course, is that children need help in understanding those symbolic representations – such as language and reading – that give meaning to life.

Unlike Piaget, Bruner was interested in the implications of learning theory for teaching strategies, and he advocated the use of *scaffolding*. Thus, if a child did not understand something, Bruner advocated giving him or her the most appropriate (or what he called 'contingent') level of support. By the teacher providing an appropriate piece of the 'scaffold', Bruner argued that eventually the child would be able to undertake the task without its aid. Clearly, this was an optimistic view of the teaching and learning process; this idea of *levels of support*, as well as the idea of a *spiral curriculum*, where the child builds upon existing (or known) knowledge, has become profoundly influential in educational thought (see Wood, 1988). One phrase from his famous book *The Process of Education* (Bruner, 1960) that has become particularly well known is that any subject could be taught to any child at any age in some form that was intellectually honest. What matter, says Bruner, are the processes, contexts and methods that are employed in order to promote understanding and learning.

Howard Gardner, the theory of multiple intelligences and accelerated learning

Whereas many of the ideas of Piaget, Vygotsky and Bruner have been discussed and, in varying degrees, implemented over many decades, the work of Howard Gardner has become influential relatively recently, even though his ideas first emerged in the1980s (Gardner, 1983, 1994). This may be a sad reflection of the policy- and performance-driven climate in which educational discourse took place at the end of the twentieth century. Yet, as we shall see, Gardner's ideas about how children learn have profound implications for teaching, planning and assessment.

Gardner drew inspiration from his dissatisfaction with the way in which psychologists had become transfixed with traditional measures of cognitive intelligence, such as IQ tests. Gardner drew upon psychology, but also other disciplines such as neurobiology, anthropology, philosophy and cultural history, to suggest that 'intelligence' needs to be defined, evaluated and assessed differently. Indeed, Gardner argued that instead of viewing people as possessing a singular 'intelligence' we need to consider plural 'intelligences', and identified seven of them, each with different characteristics:

1. *Interpersonal*: works well in teams; effective verbal and non-verbal communicators; good listening skills; ability to see things from a wide range of perspectives.
2. *Intrapersonal*: conducive to feelings and thoughts; values personal growth and development; seeks to find solutions to broad philosophical questions.
3. *Kinaesthetic*: likes to explore through touch and movement; learns by doing; appreciates field trips, visits and role-play.
4. *Verbal-linguistic*: learns through listening, writing, reading and discussing; good at written and spoken communication.
5. *Mathematical-logical*: familiar relatively early on in life with concepts such as time, space, number, cause and effect; good at solving puzzles and working out sequences; likes harmony and order.
6. *Visual-spatial*: able to visualize things easily; good at manœuvring through space; able to construct 3D objects.
7. *Musical*: able to discern patterns in sound and enjoys experimenting with them; sensitive to moods in music; enjoys playing and improvising with various sounds; sense of rhythm.

There are some aspects of Gardner's work that are controversial (see White, 1998), such as the implication that some people – for example young children who are gifted in mathematics or music – are 'born' with certain talents (Gardner himself often uses the terms 'intelligences' and 'talents' interchangeably). This goes to the heart of traditional and long-established 'nature versus nurture' debates. However, if we accept Smith's view that 'most learners have a "jagged" profile, meaning that they will be high in some areas and low in others' (Smith, 1996, p. 53), then the implications for teaching are quite profound. For if teachers are always teaching according to their own strengths or intelligences, then they will, by definition, be excluding a very considerable proportion of their pupils who, according to Gardner's theory, have different intelligences.

History teachers may well have interpersonal and verbal-linguistic intelligences in abundance, but if they repetitively use methods of instruction such as verbal exposition and written work all the time, this may disenfranchise some pupils or even a sizeable proportion of their classes from the learning process. This may partly account for high levels of disaffection in some schools. The implication for teaching is clear: if teachers are to meet the needs of pupils they have to plan for a *variety* of teaching and learning activities and experiences.

The movement known as 'accelerated learning', associated with the work of teachers and educationalists such as Smith (1996), Dickinson (1996) and Hughes (1999), has been directly influenced by multiple intelligences and the work done by Fisher (1990, 1995) on thinking skills. These teachers and educationalists have shown ways in which Gardner's and Fisher's ideas can be applied in a wide variety of contexts and subject areas to improve the quality of learning.

Conceptualizing history teaching: Booth, Shemilt and new history

Piaget, of course, posed both opportunities and challenges to history teachers (see Chapter 2 and Cooper (1994) for a fuller discussion of this). Child-centred and activity-based learning provided exciting prospects but his 'ages and stages' theory meant that, because history contained many abstract and demanding concepts, the subject could potentially be considered too difficult for younger pupils. This was confirmed by the work of Peel (1960) and Hallam (1970), parts of which seemed to suggest that pupils needed a cognitive age of 16 before they could begin to think hypothetically or deductively, which was essential for conceptual understanding and for the ability to appreciate historical methodology and source evaluation. As Gunning remarked, Piagetian theory led rather unsurprisingly to caution in history teaching:

> a proposition like 'the peasants attacked the aristocrats' might once have been seen as a very straightforward piece of information to be learned. We are more likely now to see it as a sentence containing two concepts, which are both likely to be less than fully understood by many students in almost any age–ability group.
>
> (Gunning, 1978, p. 11)

The work of Martin Booth (1980, 1987), however, provided an invaluable critique of the application of Piagetian developmental theory. Booth argued that we needed to consider more carefully how children thought historically. If this was done, techniques, strategies and contexts could be used to help pupils develop more advanced, historically based conceptual ideas at a relatively young age. Following Vygotsky and Bruner, Booth realized that the selection of teaching methodology was vital for learning. By concentrating more attention upon how historians construct arguments and judgements and, equally important, by organizing his classes in ways that allowed pupils to discuss, share information and make decisions together, Booth (1980, p. 246) found that 'not only can fourteen- to sixteen-year-old pupils think in a genuinely historical way but that learning history can make a significant contribution to their ability to use evidence and to conceptualize' at relatively sophisticated levels. Booth went on to conclude that 'the results of this research programme is one of optimism' (see Vermeulen (2000) for a discussion of Booth).

Another potential challenging implication posed by child-centred education was the belief that discrete subjects, like history, were not thought necessary. Rather, integrated topic work was more conducive to learning, a view that dominated primary education in the three decades prior to the National Curriculum. Bruner, however, provided a rather different perspective. First, of course, Bruner's work had demonstrated that pupils could understand difficult concepts at a relatively young age, depending upon the support (or 'scaffolding') provided by the teacher. Second, Bruner had also placed emphasis upon what he termed 'the structures of subjects', in other words those characteristic features of the subjects, such as the skills, concepts and methodology of a particular subject. Thus, as Gunning argued, this led to the idea that:

> the central goal of a learner who is 'doing' history is to learn the characteristic procedures of a professional historian and to master the central concepts of the historical discipline, like 'evidence', 'source', and the notion of the tentative, provisional nature of historical judgements.
>
> (Gunning, 1978, p. 12)

This, of course, provided much of the intellectual justification for the SCHP. One should recall from the previous chapter that history was 'in danger' in the late 1960s

(Price, 1968; Booth, 1969) not only from integrated courses but because there was real evidence to suggest that pupils were becoming disaffected by the subject: in short, they found history boring and irrelevant. It was time, literally, for 'A New Look at History' (SCHP, 1976). In this publication, the SCHP set out a very clear rationale for the Project. Making direct reference to Price (1968), the SCHP argued that history had to meet the needs of individuals. The Project questioned strict Piagetian applications to history and made reference to another Schools Council initiative, namely the 'History, Geography and Social Sciences 8–13' Project, which showed that pupils could develop conceptual understanding by handling historical evidence. Difficult concepts had to be explained carefully and in order to do this, the SCHP made reference to the usefulness of Bruner's spiral curriculum, his belief in teaching in an 'intellectually honest form' and that the use of certain teaching methods could meet pupils' diverse needs.

Fines (1980) emphasized Shemilt's and the SCHP's contribution in helping history teachers overcome the limitations of Piagetian approaches in history; he stressed that it was possible to challenge pupils to make progress in history in an appropriate manner and that he had shown how history could be active, exciting and relevant. Shemilt and the SCHP's Project initiated an enormous amount of discussion about the nature of pupils' learning, reflected in the pages of *Teaching History* and also in the publication of some very important books (see Dickinson and Lee, 1978; Rogers, 1979; Dickinson *et al.*, 1984). Their ideas influenced a generation of history teachers and, as we shall see in the next chapter, many of the ideas it generated are still profoundly influential. A former HMI probably summarized it most accurately by claiming that it was:

> the most significant and beneficial influence on the learning of history and the raising of its standard to emerge this century. It gives young people not just knowledge, but the tools to reflect on, critically to evaluate, and to apply that knowledge.
>
> (Slater, 1989, p. 3)

Practitioner-initiated research since 1988

Influenced mainly by the work of Ball (1990), I argue in *History Teaching, Nationhood and the State* (Phillips, 1998a) that the National Curriculum represented a return to traditional pedagogical values. Endemic within New Right ideology, which influenced the ERA in 1988, was a profound distrust of theory and research-orientated approaches to teaching (see Chapter 2). Despite this, the 1990s saw the emergence of a new generation of thinkers, whose work has helped make history teaching and learning vibrant and interesting.

Yet the period immediately after 1988 did not bode well for the future. Most teachers, labouring under the pressure of inspection, league tables and assessment, seemed to be understandably preoccupied with implementing the National Curriculum and this is reflected in much of the research, which, as Swinnerton and Jenkins (1999) have shown, was concerned mainly with policy-related issues such as evaluating teachers' perceptions of the National Curriculum (Phillips, 1991, 1993) – or aimed to consider how history could be most adequately assessed (Teaching History Research Group, 1991). A teacher in one of my surveys described the National Curriculum as the 'sword of Damocles' (Phillips, 1992b).

Gradually, however, as the National Curriculum became more flexible and as teachers became more confident, so a new generation of teachers with interesting ideas has emerged. This has been reflected, for example, in the pages of *Teaching History*, which contain a wealth of new, exciting ideas, as well as in the production of books that seek to examine aspects of pupils' learning in the post-National Curriculum period (Grosvenor and Watts, 1995; Farmer and Knight, 1995; Haydn et al., 1997; Arthur and Phillips, 2000). I want to focus upon three important ideas that have emerged in recent years.

The first relates to the methods of encouraging pupils to write in analytical and discursive ways, chiefly associated with the work of Christine Counsell (1997). One of the principal weaknesses of history, particularly in the early years of the secondary school, was the view that teachers did not encourage pupils to write at length about issues. This was not helped by the attempt to devise tasks that initiated relatively short responses geared towards the levels of the National Curriculum (Booth and Husbands, 1993), and similar sorts of tasks set in textbooks (John, 1993, 1994). Influenced mainly by the work of Wray and Lewis (1996) on literacy and the use of writing frames, Counsell argued persuasively that it was indeed possible and desirable to encourage pupils to write at length in history about complex issues. In many ways, these techniques, such as the use of writing frames, represent the fruition of Bruner's notion of scaffolding. The work of Counsell and others is discussed at length in Chapter 8.

The second major initiative in recent years is the notion of 'Outline' and line of enquiry, mainly associated with the work of Michael Riley (1997, 2000). Riley and others became convinced that the difficulties faced by pupils when confronting a topic, period or issue in history were interconnected, namely that pupils need an overview or frame of reference, as well as a clear line of enquiry, in order to facilitate understanding. Riley devised clever 'overview' activities, related to 'big questions', which helped pupils see large historical topics in totality. He found that these outlines were useful for:

- enhancing 'in-depth' analysis of history by cultivating a wider historical context, from which pupils were able to draw;
- demonstrating connections between events, changes and key features, both within and between periods;
- developing a deeper appreciation of change, cause and consequence;
- reinforcement of understanding of important historical terms and concepts;
- encouragement of a meaningful evaluation of evidence and interpretation.

Both Counsell (1997) and Riley (2000, p. 8) emphasized the importance of the 'carefully crafted enquiry question' not only for outlines but also for effective planning in general (see Chapters 5 and 6).

A third important and influential idea that has emerged in recent years complements the 'outline', namely the idea of a 'depth' study. When used in combination, 'outline and depth' provide a very useful learning tool. My own empirical research on teachers' views of the National Curriculum in the early days of implementation demonstrated that they were particularly unhappy with what they termed the 'rush through the ages' approach, without having enough opportunity to analyse things in sufficient depth (Phillips, 1993). Dale Banham's (1998) excellent 'depth' study of King John shows how the richness of detailed, depth studies can provide quality teaching and learning opportunities, and in the process greatly enhance pupil understanding. He has developed innovative and clever ideas for promoting discursive writing (Banham, 1998, 2000; Banham and Dawson, 2000).

Through our own *Total History Experience* Project (Phillips, 2002a; Phillips and Cunnah, 2000) based at the University of Wales Swansea, we have been attempting, since 1998, to evaluate the use of outline, depth and discursive writing, as well as our own idea of what we call Initial Stimulus Material (ISM) (see Chapter 6 and Phillips, 2001b). We have also devised tasks that have been related to Gardner's 'multiple intelligences'. This research project, as well as the research described above, is referred to often throughout many of the chapters in this book, to demonstrate the ways in which research ideas can be used to produce innovative, challenging and effective teaching strategies to enhance pupils' learning.

CHAPTER 4

So what does it mean for us? Using research for historical knowledge, understanding and progression

> It is in our imaginations that we are fulfilled; it is there that we dream and become truly human. There are many dimensions to imagination, but one is surely the historical dimension. It is not a matter of the dates of battles or kings or the causes of revolution – important as these are – but about registering the essential otherness of the past or rather the otherness of all pasts.
>
> (Davies, R., 2001)

Introduction

This chapter (and the next three chapters) demonstrates ways in which the research described in the previous chapter can be put into practice. It starts from the premise that although many of the ideas described earlier sometimes appear contradictory, they provide an exciting menu of effective teaching strategies when used selectively and cleverly. Indeed, like others (Shayer, 1997), I want to argue that we need to synthesize many of the ideas described in the previous chapter. I focus first upon knowledge and understanding in history; in particular, I demonstrate how the concepts associated with historical knowledge can be taught in ways which facilitate pupils' understanding. Specifically, I show below how history can be taught in effective, progressive ways. I want also to suggest that these techniques should be viewed essentially as generic – that is, that they can be applied to a range of different contexts across all the key stages. The chapter attempts to show ways in which history teachers can become 'professionally creative' (Ashcroft and James, 1999; Postlethwaite, 1999).

Chronology, change and continuity

One of the most controversial aspects of the debate over history within the National Curriculum centred upon the teaching of chronology. There was a view that chronological understanding had been relegated by new history and thus the HWG was keen to stress that 'chronology provides a mental framework or map which gives significance and coherence to the study of history' (DES, 1990, p. 9). Similarly, Lomas (1993) and Wood (1995) have stressed the importance of chronological awareness for historical understanding. Chronological awareness thus figures prominently in the current

The 4T's	Definition
T1	The mechanics of time, including the conventions of chronology such as dates, terms like 'BC' and 'AD', the names of periods, epochs and ages (medieval, early modern, modern, etc.).
T2	The framework of the past, this involves understanding the 'map of the past', including a knowledge of the strands and themes of history, for example, monarchy, transport, society or warfare over time.
T3	Sequence of the past, including an appreciation of the sequence of events, for example the religious changes of the sixteenth century, the main battles of the First World War or the major turning points of the twentieth century.
T4	'Deep time', giving pupils an appreciation of the scale of the past, for example appreciating the time involved in 'prehistory', as well as clarifying misconceptions and anachronism.

Figure 4.1 *Definitions of chronology based on the notion of the 4Ts* (Haydn et al., 1997)

National Curriculum (DfEE, 1999b; ACCAC, 2000) and in the GCSE and A/S level criteria. Issues relating to change and continuity also feature significantly in the National Curriculum, including the requirement that pupils are taught to:

- explore the interrelationship and connections between periods and societies studied;
- appreciate the reasons for, results of and significance of historical change;
- identify trends both within and across different periods;
- consider the significance of the changes studied.

One of the best research-based definitions of chronology is provided has been Haydn *et al.* (1997, p. 89); they summarize it around the notion of the '4Ts', as shown in Figure 4.1.

It would be useful here to note the importance and significance of the HWG's definition of 'history as understanding' (see Chapter 2). Note how each of the 4Ts in Figure 4.1 are useless without a wider contextual understanding; even T3 – such as a grasp of the dates of the many religious events of the sixteenth century – would be fairly useless without understanding why these happened, their significance and the complex, far-reaching nature of the changes – social, political and even economic, as well as religious – that they initiated. As Lomas (1993, p. 20) rightly points out, without an appreciation of chronology and time 'there can be no real understanding of change, development, continuity, progression and regression'. One of the best pieces of research-based analysis on the issue suggests that 'we do not want children merely to develop the ability to construct chronicles of the past, we want them to be able to fashion coherent explanations, and to begin to understand other relationships between events other than temporal ones' (Stow and Haydn, 2000, p. 86). Research on children's development of chronology has emphasized the following:

- Although intellectually demanding, children can grasp quite sophisticated chronological concepts at a relatively young age. The work of Harnett (1993) and others demonstrate that the context of learning is vital here (see below). This was also confirmed by the work of Shemilt (1980) and the SCHP (1976) and by the work of CHATA (Concepts of History and Teaching Approaches 7–14) (Lee *et al.*, 1996). As Stow and Haydn (2000, p. 93) argue 'research indicates that a range of methods should be used to scaffold children's thinking about time'.

- Explicit care and attention needs to be given to the type of language and vocabulary used when discussing chronology-related issues with pupils (see Wood, 1995 for an excellent discussion, and also Chapter 8).

- Sequencing chronological events becomes far easier when visual materials are used (Lynn, 1993; Harnett, 1993).

- Concrete-kinaesthetic approaches such as the use of artefacts, the study of buildings and architecture, as well as site visits can also improve pupils' sense of chronology (Andretti, 1992; see also the discussion of other strategies in Stow and Haydn, 2000).

- Display work is extremely useful for cultivating, consolidating and developing pupils' awareness of time and chronology – in relation to dates, sequence and period – in a wide variety of ways (Cooper *et al.*, 1996).

- Nichol (1995) suggests that empathetic-type approaches – for encouraging pupils to penetrate written and visual sources deeply by inviting them to 'hear, smell, touch and feel' – may help develop chronological awareness, as well as reduce the possibility of anachronism.

- Iconic representation through timelines can be useful (Chapman, 1993; Hoodless, 1996).

Similarly, research on pupils' understanding of change and continuity has stressed that:

- Pupils need to be shown the ways in which cause, change and effect are linked (Shemilt, 1980).

- Pupils also have to be shown the importance of changes to people at the time, in order to encourage them to grasp the meaning – or significance – of changes (Shemilt, 1980); thus activities that encourage a deep penetration of past situations, such as role-play, may be important here.

- Haydn *et al.* (1997) stress that pupils need to be encouraged to appreciate that the past is not all about change, that continuity also plays a part in the dynamic of history (SCHP, 1976). Similarly, opportunities need to be provided to discuss the notion of 'progress'. Pupils' preconceptions that all change involves 'progress' need to be challenged.

What specific teaching strategies, based upon the messages derived from this research, are useful for developing chronological awareness and an appreciation of change and continuity? Put another way, using Stow/Haydn/Bruner reference above, what methods are needed to 'scaffold children's thinking about time', as well as historical change? Some practical suggestions are identified below.

Concrete past/present analogies
We saw how the SCHP used the 'present' example of Mark Pullen to illustrate the importance of order and sequence; similarly, Shuter *et al.* (1989) provide an excellent past/present analogy involving pupils piecing together how and why a school window

was smashed during a lunch-break (also useful for causation, as discussed). These examples can then be related to sequencing activities in a specific historical context.

Sequencing

Many textbooks, particularly teacher resource packs, provide sequencing activities with pupils being asked to place historical events in the correct chronological order. These can be written or visual. Based upon the research evidence above, the most effective are those that combine visual and written (e.g. through labelling exercises) activities. Also, be aware of 'death by too many sequence cards'. Probably five or six is an optimum number for an effective sequencing activity (see Haydn *et al.*, 1997 for some further examples).

Timelines

As with sequencing, many textbooks provide timelines to assist chronological awareness. These can either relate to specific events or whole periods. Hoodless (1996) argues that timelines can be used in a wide variety of contexts, from simple timelines with visual support, to more complex ones providing, for example, local, national and international dimensions. Pupils can also be encouraged to construct their own timelines. Some of the accelerated-learning research, particularly in relation to the influence of 'left brain/right brain' factors (see Smith, 1996), as well as research on dyslexia, suggest that the presentation of timelines may be important – horizontal may be more effective than vertical timelines – but this needs further empirical research.

Repetition, revisiting and familiarity

As with so many concept-related activities, it is vital that the sorts of teaching and learning tasks and methods described above are used constantly throughout the child's experience in school in order to encourage progression. Nothing is more powerful in learning terms than the ability of the teacher to be able to say 'remember when we did . . .?' and then repeat the exercise in a different context. This explains the power and effectiveness of the 'outline' method described in detail below.

The use of the 'outline' or 'overview'

Riley (1997) advocates the use of outline activities to promote chronological awareness by encouraging a wider, overview knowledge, demonstrating connections between events and for reinforcing key historical terms and concepts, including chronological conventions. He also argues that outlines or overviews promote a deeper understanding of change, cause and consequence, as well as encouraging a more meaningful evaluation of evidence and interpretation. Riley advocates a variety of outline activities for different purposes, which are discussed in some detail below.

Haydn *et al.* (1997, pp. 107–11) provide some outstanding suggestions for developing an understanding and appreciation of change and continuity; in addition to the 'overview', they advocate the following activities (which you will notice are rightly very much influenced by Shemilt's (1980) research).

- Use of diagrams, charts, flow charts and timelines.
- Comparative exercises, which encourage pupils to note the similarity and difference between historical situations; the notion of a 'then/now' comparative analysis is particularly useful.
- Comparison activities that stress the importance of changes to people living at the

Overview	Definition
O1	A short overview at the start of a series of enquiries to engage interest, frame a hypothesis (via a key question) and provide key vocabulary. It can also be used at the end of the series of enquiries to test the hypothesis.
O2	Overviews to provide chronological context for a particular in-depth enquiry.
O3	Different groups working on 'in-depth' studies to provide an overview.
O4	Two or more thematic overviews built up as pupils pursue depth studies.

Figure 4.2 *The use of overview* (based on Riley's (1997) work on outline and overview)

time; this can be done particularly usefully by focusing upon a specific region, village or family via case study, in-depth analysis and role-play.

- Speculation exercises, which encourage pupils based upon what that they have studied (such as the factory system) to speculate about some of the changes that may occur (for example, in relation to the number and types of jobs) in subsequent decades.
- Hypothetical questions ('What would have happened if X had not occurred?') are useful for demonstrating the significance of change (or lack of it).
- Sequencing activities, such as those suggested in relation to chronology (above) and causation (below); categorization activities are also useful here, of course, for identifying the different types of change (e.g. political, social, economic, religious, artistic, cultural, etc.); acronyms help pupils make sense of these (see below).
- Identifying and justifying turning points in relation to a topic, theme or period; this entails an appreciation of significance (see below).
- 'Spot the anachronism' activities provide not only the opportunity for a serious identification of change, but also an opportunity for light relief.

I now want to spend some time analysing Riley's (1997) work on outline and overviews in further detail, for this work, as we shall see, is immensely useful not only for encouraging a sound appreciation of chronology, change and continuity, but also other key elements within history, such as cause and consequence, significance and interpretation. Riley suggests that overviews can be used in a variety of contexts; I refer to these as 'O1–4' in Figure 4.2.

Riley has suggested a series of exciting outline activities for different purposes:

1. 'The hunting game' for identifying key features of a period.
2. 'Before and after snapshots' to develop a grasp of outline chronology or change.
3. 'Interlocking stories' to develop an understanding of change.
4. 'Contrasting images' in order to cultivate an appreciation of different interpretations of a period.
5. 'Immediate context' for providing a brief introduction to a more 'in-depth' study.
6. 'National context' for providing contrasting national situations relating to a particular theme.

7. 'European or world context' for providing a wider global context within which British developments can be understood.

In our *Total History Experience* research (Phillips, 2002a; Phillips and Cunnah, 2000), we decided to test the effectiveness of Riley's outline thesis but also we used the research project as a means of devising a series of distinctive overviews to meet the specific context of the core history units within the history National Curriculum in Wales. Like Riley, the outlines were devised for a range of purposes and contexts. What was very apparent was the versatility of each of them, and their great utility:

Outline 1: Middle Ages through a wide range of vivid, colourful images

This was modelled directly on Riley's ideas. A series of interesting images were selected to represent the major features of the Middle Ages, particularly in Wales. These included pictures relating to conquest and invasion, castle building, social life, feudalism and religion. Pupils were divided into groups, and were instructed to match up labels to each of the images. They were then asked to devise a key question that summed up each of the topics and to prepare a brief presentation to the rest of the class. Every pupil was given what we termed a 'concept wheel' to sum up the key questions, words and concepts of the medieval period. Finally, pupils were given a small (A5) summary sheet and were told to stick it in their books for future reference.

Outline 2: Tudors through a small selection of colourful images

As a contrast to the above, all pupils were given just four images of the Tudor period, including copies of Holbein's well-known painting of Henry VIII, the Henry VIII/ Edward IV succession picture, the Armada portrait and a very interesting image of a Tudor nobleman called Sir Henry Unton (displayed in the National Portrait Gallery). Pupils were asked to work in pairs. Each of the pictures contained important messages about the Tudor period. Pupils were given carefully constructed prompt (or 'scaffolding') questions that drew pupils' attention to these important features. Thus, pupils were asked to consider what Henry VIII's posture told them about Tudor monarchs (power and strength); the succession picture revealed interesting things about the attitude towards Catholicism; the Armada portrait provides a wealth of information about power, exploration and discovery; finally, the image of Henry Unton gave pupils a wide range of clues about Tudor life, including the centrality of religion. Again, they were asked to sum up the Tudor period around key questions; as with all the outlines, an A5 summary sheet helped them to review the period.

Outline 3: Chronology of the Stuart period

This was a conventional chronology exercise. Again asked to work in pairs, pupils were told to arrange each of the pictures in chronological order, using the appropriate labels. But the chronology also served other purposes: pupils were asked to identify causes, changes and to justify what they thought was the most significant event of the seventeenth century. The outline was also designed in such a way that it could be used later, for example, to re-examine the causes, changes and significant events from a slightly different perspective – they had studied the period in depth – in what Riley refers to as 'challenging the original hypothesis'. Outlines can therefore be used as summaries as well as introductions.

Outline 4: The Industrial Revolution 'bidding game'

Many teachers feel that the Industrial Revolution is one of the least interesting topics for pupils. This, in my view, is unfounded; nevertheless, we did want to devise a particularly interesting and innovative Industrial Revolution overview, similar to Riley's 'interlocking stories' outline. This is vital not only to demonstrate the nature of the industrial changes in Wales, but also to show their connections with the 'bigger picture' of Britain and the rest of the world. Our outline involved having all the pupils around a large table with, initially, two big pictures in the middle: one of Merthyr Tydfil in *circa* 1700 (rural, idyllic) and the other, a contrasting image of the same town in 1800 (industrial, polluted). Immediately, after discussion, pupils were clear that this 'big change' is called the Industrial Revolution and that the purpose of the task was to explore the major features of it. Big headings were then put on the table in a circle around the central images: population, agricultural revolution, inventors, factory system/industry, transport, urbanization, poverty and disease, wealth and finally, Empire. Each pupil was then given approximately three small pictures each, with a label on the back describing what each of them was. They were then asked to 'bid' to place their pictures next to the appropriate label; in order to do this, they had to justify their choice to the rest of the class. The end result was a fascinating and detailed illustrative summary of the major features of the Industrial Revolution. Pupils were then asked to discuss the order of the big headings: could we have started with 'empire' instead of 'population' or 'agricultural revolution', encouraging pupils to think about the developmental as well as the contingent nature of the Industrial Revolution. Finally, they were asked to speculate about 'what would have happened if X or Y had not been present? In what ways would history have turned out differently?'

Outline 5: A 'key image' and 'building blocks' – the First World War

This was designed to evaluate Riley's hypothesis that outlines do not just have to relate to whole periods but instead provide immediate, national and world contexts. Pupils were shown, on an OHP, an image that best summed up the key feature of the First World War, namely trench warfare. In pairs, they were then asked to identify the trenches, men going over the top, barbed wire and their weapons. They were then given two A3 sheets, the first of which contained images relating to where the Western Front was located and the second containing pictures of the tactics and strategy of trench warfare. Pupils were also provided with two sets of labels and told first to use the blue labels to match up to each of the pictures. This provided a basic understanding of where the fighting took place and the major tactics employed. After a whole-class discussion to clarify the main points, pupils were then asked to use the orange labels, which gave them further information about the War. This method has the advantage of building up pupils' knowledge and understanding in manageable blocks, so that they are not overwhelmed with information initially.

Outline 6: Combining chronology, change, significance and interpretation – the twentieth-century world

We were also keen to develop outlines that can, as Riley suggests, cultivate other conceptual awareness and understanding – for example of significance, evidence and interpretation – as well as focusing upon chronology, change and connection. The final outline involved selecting five key images of the twentieth century (see also Brown *et al.*, 2000) to sum up five discrete periods within it: the suffragettes (beginning of the century); trench warfare (era of the First World War); Hitler and Churchill (era of the Second World War); the Beatles (1960s); and the Ethiopian Famine (end of century). These were placed on a whiteboard so that all pupils could see them. Pupils were then divided into five groups each assigned a sub-period to explore in greater depth, involving images and labels. Consequently, these were used as the basis of a presentation to the rest of the class, with further images added to those already displayed on the board. Pupils were then asked to categorize the major changes of the period using an acronym REPEATS, which stands for Religious, Economic, Political, Environmental, Artistic/Cultural, Technological and Social (acronyms are very useful, as I illustrate below). Finally, they were asked to decide who was the most significant personality of the twentieth century and to consider whether the twentieth century should be given the title 'Century of Conflict' or 'Century of Progress' and to justify their choice. A lively discussion ensued!

We displayed each of the outlines on the wall of our teaching room in Swansea, so that pupils (and student teachers!) were regularly reminded of what they had done and what was learned. Research has shown the importance of display in the classroom (Cooper *et al.*, 1996) and I still use them now when I introduce historical content at the beginning of my PGCE course and throughout the year when we discuss language, vocabulary, key questions, concepts and ideas. We also found the 'little A5' summaries extremely useful both for pupils and student teachers, for they provided:

- Clarity and a definitive summary, which could be used time and again for reference by pupil and teacher
- Learning objectives
- Key questions (hypothesis)
- Major themes and concepts to be studied
- Main vocabulary and terms required.

In effect, they turned out to be 'mini-schemes of work', which were pasted into pupils exercise books and referred back to frequently. Overall, the outlines proved extremely effective and met virtually all the claims suggested for them by Riley. (For a more detailed discussion of the research, see Phillips, 2002a.)

Teaching historical significance: the forgotten key element?

I have argued elsewhere that the notion of significance has not received the attention that it merits in history teaching (Phillips, 2002b). This may seem rather odd because the notion of historical significance or resonance lies at the very heart of the subject. Perhaps one main reason for this is that significance has not been properly theorized and consequently has not been considered explicitly enough. An excellent contribution by Hunt (2000), using the work of Partington (1980) and others has started to address this shortfall. Partington argued that significance was a vital element of historical education, but that in order to understand what it meant, it was vital to understand what made an event significant; this, he argued, was dependent upon the following factors:

1. Importance – to the people living at the time.
2. Profundity – how deeply people's lives were affected by the event.
3. Quantity – how many lives were affected.

4. Durability – for how long people's lives were affected.
5. Relevance – the extent to which the event has contributed to an increased understanding of present life.

Thus, if we apply these criteria to the study of the First World War by focusing upon the big enquiry question of 'Why was the First World War so significant?', then our study of the War is likely to be greatly enhanced, say, if we were to consider some 'little questions' based around each of Partington's criteria:

1. Importance – by studying the main events of the First World War, we can consider questions such as 'Who was affected by the War?'.
2. Profundity – by analysing a diverse range of contemporary accounts from the First World War, we could ask: 'How were people's lives changed?'.
3. Quantity – by analysing both the Western Front and the Home Front, we could consider 'How many people were affected by the First World War?'.
4. Durability – by studying newspaper accounts of the anniversary of the First World War or by analysing local memorial stones to the soldiers who died during the war, we may want to ask 'Why is it important to remember the First World War?'.
5. Relevance – by considering the long-term effects of the War, we may wish to ask 'Why is it important to study the First World War?'.

Indeed, this last question provided the primary motivation behind another aspect of our *Total History Experience* research (Phillips, 2002a). We were conscious that significance had been an under-represented concept in history teaching and to this extent one of the Project's aims was to find ways of teaching the concept more effectively. We therefore devised a teaching pack based upon the study of the Battle of Mametz Wood, July, 1916 (part of the Battle of the Somme: see Phillips, 2002c), which actually began with an attempt to encourage pupils to consider why the First World War – and the Somme in particular – is still commemorated today. Newspaper articles describing the 80th anniversary of the armistice was used as Initial Stimulus Material (see Chapter 6 for more on ISM) for this. A further (particularly oblique) ISM – a pack of jelly babies no less – was also used as a concrete way of bringing the concept of commemoration home (jelly babies derive from 'peace babies', which were given in schools at the time to mark the armistice: see Chapter 12 for further discussion of commemoration).

We decided upon the following as our 'big question' to guide our analysis: 'Why was the First World War called the Great War?' After studying Mametz in some detail, and then going on to analyse other aspects of the War, including the impact upon the Home Front, pupils were given the final group work exercise (Figure 4.3), which helped them answer the 'big question' directly. Note how its design was influenced – very explicitly – by Partington's (1980) criteria, as well as the use of another acronym to help pupils appreciate the concept.

One of the most interesting aspects of the *Total History Experience* research, in fact, was the way in which it showed the usefulness and effectiveness of significance for really sharpening the study of certain topics. We therefore devised a range of significance-related tasks on topics that teachers have traditionally perceived either to be dull, difficult or both. The following activities were designed, with accompanying 'big questions'. Again, note how each of the exercises are influenced directly by Partington's (1980) criteria:

Why was the First World War called the Great War?

- In order to answer this question you need to analyse the *significance* of the War
- To start with, you might like to consider what we mean by the word **GREAT**:

G	Groundbreaking
R	Remembered by all
E	Events that were far-reaching
A	Affected the future
T	Terrifying

Task 1

- On your table you will find a set of cards describing and illustrating aspects of the First Word War, and four cards with headings.
- Your first task is to place each card under one of the 4 headings.

Task 2

- Now look at the cards in more detail.
- Decide whether each card had *long-term* or *short-term* consequences.

(Notes: pupils were then given a writing frame to help them answer the big question.)

Figure 4.3 *Group work exercise on the significance of the First World War*

'*Robert Owen – different from the rest?*' Significance, of course, lends itself very well to the study of individuals in history (see below for a fuller discussion of this). We decided upon 'Robert Owen – different from the rest?' as our key question, thus providing the opportunity to link significance with interpretation. Pupils were given opportunities to study Owen's multivarious role as entrepreneur, factory owner, social reformer and trade union activist. They were encouraged to consider Owen's importance at the time and today. The final activity involved pupils designing an entry for Encarta about Robert Owen.

'*Olaudah Equiano – a role model for today?*' Equiano's extraordinary life story provides an excellent opportunity to demonstrate his contribution to the anti-slavery movement. This exercise involved breaking down the chronology of his life, and encouraging pupils to discuss the most significant events which influenced him. Cards were then provided showing aspects of Equiano's life, which the pupils were asked to sort into the short- medium- and long-term significance in terms of the contribution he made to the campaign against slavery. This was used as the basis of the extended piece of writing (see Chapter 12 for a further discussion of this exercise in relation to anti-racist education).

'*The Industrial Revolution – how important is it to our lives today?*' Earlier we saw the importance of an outline as a way of introducing a period, large topic or theme. This significance-related exercise provides a way of summing-up (as with the Great War exercise in Figure 4.3) a large topic. In order to help them investigate the 'big question' directly, pupils were given cards containing evidence relating to industry and inventions, agriculture, transport, social change and 'Britain and the World', which they were then asked to categorize under the titles of 'Before the Industrial Revolution', 'During the Industrial Revolution' and 'Our World Today'. A summary table was provided for them to note the key points, which was then used as the basis for a final activity that involved pupils either (a) preparing a TV programme script showing the importance of the Industrial Revolution to our lives today or (b) designing their own 'commemorative plate' of the Industrial Revolution, to demonstrate its significance (paper plates were provided, which could then be displayed on the wall).

'The Tudor period – was it a bridge to the modern era?' This was stimulated by a wonderful illustration from a book by Peter Moss (1976). Pupils were given a picture of a bridge being crossed by Tudor figures carrying flags, with the letters S P E A R on them (one letter per flag). Pupils were then given key features of the Tudor age, relating to the SPEAR acronym: Social, Political, Economic, Artistic Cultural and Religious. They were asked to sort and categorize the cards under each of the flags. A writing frame was then provided in order to answer the 'big question', encouraging pupils to consider the most significant changes of the Tudor period, but also to evaluate some of the features of life that stayed the same.

Causation and consequence: contingency and connections

Few concepts in academic history are more keenly debated than causation; when we consider some of the most controversial historiographical debates of the twentieth century – for example, relating to the English Civil Wars or the Second World War – we find that most of the historical debate focuses upon the question: 'What caused these events to happen?' One of the major reasons for debate here is that causation is rooted in contingency and uncertainty. Historians can argue that X and Y caused Z, but what if Y had not been prevalent, would X have caused Z to happen anyway? Thus, one of the most contingent features of British life – the weather – has had a notorious impact upon the outcome of British history. What if the weather had been against the fortunes of William I when he set sail for England? What if the Spanish Armada had not been blown off course? In what ways would history have turned out differently?

Scott (1990) and his colleagues define causation as

> an understanding of the difference between long-term and short-term causes; an understanding that some causes are likely to be more important than others; an appreciation of the difference between, and the interdependence of, motivatory and enabling factors; and an understanding of the inter-relationship of different causatory factors.
>
> (Scott, 1990, p. 9)

It is this very complexity and contingency that Shemilt (1980, p. 30) argued was one of the major reasons why the pupil 'frequently misconstrues even the most apparently self-evident features of the causality concept'. Shemilt's research demonstrated that although pupils could grasp the idea that a historical cause was something with the 'power to make something else happen', they often could not identify, articulate or understand the direct connection – the causal link – between cause and effect. This problem was compounded by the fact that Shemilt also demonstrated that pupils found motivation difficult to appreciate, mainly because they saw history 'as a record of what happened to people rather than of what they made happen' (p. 32), a feature of adolescent thinking confirmed by the CHATA research (Lee and Ashby, 1998).

Using the work of Shemilt (1980), Scott (1990) and Haydn *et al.* (1997), we can summarize some of the chief conceptual challenges faced by pupils when assessing causation:

- Mistaking events and facts for causes and consequences
- Not being able to identify connections between cause and effect
- Only appreciating monocausal/consequential, rather than multicausal/consequential factors
- Not being able to appreciate different significance of causes and consequences
- Not being aware of categories (e.g. social, political, economic)
- Not being able to distinguish between long- medium- and short-term cause and consequence
- The tendency to accept inevitability and to dismiss contingency
- Failing to understand the complexity of motivation in history.

As is so often the case in this book, identifying the challenges (problems) faced by pupils should always be seen as a means by which teaching opportunities (solutions) can be identified, based upon the ideas discussed in the previous chapter. A brief description of some research-based ideas for teaching about causation is now presented.

Past/present analogies

The idea of cause and consequence lends itself to past/present analogies. In Shuter *et al.*'s (1989) textbook, pupils are given a set of jumbled-up scenes relating to an incident in the schoolyard. A classroom window has been broken and pupils have to piece together what happened. This provides the opportunity not only to place the events in the correct chronological order (see 'Chronology, change and continuity' section at start of this chapter) but also to consider who was responsible for the window being broken. Was it because the pupils had been playing football in the yard? But they had been given permission to do so by the teachers. And the window in question was the only one without wire gauze to protect it, as the older one had rusted through and had not been replaced by the caretaker. What would have happened if the gauze had been there? Would the window have been broken?

Another way into this exercise would have been simply to give the pupils a picture of a broken window and encouraged them to speculate about what had caused it to occur. Speculation is useful for raising awareness of contingency and multicausality. For example, most pupils are aware of the sinking of the *Titanic*. A discussion relating to how and why the ship sank, causing the death of so many, could lead to a multitude of possible factors: the design of the ship, incompetence, bad luck or stupidity. Scott (1990) discusses the use of similar 'past/present' analogies to promote understanding of cause and consequence.

Concrete/iconic mind pictures

Given the particularly conceptual, contingent and complex nature of causation and consequence, concrete mind pictures are particularly useful and relevant. Here are some examples:

- Pyramids – to present causation in the form of a pyramid not only provides a concrete image but offers a good opportunity for identifying categories.
- Icebergs – pupils can be shown in a concrete way that historical events are often 'the tip of the iceberg', caused by other events that lie below the surface.
- Volcanoes – with the consequences spewing out of the top, what caused the 'volcano' (after years of lying dormant) to suddenly erupt?
- Powder keg – as with the example above. What was the 'spark' (the short-term cause) that ignited the 'fuse' (longer-term cause)?
- Steps and a diving board – what were the 'steps' (causes) that had to be taken before reaching the 'diving board' (event)?
- Ripples – what happens when someone dives into a pool? Ripples occur, which are excellent for demonstrating short-, medium- and long-term consequences.
- Chains and links – a particularly good, concrete way of illustrating connections and for demonstrating contingency, as against inevitability: what if one element of the 'chain' was broken?
- Snakes and ladders – useful for showing short- and long-term cause and consequence.
- Trees and branches – probably the most versatile mind picture. The multilayered, deep and surface 'roots' (causes) lead to the 'tree' itself (the events), which (consequently) are attached to an array of 'branches'.
- Rollercoaster and grand prix – the religious changes of the Tudor period can be portrayed as a 'rollercoaster' and, of course, Banham (1998, 2000) describes the way he takes his pupils through the interpretive 'grand prix' of King John's reign.

Role-play

This is also an effective means of demonstrating the contingent nature of historical causation and consequence, as well as the complexity of motivation (see Towill, 1997; Luff, 2000; and for a fuller discussion of role-play see Chapter 9). Dawson (1996, p. 19) describes a fascinating way of showing pupils how the outcome of the Battle of Hastings could have been different. Using 'some sugar paper and a hairdryer', Dawson's role-play takes the pupils through the options presented to William and Harold and gives pupils 'a good grasp of the sequence of events, of the fact that things could have happened differently, of the difficulty of the decisions and why they were made'. In our *Total History Experience* research (Phillips and Cunnah, 2000), we devised a role-play to illustrate a very conceptual (and contingent!) issue, namely the alliance system prior to the First World War. Pupils were divided into countries and the complex and intricate linkage between them was shown using a piece of string.

Sequencing, sorting and categorizing exercises

Counsell (1997) argues that two inter-connected difficulties confront pupils as far as writing about causation and consequence are concerned, namely selecting which factors are relevant, and then sorting or categorizing them in a meaningful manner. She argues, therefore, that well managed, concrete sorting activities are essential to help them understand concepts like cause and consequence more effectively (see Chapters 8 and 9 for a detailed description of these strategies and Haydn *et al.* (1997) for further suggestions).

'Spider-links'

This involves a jumbled list of causes, with a parallel list of consequences. Pupils are asked to link, in pencil, the appropriate cause and consequence, and to justify their choice.

Understanding 'characteristic features' of the past: the 'E-word' by another name?

Few aspects of history teaching in the late twentieth century became more hotly debated and contested than the teaching of empathy (Knight, 1987). As I suggested in Chapter 2 and in *History Teaching, Nationhood and the State* (Phillips, 1998a), empathy was particularly singled out within the 'discourse of derision' of the New Right – by politicians and the media – as the epitome of the apparently misguided, woolly and ideological new history. Subsequently, empathy was officially disestablished from the liturgy of the National Curriculum and the GCSE in the 1990s. Furthermore, because of the controversy associated with empathy, many history teachers lost confidence in seeking to teach anything that could be construed as the 'E-word'.

In my view, this is a tragedy and reveals much about the absurdity of the politics and policy-making surrounding education in the last quarter of the twentieth century (see Phillips and Furlong, 2001). Like R. Davies (2001), cited at the beginning of this chapter, my essential argument here is that, if history teaching is not at the very least about trying (within obvious constraints) to show children what the 'otherness of the past' was really like, what is it about? (see also Lang, 1996). This is a particularly complex issue and before we can really understand the merits and demerits of the respective arguments, we need to define historical empathy and to examine its pedagogical origins.

Ever since the work of Keatinge (1910), teachers have seen the need to devise methods of reconstructing the past in order to encourage pupils to understand it. Yet historical empathy, like many other historical concepts, did not become institutionalized in history teaching until the 1970s and 1980s through the SCHP and the GCSE. The SCHP's development of empathy as an important aspect of history teaching stemmed from the belief that in order to meet adolescents' needs, history had to 'offer them the opportunity to experience vicariously an immense range of real human life and endeavour' (SCHP, 1976, p. 13). The belief was that by comparing their lives to people in the past, pupils would be able to find a clearer sense of their own identity.

Empathy became a central element of the GCSE, although the criteria did not actually use the word, but referred instead to 'an ability to look at events from the perspective of people in the past' (DES, 1985a, p. 3, par. 3). The Southern Regional Education Board (SREB) (1986, p. 13) defined it as an 'attempt to get to grips with the strangeness of the past'. This started from the premise that the past was a foreign country to students (see Cunnah *et al.*, 2001). Subsequently, HMI (DES, 1985b, p. 3) defined it in terms of thesis and anti-thesis: thus empathy could be viewed as 'the ability to enter into some informed appreciation of the predicaments or points of view of other people in the past', but there was also the warning that 'empathizing is not the same as identifying with, still less sympathizing with, people in the past'. Many recognized that empathy was a notoriously difficult concept both to define and achieve, but essentially it should be seen as 'the heart of historical understanding' (SREB, 1986, p. 13). Indeed, as Portal (1987a, p. 89) pointed out, empathy derived its name from the German 'einfühlung', meaning (essentially) an understanding of the world (see also Lee, 1984).

From the outset, researchers stressed that empathy should not be viewed simply as an opportunity for imagination, most commonly expressed in the form of the 'Imagine you are . . .' type exercise, which lent itself to historical anachronism, stereotyping and profound misunderstanding. The SREB (1986) publication (as above) stressed that historical empathy was very intellectually demanding, as it was concerned mainly with exploring motives, beliefs, ideas and situations in the past. It also suggested that pupils' understanding of empathy developed in the following way:

- Pupils first merely viewed sources as information about people in the past: *no empathy*

- Pupils then started to apply twentieth-century ideas to the past: *everyday empathy*

- Pupils then began to understand viewpoints in the past but this understanding was limited; for example, they were unable to appreciate that people had different viewpoints: *stereotypical empathy*

- Pupils could eventually begin to appreciate that people in the past not only held different views, ideas, beliefs and motives from their own, but that these could be complex and varied, with individuals possessing many different points of view: *differentiated empathy.*

Research by Ashby and Lee (1987), utilizing the work of Shemilt (1984), found similar patterns in pupils' understanding of historical empathy; at the lower levels, they identified what they termed 'the divi past', where pupils saw the past as unintelligible and essentially viewed people from the past as 'stupid' or 'thick' because they did things so differently from themselves. In order to achieve differentiated empathy – or what Ashby and Lee call 'contextual empathy' (Wineberg and Fournier (1994) also refer to 'contextualised thinking') – the researchers found that not only did teachers need to provide a rich variety of sources of evidence, they also had to provide a wide range of activities including varied source work and simulation exercises such as drama, role-play, letter writing and so on.

It is easy to see how empathy became such a subject of derision by the New Right and the media. As I have demonstrated elsewhere (Phillips, 1998a) it is little wonder that there were obviously problems teaching and assessing empathy (see Low-Beer, 1989), given the relative lack of research on the concept and the fact that all the research that had been done on it confirmed that it was difficult to achieve. There is evidence to suggest that many teachers did, in fact, resort to 'Imagine you are . . .' exercises and these were often highlighted by the press. New Right critics of history such as Deuchar (1989) Partington (1986) Lawlor (1990) and others launched into an attack on empathy with vigour. Given this attack, it is little wonder that the 'E-word' was not only left out of the National Curriculum and the revised GCSE, but also, as I have previously said, undermined the confidence of some teachers in using empathy-related tasks.

So, to repeat the question in the title of this chapter, 'what does it mean for us?'. Does it mean, in the words of Clements (1996), that historical empathy should 'rest in peace?'. Even the most cursory glance at the current National Curriculum, as well as GCSE and A/S level criteria, will demonstrate that this is not the case. There are obvious references to what we would recognize as historical empathy – based on some of the definitions used earlier – in a number of clear statements in the National Curriculum (DfEE, 1999b). Note how they relate closely to the HWG's definition of 'knowledge as understanding' (DES, 1990), stating that pupils should be taught:

- the 'range of ideas, beliefs, and attitudes of men, women and children in the past';
- the 'social, cultural, religious and ethnic diversity' of the past;
- to 'analyse and explain the reasons for, and results of, historical events, situations and changes'.

These all relate to elements of the SREB's (1986) idea of 'differentiated empathy' and Ashby and Lee's (1987) idea of 'contextual empathy'. But elements of historical empathy can also be seen in the reference to significance, which as we saw earlier involves pupils appreciating why certain events were important to people living at the time. In fact, if we take empathy to mean an attempt to understand the past, then it clearly is still at the heart of history teaching in the early twenty-first century and, as I made clear earlier, in its rightful place. This was reflected, for example, in the 100th edition of *Teaching History* entitled *Thinking and Feeling*, which contained a number of interesting suggestions and contexts through which pupils could think, feel and understand the past; these included role-play (Luff, 2000), in-depth analysis of values in the past (Illingworth, 2000), site visits (Wiltshire, 2000) and even drawing (Sheppard, 2000).

One of the most obvious ways of encouraging deep, contextual understanding of the past is by encouraging pupils to write – using Gardner's (1984) term – in 'intrapersonal' ways through letters, diaries, speeches and other genre located in the past (see Chapter 8 for a lengthy discussion of literacy and extended writing). Drawing upon the research of Counsell (1997) and Haydn *et al.* (1997, p. 100), it is important to emphasize that in order to avoid anachronism, generalization, stereotyping and misunderstanding, attention must be given by the teacher to:

- *Context* – ensuring that the pupils have access to the historical evidence in order to undertake the task in a rigorous and historically meaningful way
- *Purpose* – emphasizing that the objective of the task is to express the views of people at the time, thus avoiding anachronism
- *Structure* – little things matter; for example, if setting a letter writing exercise, care and attention must be taken over the name, address, precise date, starting and ending the letter, language and phrases used, and so on.

These sorts of guidelines should ensure that pupils do not view people in the past as 'divis' (Ashby and Lee, 1987; Lee *et al.*, 1996). They can also generate the type of contextualized thinking amongst pupils (Wineberg and Fournier, 1994) that is fundamental to acquiring the knowledge and understanding of events, people and changes in the past and that should be at the core of good history teaching at all levels. At A level, for example, Lang rightly argues that:

> until we really feel we know the characters we study, how can anything they did make sense? It is this leap of thinking, to get into the minds of the people we are studying, which constitutes the empathy which is the hallmark of good historical understanding.
>
> (Lang, 1996, p.7)

Following R. Davies, (2001) we need to be reminded that imagination – including historical imagination – is a vital element of teaching and learning (see Egan, 1992).

CHAPTER 5

Organizing, managing and planning the teaching and learning of history

> You don't realize what's involved in teaching until you've tried it. I realized after a term in school that actually teaching in the classroom is just the tip of the iceberg. You don't see the organization and planning that lies underneath it.
>
> (Student teacher, University of Wales Swansea, 2000)

Introduction

This chapter considers some of the vital organizational issues that relate to the teaching and learning of history. As we saw in the previous chapter, research indicates that one of the major concerns felt by many student history teachers is classroom management and control, with the foremost thought at the start of the course being: 'Will I be able to control my classes?' It needs to be said immediately that even the most gifted and experienced classroom teachers at some time experience challenges relating to classroom control. Yet for the vast majority of the time, these teachers organize their teaching and learning in such a way that classroom control does not become a preoccupying challenge. This chapter focuses upon some of their attributes and techniques. It starts from the premise, however, that classroom control is closely related to effective teaching and learning. In other words, if we can plan teaching activities that are interesting and appropriately challenging, we create a learning atmosphere that is conducive to learning, as opposed to disruption. A boring history classroom is invariably also a disrupted history classroom. *Plan lessons well – classroom mgmt becomes less of an issue.*

What is 'effective teaching'? Knowledge, skills and qualities

The notion of what constitutes an appropriate definition of 'effective teaching' is a challenging one, which has exerted the interests of researchers for some time (Cooper and McIntyre, 1992; Stephens and Crawley, 1994). The most comprehensive and systematic of the issues is in my view provided by Kyriacou (1992, 1995). Like John (1991, see also Chapter 1), Kyriacou argues that 'effectiveness' depends upon range of knowledge, skills and attributes, which he calls 'holistic qualities'. He argues that it is impossible to define effectiveness too precisely (a weakness of the Standards perhaps?) because there are a 'number of different ways in which teachers may be effective, and these different ways appear to rely on different characteristics' (Kyriacou, 1992, p. 108). However, after interviewing and observing many different teachers and doing an exhaustive search of the literature, Kyriacou identified a 'set of qualities' that seemed to be generic to most 'effective' teachers. These include:

- *Preparedness*: including good organization, structure and sense of purpose
- *Pace and flow*: keeping pupils involved and attentive, as well as dealing with the unexpected
- *Transition*: gaining attention at the start and then maintaining attention when moving from one activity to the next
- *Cognitive matching*: gearing lessons to pupils' abilities and interests, setting work that is appropriately challenging and catering for individual differences amongst pupils
- *Clarity*: teacher instructions and explanations are clear and pitched so that pupils can understand
- *Business-like*: relates mainly to the impression created by the teacher, including a sense of authority, firmness and confidence; reaction to misbehaviour; and positive expectations of the quality of work and behaviour required
- *'Withitness'*: perhaps the most difficult to define, this relates to alertness, the ability to anticipate difficulties and to pre-empt misbehaviour or take swift action when it occurs; 'withitness' also involves sensitivity to pupils' inattention and inability to do the work set, and to take action accordingly
- *'Encouragingness'*: the ways in which teachers use a mixture of praise, instructive criticism, enthusiasm and humour to create a positive atmosphere and good pupil–teacher relations.

The descriptions of what constitutes effective teaching provided by HMI, OFSTED and ESTYN, on the whole, mirror Kyriacou's research. The OFSTED (1993) criteria for effective teaching, for example, stressed the following qualities:

- Teachers have clear objectives
- Pupils are aware of the objectives
- Teachers have a secure command of the subject being taught
- Content is suitably selected
- Activities are planned to promote learning
- Teaching is engaging, motivating and challenging
- Assessment is used to promote the above
- Lessons are conducted at a suitable pace.

As Kyriacou (1995, p. 8) suggests, although 'there is no blueprint for the perfect lesson', inspectors over the years have 'expressed certain preferences', namely:

- Lessons should be purposeful, with high expectations
- Pupils should be given opportunities to organize their own work, as opposed to lessons being dominated by teacher-led activity
- Pupil interest should be promoted by making lessons relevant and challenging
- Work needs to be appropriately well-matched to pupils needs and abilities
- The language used by pupils needs to be extended, with teachers' questioning techniques being important in this respect

- Teachers should utilize a variety of teaching and learning activities
- Classroom control needs to be based upon involving pupils in the lesson and mutual respect between pupil and teacher.

Clearly, in order to achieve these sorts of characteristics and qualities, teachers need to develop certain skills and abilities. Kyriacou (1995, pp. 10–11) identifies the following 'essential skills' in teaching:

1. Planning and preparation: The ability to select aims and objectives, as well as the best means of achieving them.
2. Lesson presentation: The ability to engage pupils in the learning process via instruction.
3. Lesson management: The ability to organize and manage teaching and learning activities that maintain pupils' attention and interest.
4. Classroom climate: The ability to maintain positive attitudes in the classroom and to motivate pupils towards learning.
5. Assessing pupils' progress: The ability to use assessment (both formative and summative: see Chapter 10) to promote learning.
6. Reflection and evaluation: The ability to reflect on one's practice in order to improve it further.

Using this research, the Standards and my own experience, at Swansea I offer my students the definition shown in Figure 5.1 of what it means to be an effective and reflective ('E & R') history teacher. (Note: these characteristics should be read within the context of the previous chapter and by making reference to the Standards themselves.)

I now want to focus upon each of the skills shown in Figure 5.1 in more detail. Planning, presentation skills, and lesson management issues are considered below, while assessment is dealt with separately in Chapter 10. You will find that the issues relating to 'classroom climate', as well as the capacity to 'reflect and evaluate' permeate this book.

Lesson management, control and organization

Issues relating to the management and control of lessons are priorities for student teachers. It would be foolish to claim that in a short section like this, I can cover 'all you need to know' about class management and control – this requires direct obser-vation in the classroom, practical experience and further reading (e.g. McManus, 1993; Robertson, 1989; Smith and Laslett, 1993; Wragg, 1993). But at least I can begin with some sound advice, based upon what some of this extensive research tells us. A good starting point is to consider the structure of 'typical' lessons. Although Kyriacou (1992, 1995) and others rightly suggest that there is a danger in attempting to define the 'typical lesson' too rigidly, nevertheless it is clear from observation that the majority of lessons have the following structure:

- *'Lesson introduction'*: This is perhaps the most crucial point, when the tone for the rest of the lesson is often set. Here, a range of factors come into play, from practical issues such as how the pupils enter the room and the ways in which the teacher imposes control, to more technical issues such as the way in which the teacher outlines the aims and objectives of the lesson and gains the pupils' attention.

- '*Main part*': This is where teaching aims are converted into learning activities via a range of tasks and activities. The success of this part of the lesson depends upon a range of variable factors, for example, how appropriate the selected tasks and activities are for the pupils, whether they know what is expected of them, whether the work is being monitored effectively and what methods are being used to ensure that pupils are kept 'on task'.

- '*Conclusion*': Lessons have to be properly concluded, where opportunities are provided for summarizing what has been achieved, assessing whether objectives have been met, providing opportunities for homework and ensuring that the class departs in an orderly fashion.

Clearly, the transitions in the lesson provide opportunities for potential disruption, pupil misbehaviour and subsequent loss of control. It is therefore clear to see why Smith and Laslett (1993; pp. 3–13) argue that there are essentially four major stages and accompanying 'rules' of effective classroom management.

Rule 1: 'getting them in'
Rule 2: 'getting on with it'
Rule 3: 'getting on with them'
Rule 4: 'getting them out'.

One of the most important things to consider as a student teacher is: what causes pupil misbehaviour? Capel *et al.* (1997), building upon the work of Kyriacou (1995), argue that the following factors account for most pupil misbehaviour:

- Boredom
- Excessive intellectual demands
- Frustration
- Low self-esteem
- Attitudes ('what's the point?')
- Emotional difficulties
- Lack of pastoral support in school
- School ethos
- Peer pressure
- Dislike of the teacher.

The analysis above shows that student teachers need to be aware that many of the factors that cause disruption and misbehaviour in the classroom are sometimes beyond their control. Equally there are many other factors that *are* within their remit to control. Most of the research literature suggests that conveying a sense of authority is vital for class management and control. Again, however, this puts student teachers in something of a predicament, because they lack some of the vital ingredients – such as reputation and status – that experienced teachers possess. That is why expert teacher educators and trainers, such as Furlong, advocate a 'phased in' approach to the classroom, as opposed to student teachers being 'thrown in at the deep end' or thrust into the lion's den! Nevertheless, although student teachers do not possess 'situated status' (held by experienced teachers), research conducted by Wragg (1984), Robertson (1989) and Kyriacou (1992, 1995) suggests there are a number of things that can be done in order to increase a student teacher's authority:

Features of effective and reflective ('E & R') history teachers

Knowledge and application

- The subject knowledge of the history teacher is good but it can also be packaged and applied effectively
- Key elements are used to inform planning

Planning

- Lesson plans are detailed, innovative and thorough
- Learning objectives are very clear and achievable
- Tasks are carefully matched to pupils' individual needs (differentiation)
- Resources are produced to supplement departmental resources

Teaching and learning techniques

- Lesson introductions are exciting, grab the attention and are varied
- Instructions, explanations and demonstrations are vivid, precise and informative
- Questioning technique is varied, correctly pitched and involves the maximum number of pupils
- Tasks are carefully managed in order to ensure maximum amount of time spent 'on task'
- Teaching methods are varied and appropriate and are always geared towards pupils' learning needs
- Full use is made of a variety of teaching aids
- The pace of the lessons is brisk and time is used efficiently
- Enough time is devoted to lesson endings in order to conclude and sum up key points

Class management and control/relationship with pupils

- Lesson introductions, transitions and endings are well managed
- Awareness and vigilance is always maintained
- Control of noise and talk is appropriate to learning tasks and outcomes
- Praise and encouragement are used appropriately
- The quality of relationships with the vast majority of pupils is good and based upon a healthy mutual respect

Monitoring and assessing pupils' progress

- Awareness is displayed of pupils' learning needs and frequent attempts are made to check pupil understanding
- Time is devoted to checking that learning objectives have been met
- Regular and appropriate feedback is given to pupils so that they can progress

Effectiveness

- Effective approaches are used for whole-class, group, paired and individual teaching
- High expectations are set for work and behaviour – pupils are challenged appropriately (progression)
- Discipline is sound
- Enthusiasm is displayed
- The quality of pupils' learning is given maximum priority

Professional qualities

- Awareness of pupils needs, over and above the needs of the teacher
- Organization
- Appropriately self-critical
- Research-orientated
- Able to accept objective advice
- Able to take on new ideas and pass on new ideas to others
- Awareness of wider professional issues
- A desire to learn new ideas to improve pupils' learning

Figure 5.1 *Definitions of what it means to be an effective and reflective ('E & R') history teacher*

Acting

Lack of 'situated status' can be compensated for by at least acting as though we possess it. Teaching is often compared to acting, so why not 'act' as though we possess status? The way we present ourselves, communicate with pupils and organize the classroom are vital. Even though we may not feel confident, it is *vital* that we attempt to present a sense of confidence to the pupils. Flores (2001) and Weber and Mitchell (1995) contain fascinating discussions on the traditional 'image' of the teacher, and the ways in which student teachers have to adapt.

Non-verbal communication

Conveying authority and status does not have to be done by shouting; often the most effective teachers are those that exert authority and maintain control via non-verbal techniques (Neill, 1991) and body language (Neill and Caswell, 1993). For example, it may be appropriate to stand in front of the class at certain times but then walk around the room at others. Hand gesticulations used to convey enthusiasm or to make demands, for example folding one's arms when waiting for silence. Eye contact is also essential, either in terms of 'scanning' as many pupils as possible or the use of the occasional sharp 'glare and stare' to demand a change of behaviour (see below).

Monitoring techniques

Capel *et al.* (1995, 1997) and Kyriacou (1992, 1995) advocate the following:

- Scanning: Position yourself appropriately and frequently look around the room
- Circulating: Do not stand in the same place all the time; anticipate problems and check pupils are 'on task'
- Eye contact: Address the whole class, not just certain individuals
- Asking questions: To involve as many pupils as possible (see below)
- Using space: Either to circulate amongst pupils or to separate pupils when necessary
- Supporting: Giving appropriate help, encouragement, rewards and motivation
- Changing activity: Checking that pupils have finished or signalling what to do next

- **Encouraging individuals:** Ensure that pupils know that you are aware of their progress; getting to know pupils as individuals is absolutely vital, starting with remembering their names!
- **Acting:** Insist on 'ground rules' (see below).

It should be emphasized that these measures are not just vital for control but also for effective learning. Thus, Mercer (1995) describes in detail the ways these techniques can be used to promote what he terms 'the guided construction of knowledge'.

Laying the ground rules

Observation is particularly vital in relation to all of the above; student teachers should ideally spend time observing the common rules and regulations in use in the classroom, so that they get to know the routines with which the pupils themselves are familiar. The extensive research of Wragg and Wood (1984, p. 67) demonstrated that the following rules were the most commonly used in the classroom (in order of frequency):

- No talking when the teacher is talking
- No disruptive noises
- Rules for entering, leaving and moving in classrooms
- No interference with the work of others
- Work must be completed in a specified way
- Pupils must raise their hand to answer, not shout out
- Pupils must make a positive effort in their work
- Pupils must not challenge the authority of the teacher
- Respect should be shown for property and equipment
- Rules to do with safety
- Pupils must ask if they do not understand.

As was said in Chapter 1, observation is vital here; if the student teacher is not aware of the 'routinized' rules and regulations that are familiar to pupils and starts using entirely different ones, this may have a profoundly negative impact. On the other hand, there is scope for limited mediation; all teachers are different, favouring slightly alternative methods and the student teacher needs to decide, within reason, upon tried and tested strategies that are best suited to him or her. The important thing is that these rules and regulations need to be articulated to pupils, repeated and implemented consistently.

Pre-empting and dealing with misbehaviour

I started this chapter with the claim that if we teach history in a way that arouses curiosity and prevents boredom, then pupil misbehaviour is likely to be reduced and I want to reiterate that point here. In addition, the non-verbal and monitoring techniques, as well as the ground rules above, will assist in this process. Nevertheless, misbehaviour will still occur and in order to deal with it, the following advice on reprimands by Capel *et al.* (1995, pp. 112–14) is probably some of the best informed by research; this needs to be considered within the context of their list of causes of misbehaviour cited above:

- Reprimands should be conducted, wherever possible, in a 'low level' way; when reprimanding a pupil, the rest of the class should be allowed to continue working

- Avoid anger but emphasize other features such as concern and disappointment
- Avoid confrontation – private rather than public reprimands mean that pupils do not 'lose face' in front of the rest of the class
- Do not debate with pupils – if necessary, state that you will discuss the matter after class
- Avoid personal criticisms or comparing certain pupils to others
- Direct comments to the pupils' work
- Avoid 'blanket' reprimands or sanctions to the whole class, which alienate many pupils
- Maintain consistency and fairness when handing out sanctions
- Be aware of the school's policies on sanctions and use them in a hierarchical way
- Do not be afraid to use the support network in school.

This last point needs to be mentioned for, if the student teacher has attempted all the strategies mentioned in this section, then it is only fair – and should not be perceived as a sign of weakness – that other teachers and whole-school mechanisms, should be used to help. One thing should have been apparent from the above, however; that planning and preparation are vital for organizing and controlling classes effectively.

Planning for effective teaching and learning in history

Planning is probably the most important aspect of effective history teaching and learning. This may seem a fairly obvious statement to make, but many experienced history teachers who possess implicit professional craft knowledge in abundance often seem to the inexperienced observer to plan 'on their feet' so to speak. This is a gross simplification, as teachers draw upon a vast array of professional craft knowledge when planning (John, 1991). Inexperienced practitioners, on the other hand, do not have this wealth of knowledge on which to draw and their planning therefore has to be very explicit and carefully constructed. The remainder of this chapter suggests a range of ways in which history lessons can be planned to make the subject interesting, accessible and appropriately challenging in a wide variety of contexts. One of the first questions we need to consider is: *what are we planning for?* The previous chapter argued that the central imperative in the teaching process is to recognize the learning needs of pupils, and it follows that the main objective of the planning process is to ensure that the most conducive atmosphere is created for pupils to learn effectively.

Before we evaluate the main ways of achieving this, it may well be worth while considering the particular challenges facing student teachers as far as planning is concerned. Given that students teachers lack the professional craft knowledge of their more experienced colleagues they are faced with a number of particular challenges. Haydn *et al.* (1997) suggest, for example, that they face the following difficulties in relation to planning:

- 'Packaging' the subject knowledge in an effective way
- Balancing historical content, concepts and skills
- Being pre-occupied with control issues to the extent where planning becomes centred upon 'coping' strategies, 'settling' activities and 'low-value' tasks

always try + challenge.

- Reconciling the needs of the history department with the needs of the student teacher
- Concentrating upon short-term rather than medium- and long-term planning.

A good starting point for overcoming these difficulties is to consider very carefully from the outset what we actually mean by 'effective teaching' (see back to the definitions of effective history teaching given in Figure 5.1). Another starting point, as Capel *et al.* (1995) suggest, is that we ask a number of fundamental questions – practical as well as conceptual – when embarking upon planning. These include:

- What am I trying to achieve?
- What has been taught before?
- How much time is available to do this work?
- What resources are available?
- How is the work to be assessed?
- How does this work fit in with other work that pupils are doing?
- What is to be taught later on?

Based upon the above, then, it follows that when planning lessons, a number of specific issues have to be considered.

1. *Specific learning objectives*: A crucial phrase that every teacher should be asking at the beginning of the planning process is 'by the end of this lesson or series of lessons, pupils will be able to do X, Y and Z'.
2. *The range of abilities of the pupils*: As we saw in the previous chapter, pupils have a multiplicity of differing learning needs; they bring particular skills, strengths and weaknesses to the classroom, which have to be catered for. Differentiation is therefore vital (see Chapter 8).
3. *The time available*: One of the most frustrating things for student teachers is to gauge, accurately, the amount of time that certain activities will take. However, this soon comes with experience.
4. *The resources available*: It is pointless planning for a range of teaching and learning activities if the resources are not available to teach them. An important piece of advice here is not to 'reinvent the wheel' as far as resources are concerned, but to supplement what already exists within the history department.
5. *Selecting appropriate teaching strategies*: These will depend, again, upon the learning needs of the pupils. In the previous chapter I argued that, given the diverse learning needs of pupils, a broad range of teaching and learning activities have to be planned for.
6. *Appropriate assessment methods and opportunities*: Experience suggests that planning can often disregard assessment. Appropriate opportunities have to be provided, particularly for diagnostic assessment, which can promote planning, effective teaching and learning (see Chapter 10).
7. *Evaluation*: Planning is necessarily informed by what has gone on previously and therefore a central, ongoing question in the planning process is: *what do pupils know now and where do they go next?*

Haydn *et al.* (1997) argue that within history teaching there are certain 'starting points' for planning:

- Certain topics lend themselves to particular approaches: Intuition and experience will help here.
- Asking questions about the topic: A good 'way-in' to any topic is for the teacher to brainstorm as many questions about a topic as possible (see Chapter 6).
- Drawing upon pupils' knowledge: It is pointless assuming that pupils possess certain knowledge about a topic; attempts have to be made to find out what they know about a topic and to cultivate this accordingly. On the other hand, a safe piece of advice here is to assume the worst!
- Making connections between the past and the present: As we saw in the previous chapter, a key to unlocking children's understanding is to connect with their existing, lived experience, so that opportunities in the planning should be provided to go from 'the known to the unknown' and not the other way around.
- Approaching the topic in an oblique manner: This is a highly effective way of captivating pupil interest; I refer to this in Chapter 6 as 'Initial Stimulus Material' (ISM).
- Resources as the starting point: This involves seeing the enormous potential in certain resources and making full use of them when planning lessons.
- Using concepts as the starting point: Sometimes we may wish to concentrate explicitly upon certain concepts in the planning process.

Clearly, there are a lot of things to think about when planning. Figure 5.2 provides a check-list of questions to help you plan effectively.

Check-list for effective planning

Before the lesson

- What am I trying to achieve?
- What do I want the pupils to have learned?
- What content do I need to teach?
- What concepts do I want the pupils to learn?
- Have I some key questions to organize the lesson around?
- What do the pupils already know?
- How much time is available to me?
- What resources, materials and equipment am I going to use?
- How am I going to organize and distribute (manage) these?
- Do I know how to use them?

Lesson introduction

- How am I going to start the lesson (using recap or ISM)?
- What questions am I going to ask?
- Will the pupils have a clear idea of what is expected of them?
- What words/difficult terms do I need to prepare for/anticipate?
- How long will the introduction take?

Main part

- What teaching/learning activities am I going to use?
- How am I going to explain the instructions?
- Are pupils going to be working as individuals or in pairs/groups?
- How am I going to differentiate?
- Do I need extension activities?
- What do I need to assess?
- How am I going to assess pupils' progress?
- How can I ensure smooth transitions?
- How long will all this take?

Conclusion

- What do I want pupils to know as a consequence of this lesson?
- How much time do I need for the conclusion?
- How am I going to conclude?
- Do I need to set homework?
- If so, how much and when is it to be handed in?
- What do I need to collect?
- Have I checked that all resources have been returned?
- How are pupils going to leave the room?
- What do I need to consider for next lesson?
- What will I want pupils to achieve next lesson?

Figure 5.2 *Check-list for effective planning*

CHAPTER 6

Making history curious: the use of Initial Stimulus Material (ISM), questions and enquiry in history teaching

> It is the learners' voices we must hear, and if they are questioning voices we should rejoice, for learning is a matter of personally engaged struggle rather than detached acquiescence.
>
> (Levine, 1981)

Introduction

This chapter relies heavily upon the findings of *The Total History Experience* research (Phillips, 2002a) and has been published in an article for *Teaching History* (Phillips, 2001b). One of the major aims of the project was to conceptualize an idea that we had been developing and experimenting with at Swansea for nearly ten years, namely the use of what we call Initial Stimulus Material (ISM). This chapter therefore provides a definition of what we mean by ISM and then goes on to consider the contexts in which it can be used in the history classroom across all key stages and at A/S. The chapter also discusses at some length the use of effective questioning in history. The central argument is that ISM, connected to lines of enquiry and key questions, can have the effect of making the subject curious, stimulating and exciting.

Towards a definition of Initial Stimulus Material (ISM)

The beginning of Terry Jones' BBC series *The Crusades* begins with a short, vivid scene of a massacre undertaken by Crusaders, which immediately arouses curiosity amongst the viewers, centring upon the question: 'Why did this event take place?' This technique, in fact, is a classic feature of Initial Stimulus Material. Essentially, ISM refers to:

- the ways in which historical material can be organized to stimulate interest and curiosity;
- the establishment of a line of enquiry or the posing of a hypothesis about a historical issue via a key question or a series of questions;
- the means by which we can outline aims and objectives in a clever, meaningful way.

As I will attempt to show here, if used correctly, ISM can have enormous dividends, not only for arousing curiosity at the start of the lesson, but for establishing the right learning environment for subsequent lessons, particularly in terms of connecting key questions or lines of enquiry with follow-up activities, including extended writing. Our research found also that ISM could be used to cultivate conceptual understanding, and help in the acquisition of vocabulary and terminology.

ISM, then, is the method of introducing an issue or topic in a deliberately 'oblique' manner (see Haydn *et al.*, 1997, p. 42). It derives theoretical inspiration and empirical research-based evidence from Piaget and Vygotsky. First, by turning Piagetian theory on its head in stressing that we 'go from concrete to the conceptual' with pupils. Second, following Vygotsky, that we emphasize the social context of pupils' learning and use teaching examples that connect with pupils' 'known' experience. This is particularly important in the cultivation of historical knowledge and understanding, which research has shown requires vicarious experiences that children do not often possess (Lee and Ashby, 2000). The following examples of ISM will give you a clearer picture of what I mean.

The execution of Charles I as ISM for the seventeenth century: a case study

During the *Total History Experience* project, we asked a group of student teachers to suggest how they would introduce the seventeenth century to a mixed ability Year 8 class. Students responded with the reasonable suggestion to start with the causes of the Civil Wars, specifically perhaps with the reign of James I. However, we explained to the students that this may not be the best way of arousing curiosity. If we take it as axiomatic that we need to engage with pupils' learning in a concrete manner and in a way that takes them from the 'known to the unknown', it may make more logical sense to actually begin the study not with causation (which is highly conceptual) but with a pivotal event, such as a battle scene or a key personality. In fact, the famous Dutch print of Charles I's execution is an excellent 'way in' to explaining many of the extraordinary events of the seventeenth century (Carter *et al.* (1989, p. 106) also use this right at the start of their section on the Civil Wars). Let me explain why this sort of source is a good starting point and, in the process, show how ISM can be managed to obtain maximum effect. I do this by making direct reference to a lesson I taught jointly with one of my student teachers.

Although visual sources are excellent as ISM, written sources are also good ISM, as will become clear later in the chapter. However, the Dutch print graphically illustrates a whole series of things that can be used to encourage a far wider discussion and level of historical understanding. Having settled down at the start of the lesson, pupils were presented immediately with the print on an OHP. We deliberately avoided telling the pupils that they would be starting to look at the seventeenth century. Instead, they were simply asked the open-ended question: 'What can you see?' After some prompting and encouragement (including asking some pupils to come very close to the OHP), pupils identified the following:

'somebody having his head chopped off'
'loads of blood'
'a bloke holding a head'
'a large crowd'
'somebody fainting'
'somebody turning his head away'.

The *oblique* nature of the ISM, as well as its context, immediately aroused the curiosity of the pupils. But ISM must always be accompanied by carefully considered questions. This is where *effective planning* is vital to the successful utilization of ISM, in order to extract maximum opportunities for learning. Note how the questions we asked (listed below) encouraged the pupils to make sense of what they were seeing and started to lead them towards a particular line of enquiry (the italicized words in brackets refer to abbreviated answers provided by pupils):

- OK, so you said that this was 'somebody having his head chopped off'. Can anyone tell me another word for this? (*execution*)
- Given that there was such a large crowd there, do you think the person being executed was ordinary or famous? (*most probably famous* – although we pointed out that the execution of ordinary people also drew large crowds)
- From this can anyone tell me what type of person was being executed? (*a King*)
- Can anyone tell me the name of the King? (eventually . . . *Charles I*)
- Can anyone tell me in which century this execution took place? (*no idea* – so we told them the century and wrote the precise date of the execution on the whiteboard)

It is at this point that the oblique nature of the ISM is made explicit to the pupils. In this case, we outlined the aims and objectives not only of this particular lesson, but what they would be studying over the next few weeks, based around a number of key questions. Even at this stage, however, we did not simply give the questions to the pupils, instead we encouraged them to think them out for themselves:

- What were the events that led up to the King's execution?
- Why was the King executed?
- What were the results of his execution?
- Why was this event so significant in British history?

Note here the ways in which key questions can be used to establish aims and objectives, lines of enquiry or a hypothesis. As far as this first lesson was concerned, we decided to interrogate the evidence further by encouraging the pupils to consider other aspects of the source. We asked them to look carefully again at the crowd, particularly at the person fainting and the other who was turning away in horror and then to speculate about why they were doing so. We also asked them to look carefully at what was happening at the top of the source. After a speculative question and discussion, pupils realized that this represented the King's soul ascending to heaven, which also led to a brief discussion on the notion of divine right.

A whole range of possibilities could have been open to us at this point. For example, we could have asked the pupils to consider whether the creator of this source was a supporter or an opponent of the King, thus raising issues of provenance, evidence and interpretation. But at this stage the intention of the ISM was to maintain curiosity and provoke questioning. One of the beauties of ISM is that it can often be used again later; indeed, as I said in Chapter 4, there is nothing more useful, in teaching and learning terms, than for a teacher to be able to say 'Do you remember when we did this?' In this case, the print could be used later as an opportunity to build on pupils' existing contextual knowledge and channel it towards an analysis of interpretation by contrasting it, say, with a Puritan view of the execution, written accounts and other sources, such as the film *Cromwell* (see Shephard *et al.*, 1992, p. 61). But for ISM purposes at this initial stage, we decided to give pupils an A4 copy of the print and then asked them, in pairs, to brainstorm as many questions about it as possible. The results showed how good pupils are at asking questions (often better, in fact, than adults):

- Why was he executed?
- Who did this?
- Why were the people upset?
- Were all people upset or angry?
- How many people were at the execution?
- Why was the King's soul going to heaven?
- What happened after the execution?

They also show that the objectives of the ISM, as defined at the beginning of this chapter, were now complete:

- pupils were curious to know how and why the King had been executed;
- a clear line of enquiry, geared to key questions, about the origins and consequences of the Civil Wars had been established;
- aims and objectives had been given to the pupils in a meaningful manner.

Managing ISM effectively: some 'do's and don'ts'

Before moving on to discuss other types of ISM, a number of essential 'do's and don'ts' about planning for ISM have to be established:

- When using a visual source, *do not give too much information away*. Remember that the power of ISM is that it is deliberately *oblique*; thus be patient. This is where an effective questioning technique is vital (see Morgan and Saxton (1991) for an excellent discussion of effective questioning: for further discussion see the 'Questioning' section later on in this chapter). The temptation is for the teacher to jump in and 'tell' the pupils all about the source, but this merely undermines the whole purpose of ISM, which is to arouse curiosity amongst pupils by helping them to ask meaningful questions about the evidence.
- *Questions* therefore have to be *carefully planned*; they have to be *realistic*, that is, based upon pupils' existing knowledge, as well as their known conceptual capabilities and understanding. A question like 'What was the precise date of the execution?' would most likely have initiated a negative response. Even a question that immediately asks for the name of the King is inappropriate because it does not connect with most children's 'known' experience. In the case study above, our initial questions related to the type of person the executed man was: pupils realized he was important and therefore concluded that he was likely to be a king. In other words, questions have to be planned in a clear order of gradation: from simple information gathering, to advanced speculative or hypothesis-generating questions (Bruner would, of course, identify this type of questioning as 'scaffolding': see Chapter 3).
- It follows that when using ISM, it is *vital not to over-estimate pupils' conceptual knowledge, understanding or vocabulary*. This is why effective planning is absolutely crucial. Questions, likely responses, key words and concepts have to be considered extremely carefully in the planning process. Moreover, to consolidate the ISM, it is also very useful, if not essential, that words, ideas, names, dates and key questions

are presented visually to the pupils in order to consolidate the aims and objectives by moving from oblique clues to explicit explanations and instructions.

- *Make the most of resources* that are available to you. ISM material does not have to be spectacular. Very often, the best ISMs are those contained in textbooks. The mistake that many inexperienced teachers make is to underutilize the visual and written resources available.

Planning to use different types of ISM for different learning objectives

It is tempting to think that only visual sources are useful as ISM, and that its purpose is only to arouse curiosity. But by thinking about ISM as a *generic* (i.e. transferable) learning concept, I now want to show how ISM can be used in a wide variety of forms and contexts and, crucially, for different learning purposes.

Written ISM

This is just as effective as visual ISM, particularly when it is used alongside other ISM material. For example, consider the types of questions that are likely to be initiated from the following description of the Black Death:

> In men and women the plague first showed itself by the appearance of swellings in the groin and armpits. Some were as large as apples or eggs. From these two parts of the body boils spread in all directions and black spots appeared on the armpits.

The same formula of questions, concepts and key words applies. But it is also important to remember that ISM can be used in combination. Here, the quotation could be used alongside other stimulus material, such as a visual image of medieval people being buried, a map showing the spread of the plague across Europe; a rat; a flea; or even the nursery rhyme 'Ring-a-ring-o' roses'! The list is endless. This sort of brainstorming, of course, demonstrates the versatility of ISM and its multifaceted nature.

Storytelling

This can also be an excellent way of arousing curiosity. Michael Riley and I have both used an extract from Thomas Hardy's *Jude the Obscure* with pupils. The extract – differentiated where appropriate and used alongside the marvellous scene from the film adaption for maximum effect – describes Jude's experience of being beaten in the fields by his farmer-employer. It provides an excellent ISM for an investigative enquiry of working conditions experienced by young children in the nineteenth century, particularly when it is contrasted, say, with idealistic Victorian paintings portraying a sort of 'Golden Age' of rural life. ISM therefore provides an excellent 'way in' to key elements and concepts, in this case the use of interpretations.

'Uninteresting' ISM

The *Total History Experience* research found that as soon as student teachers began using ISM regularly and in sophisticated ways, even the most seemingly dull things could be used to stimulating effect. One of our student teachers, for example, used a list of *War Deaths 1914–1918*, broken down into specific countries, as ISM. It is notoriously difficult at times to demonstrate to pupils the profound significance and resonance of mortality statistics. These were used alongside some visual stimulation and a strong concrete illustration comparing the number of deaths and wounded on the first day of the Battle of the Somme to the number of people at a football match at

Old Trafford. The ISM led on to a computer-based lesson comparing percentages of casualties per country, which also contributed very effectively to wider key skills. Note how the teacher used examples from the pupils' 'known experience' (the size of the crowd at Old Trafford) to help pupils grasp the true horror of that first day on the Somme.

Concrete ISM

The reference above to *concrete* examples reminds us that some of the most oblique ISM can be the most effective for promoting curiosity and stimulation. One of the best examples of this within the project was when one student teacher provided pupils with some spices, a piece of silk, pictures of concentric castles and other architectural styles, numbers and fruit, in order to demonstrate the impact of Islam upon Europe, via the Crusades, leading to a discussion of both significance, change and cause/consequence. The following fascinating extract from another student teacher's notes for the *Total History Experience* also illustrates the power of concrete examples:

> My ISM involved using the board for a comparison between Charles I (illustrated by a postcard) and Elizabeth II (illustrated by a five pound note). We looked at the dates of their reigns and, most importantly, their role and power. I led the discussions, and had the answers printed on bits of paper which I stuck up with blue tack. I tried to explain the relationship between Anglicans, Catholics and Puritans by using a carrot, a tomato and an apple. These could be divided into fruit and vegetables, to make one division, Catholicism and Protestantism. But I also wanted to emphasize that all three objects are also very different from each other (colour, texture, size, shape).

Concrete ISM is also invaluable for teaching pupils about key elements and concepts. Weighing scales can be used to illustrate 'weighing-up evidence'; the analogy of a 'volcano' is useful for demonstrating cause and effect. Counsell (1997) uses the concrete example of ripples in a pond to show the short-, medium- and long-term consequences of events.

ISM *and 'difficult' topics and concepts*

An important aim of our research was to discover ways in which ISM could be used to make particularly demanding concepts and topics easier to understand. Thus, much to their curiosity, pupils were given jelly babies at the start of a lesson on the First World War; later, it was explained to them that jelly babies originated from 'peace babies' which were handed out to children at the end of the War to celebrate the armistice (see Chapter 4). This helps to bring home to pupils a complex concept like commemoration. Another notoriously difficult concept in this respect is parliamentary reform and the struggle for the franchise. Many pupils find it inconceivable that people in the nineteenth century should think the vote so important, not only reminding us that pupils sometimes tend to see people in the past as 'divis' (see Lee and Ashby, 2000), but also reflecting pupils' apathy towards citizenship and political activity. We found that *past/present analogies* were useful here. Thus, a graphic contemporary picture from the Welsh newspaper *The Western Mail* showing Welsh farmers demonstrating through the streets of Cardiff in the late 1990s about rural poverty was used as a 'way in' to the concept of protest. The picture showed a long procession of people carrying placards behind a coffin draped with the Welsh flag to represent the 'death' of Welsh farming. The ISM led to a discussion about why the people felt so strongly about the need to protest. On another occasion, we used a role-play in which certain pupils were deliberately and unfairly disenfranchised from school decision-making, in order to show the importance of the vote and political participation. It reminded us, too, of the effectiveness of role-play in the history classroom for representing conceptual ideas in a concrete manner (see Luff, 2000). Our research found that the power of the past/ present analogy lies in its ability to penetrate the deepest aspects of the 'foreign country' that is history (see Cunnah *et al.*, 2001), including motivation and empathy.

ISM and ICT

It goes without saying, of course, that ICT is a wonderfully versatile method of utilizing ISM in an exciting manner. The Internet and PowerPoint, in particular, seem almost tailor-made for ISM. Alfano (2000, p. 43) argues that 'attention-grabbing lesson-openings, setting out a clear and exciting historical purpose to the whole enquiry, are just as important in lessons based around ICT as they are at other times' (see Chapter 11). Tape recordings are also useful; one of our mentors used a tape recording from *Braveheart* as ISM to show the noise generated by battle, a versatile resource that could be used in a variety of contexts. The project also showed that short video extracts are extremely useful as ISM. Contemporary films such as *Elizabeth*, *The Trench* (or in Wales, *Hedd Wyn*), *Jude the Obscure*, *The Land Girls* and *Saving Private Ryan* are remarkably effective for impact (again, see Chapter 11 for a more detailed discussion of the use of video).

Historical words and phrases

If history is a 'foreign country', then it also has a foreign language comprising historical words, terms and phrases that can make excellent ISMs. Ever wondered where phrases such as 'laughing stock', 'minding your Ps and Qs', 'moot point' or 'bob's your uncle' come from? Are you curious? In good ISM fashion, I'll let you find out – buy the excellent *Lock Stock and Barrel* book published by Past Times (1998) and you'll see!

The *Total History Experience* research showed that ISM is a versatile, stimulating technique that can be applied in a range of different contexts across *all* key stages and at A/S level. We found that it was very useful for motivating pupils to do extended writing and particularly good for 'choosing and planting' enquiry questions (Riley, 2000). Of course, ISM is not new: the vast majority of good history teachers use ISM every day. In one of the best articles to appear in *Teaching History* in recent years, Michael Gorman (1998, p. 23) explains how techniques were used so that 'pupils' motivation was enhanced by the fact that they could envision the end product'. He goes on to describe what he calls the 'motivating starting points' that he has used to set the scene for extended writing, including 'a detailed picture of an unusual scene, or a portrait, story, description of some gruesome facts, looking at artefacts, outside visitor, hot seating'.

As we have already discussed, the interesting thing about the 'craft knowledge' of the history teacher is that it is very often implicit. Teachers do these things intuitively, without really thinking about how and why they are effective. This is where research can help turn implicit ideas into explicit ones; these ideas then become generic and can be applied and transferred to a variety of contexts. By discussing the ways in which ISM is managed, the contexts in which it should be used and above all, by explaining why it connects effectively with pupils' learning needs, it is hoped that history teachers will also be able to use it in a wide variety of contexts.

Questioning: a clever art or a competence to be learned?

We saw above that effective questioning is absolutely vital for ISM to work properly. When embarking upon classroom observation for the first time, student teachers will soon come across experienced teachers who are extremely well versed in the art of effective questioning. Like many other aspects of the professional craft knowledge that they possess, it may seem at first glance that the questioning comes effortlessly. The correct questions seem to trip off the tongue of the teacher, pupils respond appropriately and despite a number of 'incorrect' answers, the discussion seems to flow and the children learn in the process. In fact, effective questioning involves an extraordinarily complex array of characteristic features, traits and skills (Brown and Edmondson, 1984, Dillon, 1988). Effective questioning involves:

- careful selection of appropriate questions, geared to the conceptual level of pupils;
- appropriate use of language and vocabulary;
- the use of suitable timing, involving pauses, prompts and alternatives;
- a combination of verbal and non-verbal communication.

Done well, it can help pupils feel at home in the so-called 'foreign world' of history; done badly, it can reduce history lessons to non-participative, non-communicative lessons (John, 1994; Mbenga, 1993). This is particularly frustrating for the student teacher, who lacks those vital elements of the professional craft knowledge that are essential for effective questioning. On the positive side, however, student teachers soon learn to start questioning competently and, given the right advice, many develop outstanding questioning techniques by the end of their teaching practice. Moreover, as with many other aspects of teaching, research suggests that questioning improves with experience, as intuitive skills and 'thinking on one's feet' become pronounced.

An obvious question to ask, if you will excuse the pun, is 'why ask questions?'. In a magnificent book, Morgan and Saxton (1991, p. 7) argue that effective questioning is at the heart of active learning because it has the 'power to generate vivid ideas, spur the imagination and incite both teacher and student into a shared, creative learning experience'. Postman (1979, p. 140) has argued that 'all our knowledge results from questions, which is another way of saying that question-asking is our most important intellectual tool'. Kerry (1982a) suggests that questions are important in teaching for the following reasons:

- To encourage pupils to talk constructively and on-task
- To signal an interest in hearing what pupils feel and think
- To stimulate interest and awaken curiosity
- To encourage a problem-solving approach to thinking and learning
- To help pupils externalize and verbalize knowledge
- To encourage 'thinking aloud' and exploratory approaches to tasks
- To help pupils learn from each other and to respect and evaluate the contributions of others
- To monitor the pupils' learning: its extent, level and deficiencies
- To deepen pupils' thinking levels and to improve their ability to conceptualize.

Given, then, that questions are essential for clarifying understanding, encouraging pupil involvement, maintaining class control and promoting differentiation, they need to feature very prominently in lesson plans. A key question (what Counsell (1997) calls a 'big question') or a series of key questions, provide a clear line of enquiry and contribute in an essential way to the formulation of aims and objectives; brainstorming questions relating to a subject often forms the starting point for the planning of a topic and helps to explore it in detail (see Chapter 5). However, a number of things can go wrong with questioning, especially for inexperienced teachers; here are some of the most common:

- The deathly silence: pupils simply do not respond to the questions posed by the teacher
- Limited answers and red herrings: a question is asked and the response is not what the teacher envisaged
- The brick wall: the teacher asks a series of questions, which are ignored by the pupils (this usually derives from poor class control and problems of ill discipline)
- The 'know-alls': the teacher always seems to direct questions at the same pupils, or these pupils seem to answer most of the questions posed to the class as a whole.

How, then, can we overcome these potential problems? The non-verbal techniques relating to gesture, posture, facial expressions, mannerisms, eye contact and movement around the room are particularly important. Bear this in mind when considering the solutions and strategies described below.

The deathly silence
Often, silences come about because the teacher is asking *inappropriate* questions. 'Inappropriate' here could mean that the questions are posed using language that is too difficult to understand, or that they deal with issues that are beyond the conceptual understanding of pupils. Alternatively, the questions may be totally unrelated to pupils' previous or existing knowledge and therefore over-ambitious; once again this reminds us of the need sometimes to go from the 'known to the unknown' in terms of pupils' experience. The key starting point for overcoming the dreaded 'deathly silence' is to ensure that questions are posed in ways that connect with pupils' existing/previous knowledge and that they are phrased using appropriate language. Other solutions include being patient, providing appropriate pause-time for pupils to think, offering clues, rephrasing questions, suggesting alternatives, and asking specific pupils for answers.

Limited answers
Sometimes, teachers find that the answers being offered by the pupils are very limited, often involving one or two words, or short sentences. This is frequently because too many closed questions are being asked, i.e. questions that demand only a specific, limited amount of information. In order to encourage more extensive and varied responses, teachers have to ask more open-ended questions. This will make more sense after you have looked at Nichol's (1984) list of question types in the next section.

Red herrings
When teachers ask questions they *anticipate* certain responses, which are often reflected in the planning process. Experienced teachers will often testify, however, that despite

having taught for many years, they are still astonished at some of the answers provided by pupils in response to seemingly the most 'obvious' questions. These are called 'red herring' answers. One of the worst things that a history teacher can do is to offer a negative response to a red herring, as it tends to undermine pupil confidence, particularly in the less able. The most appropriate strategy here is to try to utilize the information provided in a positive way, and to ask the pupils to think alternatively about the issues. Again, some of the strategies above are appropriate here too, such as offering clues or rephrasing.

The brick wall

Occasionally, questions posed by the teacher are simply *ignored* by the class. At first glance, this suggests that the relationship between the teacher and the class has broken down and that the pupils are out of control. This is not necessarily the case. It may be that the questioning technique used by the teacher is inappropriate. In fact, using some of the techniques suggested above can soon resolve the situation and can have a dramatic impact on overall class control. Three specific 'control' issues relating to questioning are relevant here: learning names (by using a class plan or labels to assist in the process) can have a dramatic impact upon questioning and control; insisting upon 'hands-up' before answering questions is also vital, as is calling for quiet during 'teacher talk'.

'Know-alls'

An interesting question to pose about this problem is to consider whether the teacher – through an ineffective questioning technique – is actually *creating* the 'know-all'. It may be, for example, that due to lack of confidence, lack of patience, or control problems, the teacher is either wittingly or unwittingly allowing the 'know-all' to dominate the question-and-answer session. Being conscious of the need to spread the questions widely, to involve as many pupils as possible, is essential for differentiation and in order to achieve this, all the solutions and strategies offered above apply.

Morgan and Saxton (1991, p. 7) sum up the problems and solutions above by claiming that in order to be an effective questioner, you need patience, the ability to listen effectively and above all what they call the finesse to 'send the ball back' so that 'learning is perceived by students as a dialogue in which everyone's thoughts, feelings and actions are important elements for collective and individual understanding'.

Questioning, thinking and progression

So far, our analysis in relation to questioning has focused upon how to encourage appropriate question-and-answer discussions with classes and, in the process, maintain control. I now want to shift the attention onto the ways in which appropriate questions and tasks – oral as well as written – are absolutely essential for creating an effective learning environment. In particular, I want to explore ways in which questions can be planned so that they encourage pupils to think (Fisher, 1990, 1995; Harnett, 1996, Bunyon and Marshall, 2001; see also Chapter 9) and connect effectively with key elements and historical concepts, thus promoting progression (Counsell, 2000b).

Nichol (1984, pp. 46–7) argues that 'the asking of questions is the pivot around which history teaching revolves' because it encourages pupils to think. He offers an extremely useful list of question types in history teaching, which promote certain responses and ways of thinking:

1. A 'data-recall' question (e.g. 'When was the battle of X?') requires the pupil to remember facts without putting them to any use.
2. A 'naming' question (e.g. 'What is the name of Y?') asks the pupil simply to name something without showing how it relates to any particular situation.
3. An 'observation' question (e.g. 'What is happening in the picture?') requires the pupil to describe something that they can see, without relating it to their knowledge of the situation.
4. A 'reasoning' question (e.g. 'What does X tell us about Y?') expects pupils to explain something.
5. A 'speculative' question (e.g. 'How do you think X came about?') requires pupils to speculate about historical situations.
6. An 'empathetic' question (e.g. 'How did X feel about that?') asks pupils to empathize with people in historical situations.
7. A 'hypothesis-generating' question (e.g. 'Why did X occur at that time?') requires pupils to speculate in a more advanced way, using historical knowledge.
8. A 'problem-solving' question (e.g. 'What evidence is there that X happened to Y?') expects pupils to weigh-up evidence.
9. An 'evidence-questioning' question (e.g. 'How reliable is X to tell us about Y?') asks pupils to interrogate the evidence.
10. A 'synthesizing' question (e.g. 'From what you have found out, write an account of . . .') pulls all the information together and encourages the pupil to resolve the problem.

Similarly, Husbands (1996) also discusses the notion of hierarchical questions, arguing that there are three main categories of questions:

- Questions that elicit information (e.g. 'what is it made from?')
- Questions that elicit reflection (e.g. 'was the author justified?')
- Questions that elicit understanding (e.g. 'why was this letter written?').

Note that Questions 1–2 in Nichol's list, as well as the first of Husbands' categories are essentially 'closed' question types that invite a specific answer, whilst Questions 3–10 are 'open' because they encourage a more extensive potential response. Research conducted by Brown and Edmondson (1984) suggested that many of the questions posed by teachers, including history teachers, were mainly 'low level', in other words, they fall into the first two of Husbands' categories. More recent research undertaken by John (1994) on written tasks in the classroom confirms this. It is imperative therefore that teachers think more deeply and explicitly about the nature of the questions they ask, so that they challenge pupils appropriately. In the words of Husbands (1996):

> to ask effective questions is less a matter of constructing a hierarchy of questions than about specifying the sorts of thinking which our questions are intended to promote . . . we need to organise the questions we want to ask in terms of the nature of the thinking which we ask pupils to undertake in answering them.
>
> (Husbands 1996, p. 20)

This link between curiosity, thinking and understanding explain why questioning is vital for promoting progression (see Chapter 9).

Clearly, as with planning in general, there is a great deal to take into consideration when considering your questioning technique. The following check-list is designed to help you.

Check-list: for effective questioning

Before the lesson

- What questions am I going to ask?
- What is the purpose of these questions?
- What do pupils already know?
- What don't they know?
- Who am I going to ask?
- Have I thought about the likely responses?
- How am I going to deal with these?

During the lesson

- Am I phrasing my questions clearly?
- Am I distributing my questions evenly?
- Am I involving as many pupils as possible?
- Am I using pupils' names?
- Am I allowing appropriate time and pauses?
- Am I using non-verbal communication?
- Am I prompting, giving clues, praising/encouraging pupils?
- How am I dealing with 'red herrings'?
- Am I encouraging my pupils to think?

Asking appropriate questions Think about the grading, hierarchy or progression of questions:

- **Step 1: BASIC (Low level, often closed)**

- Observation questions ('What can you see?' 'Can you describe what is happening?')
- Naming questions ('What are they wearing?' 'What does it say about?')
- Alternative questions ('Is it black or white?' 'Was it effective or ineffective – Yes or no?')
- Data-recall questions ('When was . . . ?' 'Who was . . . ?')
- Control questions ('Are you listening?' 'What did I just say?')

- **Step 2: ADVANCED (High level, often open)**

- Reasoning questions ('What does this tell us about . . . ?')
- Speculative questions ('Why did . . . ?' 'What were the reasons for . . . ?')
- Empathetic questions ('How do you think they felt?' 'Why did they believe that?')
- Hypothesis-generating questions ('What were the results of . . . ? What was the significance of . . . ?')
- Problem-solving questions ('What evidence is there to show that . . . ?')
- Evidence and interpretation-related questions ('How do we know about . . . ?' 'How reliable is . . . ?')
- Synthesizing questions ('What does all this tell us about . . . ?')

Figure 5.3 *Check-list for effective questioning*

CHAPTER 7

A certain subject? Evidence and interpretation in history teaching

> Experience is at once already an interpretation and one that needs to be interpreted.
>
> (Scott, 1991)

Introduction

Evidence and interpretation are included here together, not for any organizational convenience but because I argue in this chapter that evidence, interpretation and contextual historical knowledge are irrevocably linked and need to be considered holistically. I begin by considering the development of the use of sources and evidence in schools. Although the SCHP – and particularly Dennis Shemilt (1987) – has been rightly credited with applying the methodology associated with evidence in a systematic and rigorous manner, teachers like Keatinge (1910) were arguing for their use at the beginning of the twentieth century. Source-work, as we shall see, came under close scrutiny during the National Curriculum era and since that time, has undergone further review. Similarly, the use of interpretations has been the subject of much debate since the beginning of the 1990s. This chapter draws upon all the major relevant research to suggest practical ways in which evidence and interpretation can be used effectively and creatively in the history classroom.

Evidence, sources and enquiry 1972–1995: losing the plot?

As Aldrich (1991) and McAleavy (1998) remind us, it was Keatinge (1910) who not only first advocated the use of sources and historical evidence as a means of making history more interesting, but who argued also that it was important that pupils had a sound grasp of the methodology of historians. Yet it was the development of new history, and the SCHP in particular, that provided the catalyst for widespread use and application of source work in history classrooms, particularly from the early 1970s onwards. As we saw in the previous chapter, SHP recognized that evidence work was central to historical activity and that pupils should be introduced to the evidential methodological techniques used by historians. The period from 1972 to 1995 witnessed the publication of a vast array of school textbooks that focused explicitly upon evidence (e.g. Hinton, 1990), and an equally extensive literature that provided guidance and advice to teachers (Fines, 1983: Unit 4; Nichol, 1984; Portal, 1987b, Fines, 1988; Andretti, 1992). HMI argued that 'there is no reason why an awareness of evidence should not permeate the teaching of history for all pupils, however young' (DES, 1985b, p. 3). Even more significantly, the general criteria of the new GCSE (DES, 1985a) placed evidence at the very centre of the examination, stating that the aims of a history course were:

- to ensure that candidates' knowledge is rooted in an understanding of the nature and the use of historical evidence . . . (para. 2.3);
- to develop essential study skills such as the ability to locate and extract information from primary and secondary sources; to detect bias; to analyse this information and to construct a logical argument . . . (para. 2.6);
- to show the skills necessary to study a wide variety of historical evidence, which should include both primary and secondary written sources, statistical material, artefacts, textbooks and orally transmitted information . . . (para. 3.4):
  - by comprehending and extracting information from it (para. 3.4.1);
  - by interpreting and evaluating it – distinguishing between fact, opinion and judgement; pointing to deficiencies in the material as evidence, such as gaps and inconsistencies; detecting bias (para. 3.4.2);
  - by comparing various types of historical evidence and reaching conclusions based on this comparison (para. 3.4.3).

Shemilt (1987) undertook further extensive research on how pupils develop evidential understanding. He argued that pupils underwent certain 'stages' as far as their knowledge and understanding of historical evidence was concerned. In summarizing Shemilt's ideas, I have relied heavily upon *Teaching History*, 91 (1998, p. 14) and the article by McAleavy (1998) in the same edition.

Stage 1: Knowledge of the past is taken for granted
Here, pupils confuse 'evidence' and 'knowledge', believing that they are the same thing. They 'take as read' primary sources, and use them in the same way as they would history textbooks. They also take the view that historians know all about the past, are unable to contemplate different interpretations and believe that there are no conceptual or methodological problems in finding out about it.

Stage 2: Evidence is privileged information about the past
Pupils become aware of some of the methodological problematics of history. For example, they see that the purpose of a line of enquiry such as 'how do we know?' is a meaningful question. They start to become aware that 'knowledge' is dependent in part upon 'evidence'. On the other hand, they find it difficult to understand reliability, believing, for example, that primary sources are 'reliable' because they are 'from the time'.

Stage 3: Evidence is a basis for inference about the past
Pupils start to become aware that evidence and information are different things. They also start to recognize the problematics of evidence, such as subjectivity or 'bias'. They start to become aware that in order to find out about the past, we have to evaluate evidence.

Stage 4: Awareness of the historicity of the past
Pupils start to understand the nature and methodology of history and in particular, recognize that the conclusions drawn by historians are dependent upon the use of evidence, and that what they produce is a reconstruction of the past.

The research suggested, therefore, that evidential work was demanding for pupils and that Stages 3 and 4 could only be reached in relatively late adolescence. Pupils needed careful guidance and support when dealing with sources. One of the best school textbooks written in the early 1990s on this theme was published by Colwill *et al.* (1990), who were all experienced GCSE examiners (Shephard was also Director of SHP at the time). The book was aimed as much at teachers as pupils, and although within the context of the developments in the late 1990s it is now out of date, it still represents the best starting points for understanding the nature of evidence and the methodology needed to understand it. One half of the front cover of the book is a famous cigarette advertisement showing an artist's colourful drawing of a group of soldiers from the First World War, standing above their trench looking happy as they hand out cigarettes to each other; on the other half of the same front cover is a typically dark, grey photograph taken during the War, showing soldiers in the trenches looking tired, dirty and scared. In the book itself, there are a number of key points about the nature and use of evidence, in order to explain each of these, I will use the images from the front cover as an illustration and point of reference.

Colwill and his colleagues articulated seven fundamentals about evidence:

Utility: The usefulness of a source, or set of sources, depends upon the line of enquiry we want to ask about those sources. Therefore, if we want to ask the question 'What was life like in the trenches?', the cigarette advertisement is not particularly useful, but the photograph is.

Primary and secondary sources: It is important to stress to pupils that primary sources are not necessarily more reliable than secondary sources, as the cigarette advertisement makes clear. Primary sources, however, can provide 'unwitting' evidence; in this case, the advertisement provides interesting and invaluable information about propaganda and the persuasive techniques used by cigarette manufacturers during the War.

Bias, reliability and provenance: We have to be aware of bias in sources and understand that it is not always obvious. Reliability often depends upon provenance. In this case, the cigarette advert is not a reliable source for finding out about life in the trenches on account of its obvious bias; the photograph (housed at the Imperial War Museum) is more *likely* to be a reliable source because it shows very clearly what conditions were like. As far as the advert is concerned, provenance also influences utility: the advert is useful to find out about the nature of propaganda and persuasion, as well as to explore the minds of the people who produced such images.

Reliability and cross-referencing: Cross-referencing (including knowledge of the historical context) is important for determining reliability (and understanding). It was stated above that the photograph is likely to be more reliable, but until this is compared and cross-referenced to other sources from the time, we cannot be absolutely sure about reliability. Moreover, determination of reliability is greatly enhanced by knowledge of the historical context being studied.

Information or evidence? Asking questions about sources will transform them from simply being sources of information into sources of evidence, which we can use to answer certain questions. Thus, if we ask of the photograph 'Do the men look happy?', 'What are they wearing?' and 'What are they doing?', the answer to these questions will provide evidence to help us tackle the bigger question: 'What were conditions like in the trenches?'

Evidence as understanding: Do not underestimate the wealth of rich, interesting and valuable information and evidence that can be derived from a source. Both sources provide detailed information and evidence if we 'dig deep' into them through questions. On the other hand, cross-reference to other sources and a wider historical context are vital for a true understanding, in this case of the First World War.

Evidence sandwiches, hamburgers and lines of enquiry: towards context-related evidential work since 1995

Colwill *et al.* (1990) and others who were influenced by Shemilt's work, provided teachers and pupils with a rigorous methodology relating to the explicit cultivation of evidential skills that was required at GCSE. However, setting aside some of the extreme and altogether unintellectual criticisms of the New Right (see Chapter 2), teachers in the early 1990s such as Lang (1993) and (later) Counsell (1997) started to question certain aspects of the new history's approach to evidence. McAleavy (1998) describes the way in which the assumption that school history should be modelled upon the historians' methodology needed examination. In particular, the decontextualized nature of the 'What is History?' approach and the decompartmentalized use of skills and concepts, which sometimes led to teachers teaching 'off the peg' evidence-related answers in preparation for examinations, particularly with regard to the SHP's 'unseen' Paper II (see 'Gerry's bad habits' in Smith, 2001).

Lang (1993) claimed in particular that pupils seemed to have become obsessed with the notion of the 'B-word', namely 'bias', 'which often becomes a hackneyed catch-all, blunting and limiting pupils' evaluative work' (Le Cocq, 2000, p. 51). Thus, many source-related activities seemed to comprise of reductionist attempts to debunk the evidence, which Byrom (1998) refers to as a 'lazy cynicism'. There was also the seemingly pointless obsession with distinguishing between 'primary' and 'secondary' sources (see Smith (2001) discussed below). Rather than making history more interesting and dynamic all this seemed to make it potentially boring ('death by a hundred sources and gobbets') and increased the 'what's the point?' syndrome amongst pupils. McAleavy's (1998) illustrates this point perfectly:

> the last 20 years of classroom history has shown that to be constantly told to spot bias and to comment on the reliability of primary and secondary sources can be just as boring a being told to memorize a particular collection of facts and dates.
>
> (McAleavy, 1998, p. 13)

Above all, there seemed to be a tendency towards placing emphasis upon pupils' perception of the source material *per se*, rather than the use of sources as a means of pursuing a particular line of enquiry or reaching a conclusion. In McAleavy's (1998, p. 12) words again, given that 'the best work on sources depended on a sense of period and the ability to make interconnections', new history and SHP 'said very little about how students could deploy and organise the information they gained from this evidence'. McAleavy rightly points to the negative impact of the National Curriculum 'Mark I' (DES, 1991; Welsh Office, 1991), which separated sources and interpretation from historical knowledge and understanding. However, 1995 was a turning point in that the emphasis placed within the National Curriculum (DfE, 1995; Welsh Office, 1995) *and* the new GCSE criteria (which marked the end of the 'unseen' Paper II) meant that 'there was an increased emphasis on the need to make connections between the evidence one can derive from sources and a wider contextual knowledge of the topic in question' and that 'sources were to be used to help candidates produce valid interpretations of the past' (McAleavy, 1998, p. 15) in the shape of a reasoned and substantiated conclusion. Note the different emphasis here between the GCSE criteria of 1995 and 1985. The 1995 National Curriculum criteria (DFE, 1995) stated that syllabuses should provide candidates with opportunities to:

- Acquire knowledge and understanding of the past

- Investigate historical events, people, changes and issues

- Use historical sources critically *in their historical context* (my emphasis)

- Draw conclusions and appreciate that these and other historical conclusions are liable to reassessment in the light of new or reinterpreted evidence

- In addition, *in relation to the historical context* (my emphasis again):

  - Comprehend, analyse and evaluate representations and interpretations of the events, people and issues studied

  - Comprehend, interpret, evaluate and use a range of sources of information of different types.

There was an emphasis, too, upon historical context, and this was consolidated even further in later reviews of the National Curriculum, GCSE and A level (see Chapter 10). Note also that the 'b-word' is not mentioned here. Morgan (1999, p. 4) argues convincingly that pupils now 'need to consider the concept of bias in a way which establishes the distinction between implicit and explicit bias'. In other words, all producers of sources – speakers, writers, artists, etc. – all have subjective views to an extent, but this does not mean that they are necessarily prejudiced in the sense of being explicitly biased.

The development of context-related use of evidence, linked to a particular line of enquiry has, in my view, been one of the most positive developments in history teaching since the early 1990s. This has been reflected in exciting classroom-based research. Consider, for example, Mulholland's (1998, p. 17) 'evidence sandwich', which describes an innovative attempt to develop 'frameworks for linking pupils' evidential understanding with growing skill in structured, written argument', which, importantly, can be applied in a range of different contexts from primary to sixth form. Similarly, Byrom (1998, pp. 32–3) describes a case study of the Peasants' Revolt in order to show how 'historians construct a narrative from a range of sources', the end result of which meant that 'pupils were building an account that they felt was fair and legitimate despite the imperfections of the raw material' (see Counsell (1997) for further examples). Similarly, Banham's (1998, 2000) outstanding work on using sources in a range of different contexts (the 'grand prix') shows the benefits of constructing an in-depth 'substantiated argument' relating to King John based upon varied and often contradictory evidence.

Our actual use of evidence, then, has greatly improved since the early days of new history, and has reached a high level of sophistication (Britt *et al.*, 2000, O'Neill, 1998). Smith (2001) draws on much recent research and discussion to suggest the ways in which evidential work can be made more meaningful to all pupils, including lower attainers:

- showing pupils the purpose of sources and evidence – that they are linked to a line of enquiry;
- treating source work, not as a 'bolt-on' activity, but part and parcel of everyday historical enquiry;
- using engaging, enquiry methods that pupils enjoy, to make evidential work interesting;
- reviewing schemes of work to ensure that evidence work is integral (as opposed to supplementary) so that they are integrated naturally into the everyday investigations and enquiries that pupils undertake in the classroom;
- developing literacy strategies (such as those described in Chapter 8) to improve accessibility and readability; these might include selective adaptation, explicit discussion of language, the use of 'markers', the word-processor and particularly, the concentration upon 'key words' to demonstrate their significance (see below);
- using charts and flow diagrams (see Smith (2001, p. 10) for a specific example) and other methods such as role-play in order to help pupils visualize the past through sources and evidence;
- avoiding the preoccupation with 'primary and secondary sources' that are largely unhelpful;
- playing down the notion of 'bias' but pointing pupils to 'key words' in sources that reveal much about provenance and the motivation of the writer, as well as the purpose and usefulness of a source;
- emphasizing the importance of contextual knowledge for helping pupils understand utility and reliability;
- providing pupils with the linguistic tools through adverbs such as 'probably', 'definitely' and 'perhaps' (see also Britt *et al.* (2000) for further techniques and examples).

Le Cocq (2000) has sought to look again at how progression can be promoted within evidential work, in ways that can be more directly linked to historical context (see also Counsell, 2000a, 2001). Describing work undertaken with Year 7 pupils (she provides a useful diagrammatic summary of her findings on pp. 52–3 of the article), Le Cocq argues that it is useful to consider three main steps when evaluating evidence with young pupils:

Step 1: Comprehension: *understanding* what the source is telling you. In order to illustrate this, she describes the ways in which pupils were asked to select sources that supported three main reasons why William I won the Battle of Hastings. Through a 'sequence of underlining, feedback and discussion' pupils were asked to 'become more discriminating about what particular section of the source constituted relevant evidence for each idea. They really began to see the wood for the trees. They gained the ability to select pertinent quotations to support their points' (Le Cocq, 2000, p. 51).

Step 2: Analysis: *questioning* what the source is telling you. Le Cocq suggests that in order to do this, the teacher must deliberately avoids using the word 'bias' at all costs so that pupils can be moved on 'to a more sophisticated analysis of the reasons why certain sources may be deemed unreliable' (*ibid.*). Interestingly, she uses a concrete past/present analogy to do this (an account of the ways in which a schoolgirl is unfairly deemed 'the worst pupil in the school') to show that reliability depends upon (a) the number of sources we use (one source is never enough, we need to compare similarities and differences); (b) the difference between fact and opinion, and (c) the background of the person writing the source (i.e. provenance).

Step 3: Evaluation: *reconsidering* what the source is telling you. Le Cocq argues that 'offering final judgements about a source's value is another rung up the progression ladder' (*ibid.* p. 54) and also encourages pupils to realize that a source does not lack utility just because it is in some way partial or subjective.

Using evidence to infer understanding and knowledge about the past is also a central theme of Clare Riley's (1999) work. She draws upon the research undertaken by Portal (1987b) and Cooper (1992), as well as the messages in Lang (1993), to argue that 'when used imaginatively, sources allow pupils to develop historical knowledge' via what she refers to as 'layers of inference' (Riley, 1999, p. 6). Again, as with Mulholland (1998, discussed above), she argues that this technique can be applied generically across all key stages. The 'layers of inference' approach involves the following:

1. Explaining, showing and demonstrating how and why sources are useful. Drawing upon ideas developed by Cooper (1992), Riley advocates that pupils should ask the following questions, so that they will appreciate why sources are useful:
   - What does the source definitely tell me?
   - What can I infer from the source? (or what does the source suggest?)
   - What does the source not tell me?
   - What else would I like to find out? (or what further questions do I need to ask?)
2. Presenting the information gained from these questions in a concrete, practical manner. She did this using 'boxes' surrounding the source, which pupils had to fill in and then compare with each other (see Riley, 1999, pp. 10–11).
3. Using cards with 'definite facts' and 'inferred facts' in order to help pupils understand the notion of inference more effectively and to introduce them to the idea of 'unwitting evidence'.

Wiltshire (2000) describes an interesting application of Riley's 'layers of inference' ideas during a site visit, which was designed to use sources in order to investigate the history of the medieval church. Counsell (2000a) argues that 'the layers of inference' principle is a highly useful and adaptable tool and in order for it to be particularly effective, it needs to be revisited regularly in order to promote progression and understanding. 'Layers of inference' draws upon a long tradition of research going back to Keatinge (1910), the key messages of which are summarized in the following list of 'do's and don'ts'.

The 'do's and don'ts' of evidential work: what the research tells us

Do
1. Remember that historical sources and evidence provide exciting opportunities to enthuse pupils about the past (Keatinge, 1910).

2. Regard source and evidential work as an integral part of historical education, which requires distinctive skills and understanding (Colwill *et al.*, 1990; Portal, 1987b; Shemilt, 1987; Hake and Haydn, 1995).
3. Be aware of the conceptual challenges of evidential work in history (Shemilt, 1987).
4. Obtain the maximum information from quality sources (Colwill *et al.*, 1990; Phillips, 2001b: see Chapter 6).
5. Use sources in their historical context (McAleavy, 1998; Walsh, 1998; Smith, 2001).
6. Use sources to answer 'big questions', lines of enquiry and the key elements of history (McAleavy, 1998; Banham, 1998; Mulholland, 1998).
7. Be aware of the methodological and technical aspects of source work, but don't overplay this with pupils (Byrom, 1998; Smith, 2001).
8. Devise ways of guiding your pupils through sources in a careful and meaningful manner (Le Cocq, 2000; Riley, 1999).
9. Help your pupils get the most out of sources by asking appropriate questions (Le Cocq, 2000; Riley, 1999).
10. Use a variety of teaching and learning methods when dealing with evidence (Smith, 2001).

Don't

1. Use sources and evidence in isolation (i.e. 'context free' or 'bolt-on') without a purpose or line of enquiry.
2. Become preoccupied with the methodological and technical aspects of sources (i.e. losing the wood for the trees and forgetting what history is for).
3. Encourage a reductionist approach by overdoing exercises on reliability and 'the B-word'.
4. Bombard pupils with too many sources.
5. Underestimate pupils' capacity to become bored and discouraged by an overemphasis on source work.
6. Skip over sources without making the most of them.
7. Make false generalizations and assumptions about evidence and sources.
8. Forget the fact that evidence and interpretation are closely linked (this is considered in more detail below).

'Interpreting interpretations': towards balanced objectivity in history teaching

Few issues in the National Curriculum era have been more widely debated and discussed than the use of historical interpretation. It is probably fair to say that the use of interpretation in history teaching has led to some confusion (Bennett, 1992; Nicklin, 1992). My major task in this section is threefold: I first want to explain why the teaching of historical interpretation has been considered important; second, using the research evidence, I want to define more precisely what historical interpretation is and then, third, to consider the most effective ways of teaching it, again making reference to the best research.

We saw earlier in the book how the 'great tradition' dominated history teaching practically right up until the 1960s (Slater, 1989; Sylvester, 1994; Phillips, 1998a). Jenkins (1991) refers to this as a 'certaintist' tradition, with history viewed as narrative-based and essentially one-dimensional, with little scope for debate, dialogue or interpretation. Take, for example, the following extract from Unstead (1962, p. 111); under the title 'Bad Government in England', King John is described as 'the worst King England ever had and he probably deserved the title, for though good looking and clever in war and money matters, he was a complete scoundrel as a man and a selfish fool as a king'.

This is an essentially 'closed' text in that there is very little doubt about King John – he was obviously the most ineffective and unsuccessful King in English history! Clearly, however, history taught in this way is open to abuse and manipulation. This was recognized by the History Working Group (HWG) (DES, 1990) who emphasized the need to teach different interpretations of the past on the grounds that this would be a bulwark against political manipulation, whoever was in power. Moreover, the HWG also advocated that pupils should use secondary sources – mainly the work of historians – as well as primary sources, in order to gain a full appreciation of the past. Therefore, the use of interpretation became a fundamental aspect of the National Curriculum in 1991 and has remained so ever since. This was reflected in one of the best books on the medieval period by McAleavy (1991, p. 21), produced for the National Curriculum 'Mark I'. Under the title 'Bad King John?', McAleavy posed the following hypothesis: 'For a long time people have disagreed about King John, who ruled England in the thirteenth century. Historians used to talk about 'Bad King John'. Was John a bad King?'

In order to answer the question, pupils have to interrogate sources; note the difference between this and the other extract from Unstead (1962). Whereas the earlier example was certain or 'closed', this by contrast is essentially uncertain and 'open' to debate and discussion, based upon an analysis of the evidence. Instead of the teacher telling the pupils the 'correct' version, pupils here are invited to make their own judgement or opinion, based upon varied evidence. It could be argued that this interpretive view of history reflects contemporary society for, as Jenkins (1991) and Tosh (1984) have reminded us, everybody has different 'claims' on the past. The vast number of historical programmes on television demonstrates not only the public interest in the past, but also the desire to interpret it in certain ways.

The idea of a historical interpretation, however, needs careful definition. Whereas the HWG (DES, 1990) defined interpretations basically in terms of the different views held by historians, later documentation produced to support the implementation of the National Curriculum 'interpreted interpretations' more broadly (NCC, 1991a, 1991b). It suggested that history teachers use a wide variety of material to demonstrate how the past has been interpreted; whilst textbooks and the views of historians provide an obvious source, teachers should also consider things like museum displays, film, novels, art, advertising, theme parks, and so on. This clearly involves teaching pupils about how and why the images, opinions or interpretations about the past have been created.

Thus, the current version of *History in the National Curriculum at Key Stage 3* requires pupils to 'consider how and why some historical events, people and changes have been interpreted differently' and emphasizes that pupils should be taught to 'apply their historical knowledge to analyse and evaluate interpretations' (ACCAC, 2000, p. 10). In order to be able to do this, however, pupils need to know what interpretations are, as well as having some appreciation of the complex factors that create them. One of the best discussions in this connection is provided by George (1997, p. 63) who argues that the following factors and issues have to be taken into consideration when teaching about interpretation:

- Characters and events from the past are presented to us in many different forms.

- Different stories or representations of the past often tell us different things about the same characters or events.

- Interpretations (such as textbooks, novels or historical films) often contain a combination of fact, opinion and fiction. These can only be verified as historically accurate by reference to evidence.

- People who produce interpretations of the past (such as historians, novelists or film-makers) do so for many reasons, and this may have an impact upon the nature of the interpretations that they produce.

- In order to evaluate the historical authenticity and accuracy of a particular interpretation, we need to know something about the author, such as the person's background, his or her motivation or purpose for producing the interpretation, ideological disposition, religious or social background, and so on. In other words, using the terminology above, reliability often depends upon provenance.

- Deciding upon the quality of an interpretation relies upon judgement, which itself depends upon an analysis of evidence and historical knowledge.

This discussion of what interpretations are, how they are constructed and the methodological implications, is useful for considering how interpretation is taught most effectively. McAleavy (1993, p. 15) suggests that teachers need to consider the following questions when planning interpretation-type exercises (note how closely these relate to George's (1997) factors above):

- Which parts of the interpretation are factual and which are points of view?

- How far are these views supported by the evidence? How selective has the use of evidence been?

- What was the purpose and intended audience of the interpretation?

- How far was the interpretation affected by the background of its author?

- How plausible is the interpretation?

However, these issues raise demanding challenges to pupils (Lee and Ashby, 1998). Haydn *et al.* (1997) argue that in order to understand interpretations, pupils need:

- knowledge about the topic, theme or event being described – contextual historical knowledge;

- accessibility via language – which is sometimes particularly demanding;

- conceptual understanding – specifically, the capacity to be able to explain what an interpretation says, to evaluating, judging and analysing it;

- background information about the author – this is closely related to contextual historical knowledge above; in order to appreciate an interpretation, knowledge and understanding of the provenance is vital (see also Morgan, 1999);

- appreciation that history can be 'uncertain' – often, pupils cannot quite believe that there can be more than one view of the past!

McAleavy (1993, p. 14) argues that pupils need to be given what he calls the 'analytical vocabulary' in order to understand interpretations. His later research goes on to suggest that pupils will only really be able to understand, analyse and judge interpretations if they are able to draw upon their contextual historical knowledge, having found that there is a 'strong connection between the level of background knowledge about a historical issue and students' capacity to reflect on an interpretation' (McAleavy, 2000, p. 76). He points out that students' own interpretations of a particular historical event are a good way of introducing them to historical interpretations – for example, comparing and contrasting pictures that they have constructed based upon evidence may be a good starting point. The precise way in which interpretations are put together should also be discussed carefully and explicitly with pupils. McAleavy calls for the 'demystification' of the work of historians, museum curators, novelists, film-makers and so on. Based upon this theoretical framework, he suggests specific teaching strategies, designed to facilitate pupils' learning and understanding of historical interpretations. Pupils can be encouraged to:

- identify differences between textbooks that address the same issue;
- learn about how archaeologists interpret the past from physical remains, and then contrast this with museum representations;
- debate with each other about aspects of the past;
- reflect upon the ways in which dramatic reconstructions of the past are put together;
- discuss 'controversial' historical personalities and consider these figures from the standpoint of different opinions;
- consider commonly held views about the past and attempt to establish how accurate these views are.

Haydn *et al.* (1997) also advocate discussing explicitly with pupils how interpretations are constructed and why they may be subject to change over time (see the useful diagrams on pages 126 and 128 of their book), what they call 'explaining the purpose' of interpretations. Similarly, Harper (1993, p. 12) argues that in order to understand historical interpretations fully, pupils need to be encouraged to ask a series of questions about them. In the list below, I have slightly rearranged the order from the original; again, note how they connect with many of the ideas of George (1997) and McAleavy (1993) considered above:

- When were they produced?
- Where were they produced?
- What sources of information were used to produce the interpretations?
- Who produced them?
- What were their views or standpoints?
- Who were they written for?
- Were they produced:
  - to amuse or entertain?
  - to sell the past or an image of it?
  - to inform?

- to create myths?
- to provide truth or knowledge?
- to mislead?
• Why are some interpretations more reliable than others?

These questions are very demanding and need prompting, specific ideas and contextual knowledge. Note how all the activities advocated in this and the preceding chapters depend, ultimately, upon the construction of a hypothesis, based upon a key question, a particular line of enquiry or title: 'Bad King John?' 'Robert Owen: different from the rest?' 'What did the Normans do for us?' 'The Victorian age: age of progress or environmental disaster?' all imply an interpretive approach (see Morgan, 1999 for further examples). All the writers discussed in this chapter stress the need to link interpretations with the other key elements. As Counsell (1997) has emphasized, in order to reach conclusions about interpretations, pupils need to be provided with a range of activities and enquiries, which can often only be undertaken through 'in-depth' work and by providing opportunities to express judgement through extended activities, such as extended writing (see Chapters 8 and 9).

Probably the best analytical range of suggestions for practical interpretation-related activities, based upon research evidence, is that provided by Haydn *et al.* (1997). In an excellent chapter, they suggest a number of practical activities to help pupils understand interpretations.

Concrete past/present analogy
Haydn *et al.* suggest that teachers choose a situation that pupils can relate to, such as a football match. They then give the pupils two very contrasting views of the same game and encourage them to discuss the ways in which they are different and to speculate as to why there are differences of opinion about the same event (see Morgan (1999) for further examples).

Explaining purpose and relevance
Pupils will only be able to fully understand the purpose and significance of interpretation work if they are able to appreciate that it may help them understand the world around them. Contemporary newspaper accounts, films and television programmes may be useful in this context for again discussing how and why interpretations are produced.

The range and diversity of historical interpretation
Pupils can only appreciate interpretations if they are shown a wide range of types of interpretation. Haydn *et al.* (1977) describe an exercise involving pupils commenting upon a whole range of interpretations on the life of Beckett, including textbook, novel, play, biography, ICT, brochure, film, eye-witness account, drawings, academic study, poetic play, saga, mosaic and personal records (*ibid.* pp. 120–2). Pupils are given a sorting exercise designed to assess the usefulness of the interpretations. This connects with my discussion in Chapter 9 on the need to familiarize pupils with a range of genres of expression. Interestingly, Walsh (2001) emphasizes the importance of display work for constantly reminding pupils about the different types of interpretations that exist.

Identifying differences
Haydn *et al.* (1997) suggest providing structured, specific tasks to help pupils identify the differences between interpretations. Here, the 'analytical vocabulary' that McAleavy

(1993) emphasizes is vital. Pupils can be encouraged to identify key words that reveal much about opinion, motive, purpose and intention. Haydn *et al.* (1997) also propose 'completion' exercises, involving the use of tables, which invite the pupils to tick certain boxes in relation to sources. Thus, their example provides the opportunity to 'tick' which source refers to 'Bonnie Prince Charlie' as 'idle', 'cowardly', 'inspiring' or 'courageous'. A series of further short tasks asks the pupils to comment upon which source they believed was the most accurate interpretation.

Comparing old and modern textbooks
We saw the contrast between interpretations of King John, provided by Unstead (1962) and McAleavy (1991). Extracts like these can be used to draw out comparisons.

Using the visual
Referring to the work of Wilson (1985), Haydn *et al.* (1997) argue that visual material provides a good way of exploring the difference between fact and interpretation. They also argue that video and films like *Cromwell* provide unique opportunities for exploring interpretation.

Drama and role-play
This can be used in conjunction with visual and written sources, to particularly good effect, to illustrate the personal and individual reasons why different interpretations are created.

Culpin (2001) suggests the following teaching approaches to help pupils make sense of interpretations. He emphasizes that they are appropriate at KS3, GCSE and A level:

- 'Spot the fact/opinion exercises'
- Read out two very different interpretations of the same person
- Play the 'skittle game': some interpretations (skittles) have to be 'knocked down' by other interpretations (pin-balls)
- Select a chapter in a book then write an imaginary letter to the author offering a different point of view
- Write a text for a tourist site
- Hot-seat figures from the past
- Compare textbooks
- Role-play involving historians justifying their views.

Similarly, Laffin (2001) suggests innovative ways of making interpretations accessible to A level pupils, including the use of the interpretive 'washing-line' (see Chapter 10).

Due to the work of these teachers and researchers, our understanding of how pupils learn about interpretations has greatly improved. Banham and Dawson (2000) have drawn on many of these ideas to plan their King John textbook, which shows how far historical pedagogy has progressed since the days of Unstead! Taught in these ways, interpretation work in the history classroom can play a vital role in portraying to pupils that history is an open rather than closed text (Phillips, 1998a). In concluding this chapter, however, let me offer a slight word of warning. Just as context-free source work threatened to take the excitement and joy out of history, so 'death by a hundred interpretations' can do the same. I mentioned earlier that some pupils find the notion of 'uncertainty' demanding; we add to this difficulty if we constantly set exercises that lead to a reductionist approach, where nothing in the past is certain, significant or true (see Chapter 12 for further discussion). In order to guard against reductionism and deconstructionism, interpretation in the history classroom needs to be taught with reference to the research evidence described in this chapter.

CHAPTER 8

Making history accessible: differentiation, language and communication in history teaching

> Differentiation has rightly been described as more of an art than a science; it depends, crucially, on the skill with which the teacher manages the classroom and the learning. The process of dialogue and reflection can help clarify the sorts of learning objectives and methods required to achieve differentiation.
>
> (McAleavy, 1994)

Introduction

This chapter focuses upon a central concept in teaching and learning, namely accessibility and inclusion. It provides a definition of differentiation and then suggests strategies for achieving it in the history classroom. A central argument in the chapter is that although differentiation is vital to meet the requirements of pupils with special educational needs (SEN), it is a concept that should be seen as fundamental, integral and generic to all teaching and learning contexts. It places the onus upon the history teacher to be interactive (Collis and Penney, 1996) and creative (Ashcroft and James, 1999).

The chapter also emphasizes the importance of language and communication for making history accessible to the full range of pupils. Research has, for many years, emphasized the significance of language in promoting effective teaching and learning (Barnes *et al.*, 1990; Hickman and Kimberley, 1988; Edwards and Westgate, 1994). It will be argued that language is a particularly important consideration in the history classroom because history has a specific and discrete technical language and vocabulary of its own (Crowley, 1996). The chapter argues that in the contemporary history classroom, communication, discussion and interaction are all prerequisites for learning and it draws upon research, particularly on group work, that can be used to promote effective interaction. Because of the close relationship between differentiation, communication and progression, you will see that Chapters 8 and 9 are closely linked.

Differentiation in history teaching: meeting learning needs through variety

Differentiation can be defined as 'the process of helping individual pupils to progress in their historical knowledge and understanding in the skills and processes of history . . .

by planning in ways which are able to cater for the range of individual needs and abilities that teachers will encounter' (CCW, 1993, p. 13). This definition not only highlights the close connection between differentiation and progression (see Chapter 9), but in a sense also makes the need for a separate section on differentiation in this book redundant, for my chief aim throughout has been to articulate, via research, a variety of teaching methods that meet the diverse learning needs of pupils or, using the words of Wilson (1985, p. 28) 'the creation of a milieu that is conducive to effective learning'. In this sense, as Ware and Peacey (1993, pp. 67–8) argue, 'the aims of teaching history to pupils with learning difficulties are indeed the same as those of teaching history to any pupil' (see also Sebba and Clarke, 1991; Sebba, 1994). Moreover, 'every class is different because of its different history and the complexity of its interpersonal dynamics' (Postlethwaite, 1999, p. 28). Nevertheless, given the importance of differentiation, particularly in relation to pupils with SEN, I first want to consider how the concept of differentiation in history teaching has evolved, and then use some of the most recent research work to consider how it can be implemented effectively in the history classroom.

The word differentiation first came to be used widely in history teaching after the introduction of the GCSE in 1985. One of the major aims of the GCSE was to provide pupils 'across the ability range with opportunities to demonstrate their knowledge, abilities and achievements: that is, to show what they know, understand and can do' (DES, 1985a, p. 2). Rather than test what pupils did not know, the GCSE aimed to provide opportunities for pupils to express what they did know and in history, it was decided that differentiation should be achieved by outcome. Instead of providing different questions and tasks geared to different ability levels, differentiation by outcome involved setting open-ended questions and tasks, which could be answered in a variety of ways – from the most simple to the most complicated responses. This became known as 'levels of response' marking. Differentiation by outcome was not without its difficulties, some believing that complicated language prohibited some of the less able from answering questions, whilst others believed that the more able were not stretched effectively enough. The HWG (DES, 1990) argued for a combination of differentiation by outcome and by task – that is, setting a number of tasks of varying difficulty.

This brief discussion demonstrates 'how the terminology of assessment has significantly influenced thinking about appropriate ways of teaching and learning' (McAleavy, 1994, p. 157; also, see Chapter 11). As McAleavy points out, therefore, although careful consideration of task-setting is a central element, differentiation is really concerned with the way in which a range of teaching and learning strategies can be utilized at different times to meet the diverse learning needs of pupils. In the words of Hart (1992, p. 10) differentiation implies a 'set of judgements and procedures whose purpose is to accommodate differences in children's abilities, aptitudes and needs'. One is reminded here, of course, of the importance and relevance of the ideas of Gardner (1983). Thus, one of the most comprehensive definitions of differentiation provided by Weston (1992, p. 6) argues that:

- Differentiation is premised on diversity
- Differentiation is multidimensional
- Differentiation applies to individuals
- Differentiation applies to all learners

- Differentiation is diagnostic
- Differentiation challenges expectations
- Differentiation challenges classroom relationships
- Differentiation is an integral aspect of effective learning
- Differentiation is relevant for all teachers
- Differentiation requires a long-term, whole-school strategy.

It is clear, then, that 'pupils are motivated by a range of different learning situations and a variety of teaching methods. Varying the teaching methods is likely to benefit the range of pupil ability represented in a class' (CCW, 1993, p. 13). In this excellent publication, based upon a range of case studies, the Curriculum Council for Wales (CCW) suggested a combination of whole-class, group and individual learning situations in the history classroom:

- *Whole-class*: including 'the well-told story', question-and-answer sessions in whole-class situations and whole-class discussions
- *Group work*: including small groups with the same tasks, small groups with differentiated tasks, brainstorming, ranking and sequencing, peer-teaching and role-play
- *Individual work*: including open-ended tasks, structured tasks, extension activities and appropriate activities for pupils with learning difficulties.

The development of the concept of Special Educational Needs (SEN)

A major aim of the section above was to stress that differentiation should be viewed as a fundamental, generic concept in all history classrooms. It goes without saying, however, that it is particularly pertinent to pupils with special educational needs (SEN). Indeed, one of the positive benefits of policy changes with regard to SEN in recent years has been to encourage teachers and schools to develop teaching strategies that are 'accessible to all', particularly in the humanities (Clarke and Wrigley, 1988; Bovair et al., 1992). The term SEN has become embedded in the culture of most comprehensive schools since the mid-1980s (Dyson and Slee, 2001). This is because of a range of important pieces of statutory legislation, which we will now examine, in brief:

1978: The term SEN was first coined by the Warnock Report, which stressed that one in five pupils could be said to have a 'learning difficulty' at various points in their school careers. The notion of the 'Warnock 20%' caused a radical change in the attitude to SEN, which was no longer the preserve of the 'special needs' (or the horribly sounding 'remedial') department, but that pupils with learning difficulties were the responsibility of *all* teachers, including history teachers.

1981: The Education Act stressed that SEN pupils should have greater access to the curriculum; it also established the system of Statements, which involved evaluating the needs of pupils and then providing the means by which these needs could be met. The statements thus provided entitlement and accessibility to specialist help, support and resources.

1988: The ERA enshrined the concept of entitlement; SEN pupils had a statutory right to the National Curriculum.

1993: The Education Act and subsequent *Code of Practice* (DFE, 1994) ensured that not only the 2 per cent of SEN pupils but also the 'other 18 per cent' of SEN pupils without Statements were given adequate provision and support. This was the real fruition of the Warnock Report of 1978 because the onus was placed firmly on schools (rather than just local authorities) to ensure that the learning needs of all pupils were catered for, including drawing-up school policies for promoting entitlement, access and differentiation, managed and organized by a Special Educational Needs Co-ordinator (SENCO). The Code also made it very clear that most SEN pupils would be catered for within mainstream schools, thus articulating the concept of integration; in addition, it established a five-stage process for special educational needs, with the emphasis placed very heavily upon identifying the *individual needs* of pupils (see Ramjhun, 1996):

1. The special learning needs of the pupil are recognized.
2. Differentiated provision is established, including the drawing-up of an individual learning plan.
3. Specialist support (from outside) is used by the school if necessary.
4. Evaluation of whether a statutory assessment is needed.
5. Pupil is assessed for SEN Statement.

The 1994 Code also defined a number of categories of learning difficulties, including:

- Physical disability
- Problems with sight, hearing or speech
- Mental disability
- Emotional or behavioural problems
- Medical or health problems
- Difficulties with reading, writing, speaking or mathematics work.

1998: The New Labour government continued the consensus above by emphasizing the importance of inclusion of pupils with SEN in mainstream schools (DfEE, 1998a).

2000: As part of the 'National Curriculum Review 2000' all curriculum subjects have a list of 'common requirements', including the requirement that provision is made to facilitate pupils with SEN.

It is clear from the above that SEN pupils are to be regarded as an essential feature of the vast majority of state primary and comprehensive schools. However, the government's recent emphasis upon selection and specialization has caused some researchers to raise issues about the future in this connection. An analysis of this debate, as well as an excellent summary of the legislation above is provided by Dyson and Slee (2001) and by Farrel (2000). Clarke *et al.* (1998) provide an invaluable analysis of SEN theory and research on classroom practice, which I have found particularly stimulating.

Implications for history teaching and history teachers
Although there were some notable exceptions (see Cowie, 1979; Wilson, 1985), it is fair to say that the history teaching profession was initially fairly slow to respond to some of the challenges presented by legislation in the early 1980s. As Haydn *et al.* (1997, p. 143) point out, as recently as the mid-1990s OFSTED (1995) identified 'that 'insufficient attention was being given to pupils for whom reading and writing were

difficult, and it mentions the inappropriate use of resources and tasks for pupils with varying abilities and that history teachers do not always make best use of support staff to help provide access to the curriculum'. Haydn *et al.* (1997) also make reference to another report (OFSTED, 1993), which found that 'one of the abuses of history has been to give pupils with special educational needs mechanical and undemanding tasks, which have no intrinsically historical purpose and are in effect tests of comprehension, transcription or presentation'.

My own research in the 1990s (Phillips, 1992b, 1993) suggested that the National Curriculum 'Mark I' – specifically its complicated and inappropriate assessment structure (Haydn, 1994) – was perceived to be particularly inappropriate to SEN pupils, and largely explains the difficulties encountered by history teachers. Since then, a great deal of positive progress has been made (see Cunnah, 2000), although it is still fair to say that there is still a long way to go as far as meeting the needs of all SEN pupils is concerned.

So what do student teachers, in particular, need to be aware of when teaching SEN pupils? And according to the research, what are the strategies open to us? Based upon the research evidence, the following advice can be considered:

Ownership of 'the 20%'

Clearly, we need to recognize that *all* teachers have a responsibility to the significant proportion of pupils in history classes who have learning needs; it follows that history teachers have an obligation to develop appropriate teaching strategies and learning atmospheres to meet these needs.

Recognizing individual needs

History teachers need to recognize that pupils have a range of *individual* learning needs (see summary of DFE, 1994, above). It may be that pupils find it difficult to listen, speak, communicate, read, write, move about or sit down, touch, feel, memorize, remember, repeat or even socialize. Whatever the issue may be, it is important to recognize the difficulty. Lomas (1999) has provided a comprehensive summary of some of the most common difficulties faced by lower attaining pupils, with accompanying implications for the learning of history:

- Poor attention spans – history has a large content-base
- Lack of confidence – often reducing capacity for initiative, ability to participate naturally in group work and for making value judgements, which are important in history
- Limited vocabulary – pupils lack a sophisticated grasp of everyday language, let alone the complex demands of historical terminology (see below)
- Writing problems – involving inability to plan, poor grammar, limited style, repetition and inability to construct historical argument
- Reading difficulties – particularly with regard to long or complex words, expression and long pieces of text in history
- Absence – often the least likely to catch up in history lessons after being away from school
- Perseverance – poor concentration and commitment is often linked to failing to see the relevance of what they are doing in history

- Poor timing – either finishing work too slowly or too quickly
- Misunderstanding – even after careful guidance
- Recall – finding it difficult to link things up, make connections and to undertake what has been called 'joined-up thinking' in history (see Chapter 9)
- Lack of a good general knowledge – lacking what Lang (1996) calls the 'way of the world' (see Chapter 10) means that they find it hard to make judgements, to select what is important or recognize historical significance
- Imagination – lacking imagination can mean finding it difficult to undertake essential tasks in history such as posing questions, analysing, inferring or making links; too much imagination can lead to anachronism.

Only by recognizing this range of difficulties can we formulate strategies to help pupils overcome them (see also Lomas, 1995, 1998; Haydn, 1992).

Creating a 'supportive' environment in the history classroom

Much of this book has been concerned with exploring what research tells us about the most appropriate learning environment. Given the lack of confidence and accompanying social skills, it is particularly important to concentrate upon creating a supportive atmosphere and environment for SEN pupils in the history classroom. Using a wide range of research, and taking into consideration the list of difficulties above, Lomas (1999) has suggested that the following factors are important for creating what he calls 'a supportive environment with high challenge and low threat':

- Raising self-esteem – through praise, reward and the appropriate recognition of achievement
- 'Talking up' expectations – taking pupils beyond their comfort zone with the minimum of threat
- Engendering optimism in pupils – which can be developed by encouraging pupils to want improvement; teachers can help here by expressing confidence in the pupils' ability, showing pupils how to improve and praising them when they do
- Creating a positive learning environment – where hard work and achievement are recognized; values such as trust, openness and persistence are useful here
- Altering attitudes to the subject – research suggests that one of the main influences on pupils' attitudes to a subject is the attitude of their teacher
- Co-operation and team work – should be at the core of differentiation, with pupils sharing and exchanging information via pairs, small and larger groups, collaborative exercises, trust-building activities and encouraging ground rules for collaboration (see below)
- Focusing upon positive values and attitudes – such as concentration, listening, co-operation, mutual respect and using initiative
- Time and space – giving pupils time to think and develop their vocabulary.

Linking teaching–learning differentiation

This book has identified a range of effective teaching and learning strategies that are appropriate to *all* pupils; it is hoped that this chapter has also reinforced the powerful messages to be derived from the research of Gardner (1983). On the other hand, some pupils have certain difficulties that do require further specialist support and it is the duty of the school, through a supportive learning environment, to provide it. This may involve obtaining specialist help from the SENCO and 'in-class' support teachers; again, student teachers need to avail themselves of these support networks. The CCW (1993, p. 29) provides useful guidance for using special needs expertise:

- Vary teaching and learning methods
- Encourage discussion and debate
- Structure tasks into small, achievable but open-ended steps
- Have realistic expectations
- Use appropriate vocabulary and speech
- Carefully select content
- Provide sources in a variety of formats
- Take account of reading levels and pupils' intellectual development
- Encourage the presentation of work in a variety of formats, including ICT
- Take account of layout, language level and content of pupil materials
- Use the SENCO and support staff for all of the above where necessary.

The SENCO and other SEN staff can provide support in a variety of ways. This might include:

- providing detailed information about pupils' learning needs, such as precise reading difficulties, restricted language, perceptual weaknesses and emotional make-up;
- offering advice on schemes of work and the planning of lessons, assisting in the production of appropriate materials for pupils with learning difficulties and giving advice on marking pupils' work;
- providing appropriate equipment in class;
- arranging for support staff to assist individual pupils in class.

Because student teachers lack the situational aspects of craft knowledge that will provide the vital information about the individual learning needs of pupils, it is absolutely vital that they utilize class teachers, the mentor and, of course, the SENCO.

Differentiated resources

In response to the legislation above and calls from history teachers, publishers have since the mid-1990s produced a wide range of teaching resources for pupils with learning difficulties. One of the main aims of our *Total History Experience* research was to identify some of the most appropriate resources for meeting the needs of pupils with SEN. Like the CCW (1993) we found that the most appropriate resources and materials for SEN pupils were *instructive* by articulating very clearly what is expected; *accessible* to a range of abilities in terms of language, format and layout; and *interactive* by requiring pupils to respond in a variety of ways. In short, the CCW and our research confirmed that as far as teaching materials are concerned, pupils benefit from:

- knowing what is expected of them – through clear instructions, objectives and expectations;
- having a clear and attractive layout – particularly via ICT;

- accessible language – via differentiated resources;
- built-in support – through such things as diagrams, tables, study hints, clues and acronyms;
- achievable and challenging exercises – such as those that require sequencing, identifying, sorting and comparing;
- receiving immediate feedback – via resources, either through self-assessment or formative assessment by the teacher.

Language in history: 'paying homage'

It is clear from the discussion and analysis above that language plays a fundamental role in differentiation and in meeting the learning needs of pupils. Students on the PGCE secondary history course at Swansea since the mid-1990s will often have heard the phrase 'pay homage to language'. This is because language in many ways provides the life-blood of history and can be the key to unlocking the 'foreign' nature of the past (Cunnah *et al.*, 2001). On the other hand, used inappropriately, inefficiently and ineffectively in the history classroom, language can cause enormous problems and actually undermine the learning of the subject. A considerable amount of research has been undertaken on the use of language in history teaching (e.g. Curtis and Bardwell, 1994; Edwards, 1978; ILEA, 1979; Wishart, 1986). One of the best discussions on the importance of language in history is that provided by Husbands (1996), who outlines four different types of historical language:

1. *The language of the past* is very different from that of the present, and includes specialist terminology (e.g. 'beadle' or 'reeve') as well as shifting words (e.g. 'gentleman') which are used today but had specific meanings in the past.
2. *The language of historical time* includes words such as 'era', 'century', 'medieval' and 'modern' and is used to organize the study of the past.
3. *The language of historical description and analysis* is also used to give meaning to history but some of these words, such as 'revolution' or 'democracy', can have different meanings at different times in the past.
4. *The language of historical processes* such as 'cause', 'chronology', 'similarity', 'difference', has certain specific meanings, which historians use to communicate about the past.

Note how words in history can convey different meanings and significance. Little wonder that words such as 'church', 'state' and 'party' are sometimes referred to as *weasel* words because of the confusion that they pose for pupils. Edwards (1978) suggests that terms like 'the Black Death', 'the Peterloo Massacre' and 'the Night of the Long Knives' have certain connotations for pupils that are different to ours. According to the Inner London Education Authority (ILEA) (1979) this is because in order to truly understand the meanings of words such as 'trade', 'revolution' and 'reform', pupils need vicarious experience (what Lang (1996) calls 'the way of the world'), which they have not yet developed. Yet the mistake made by some teachers is to take this knowledge and experience for granted (Edwards, 1978; ILEA, 1979). What, then, can we do in order to help pupils make sense of this 'foreign' language?

- *Making language explicit*: history teachers need to ensure that they take the issue of language in history very seriously and 'spend time exploring historical words and concepts with pupils. It cannot be expected that their meaning – in particular, their meaning for different situations and at different times – will simply be picked up as the theme, topic or story is unravelled' (ILEA, 1979, p. 188).

- *Planning*: this needs to be reflected by making language consideration an integral element of the planning process. Key words, phrases and technical vocabulary have to be anticipated and prepared for. This provides ways for the teacher to anticipate the difficulties pupils may encounter with certain words and then to determine how to help them understand the meanings of these words.

- *Varied teaching approaches and learning styles*: we must recognize that in order to cultivate pupils' use of language, we have to use a variety of methods, as well as different genres of expression. Open questions, group work, role-play, structured writing frames, even storytelling, all play a part (see below).

- *Concrete 'mind pictures'*: research indicates that pupils will understand words far more effectively if they are given vivid, illustrative (iconic) examples to reinforce meanings.

- *Repetition and revisiting*: just like a foreign language, repetition and re-visiting consolidates understanding; we cannot expect pupils to use historical language naturally, if we don't use these words regularly as part and parcel of a natural terminology.

- *Glossaries*: simple historical vocabulary lists and glossaries provide pupils with a sort of dictionary to check meanings and to consolidate understanding; glossaries are even more effective when they are backed up with iconic representation.

- *Wall displays*: vocabulary acquisition and repetition are greatly enhanced when words are displayed in the classroom and can act as an excellent teaching tool.

- *Making Historical language come to life*: we saw how words and phrases taken from the book *Lock, Stock and Barrel* published by Past Times (1998) can be used for ISM. By arousing curiosity in this way, we can develop pupils' interest in language.

To summarize, in an excellent book Levine (1981, pp. 104–5) echoes many of the sentiments above by arguing that we can draw the following conclusions about the role of language by analysing the research:

- that concrete language helps learners learn;
- that understanding involves process and in this process learners use words with which they feel comfortable;
- that talking and listening have great potential value as a means to learning (see below);
- that a learner's acquisition of language comes with use and confidence;
- that the learner is active.

Narrative, reading and the (welcome) return of story in history

Ever since the Bullock Report (1975), it has been recognized that all subjects need to take the issue of reading seriously and, of course, this is also reflected in the National Literacy Strategy (DfEE, 1998b). Given that history relies upon an enormous amount of written material – much of it rather inaccessible even to A level pupils (see Lang,

1996) – this is particularly apposite to us. What, then, can be done to encourage effective and meaningful reading in the history classroom?

ILEA (1979) suggest that we need to select material carefully. If we resolve to use a certain (difficult) source, we need to ensure in our own minds that it is necessary for the accomplishment of the task in hand. If we decide that it is, then we could consider amending the language in the text, but this raises all kinds of philosophical and educational issues relating to whether we should 'doctor' history in this way. Some of the most apparently 'accessible' books at Key Stage 3, for example, have reading ages far in excess of the age range. Therefore, we have to devise specific reading strategies. One of the most common (and awfully overdone) methods of reading from a textbook, for example, is to ask as many individual pupils as possible to read a sentence or paragraph out loud, with the teacher clarifying understanding and meaning via question-and-answer. Experience suggests that this becomes very repetitive and boring, and so we need to develop more ingenious and creative ways of ensuring that pupils grasp the meaning of text. This could involve:

- reading in pairs, followed by whole-class clarification;
- pairs or groups assigned one paragraph each, with the task of feeding back the meaning to the rest of the class;
- encouraging pupils to summarize the meaning of a sentence or paragraph using short phrases;
- giving pupils (either as individuals, pairs or groups) specific instructions (e.g. finding out information or meaning from one sentence or paragraph);
- the use of marker pens on photocopies (sparing original textbooks!) of words that need clarification; or
- the use of marker pens to obtain information from the text (e.g. 'underline/mark all the dates on the page', 'underline/mark everything that went wrong ' or 'underline/mark words that show you how he felt').

Following the reading of text, note-taking and information-gathering exercises still have a part to play in history teaching. It is not old fashioned to believe that pupils should 'get something in their books' and that this information, knowledge and evidence is needed for more analytical, demanding and progressive tasks.

Another recent development in history education has been the reassertion by researchers of the importance of story, not only for encouraging interest and curiosity via ISM (see Chapter 6) but because of the wider educational benefits that stories and story telling have in the classroom. Bage (1999), in a passionate and fascinating book, refers to a range of research that suggests that story motivates pupils to use more sophisticated language (Fines, 1983); makes interpretations more meaningful to pupils (Little and John, 1990); improves pupils' capacity to learn factual information (Perera, 1986); and 'socializes children into wider worlds, offering youngsters access to the values and experiences of their elders' (Bage, 1999, p. 24). Little wonder that Bage sees the use of storytelling in history as a particularly effective means of promoting literacy, and reading in particular.

Bage also suggests a number of techniques for improving the readability of historical stories, texts and historical evidence, including:

1. *'Talking evidence through'*: Using group work for pupils to interrogate the text together, share ideas, ask questions, hypothesize and clarify meaning so that the

group work 'synthesizes co-operation with substantive, conceptual and discursive historical content to produce talk that makes and communicates historical meaning' (*ibid.* p. 135).

2. *'Talking documents'*: Working from either an original or simplified version, pupils use a historic document to illustrate, mime or sketch the meaning of it.

3. *'Storyboarding'*: Turning a piece of text into a storyboard of pictures to tell the story.

Work by Hoodless (1998) and Collins and Graham (2001) has rightly emphasized the value of historical fiction for encouraging curiosity and interest, as well as for using in connection with interpretations. Claire (1996) has also stressed the importance of story and historical fiction for multicultural education (see Chapter 12).

From teacher talk to pupil talk: encouraging participation

I indicated above that researchers have for many decades recognized the importance of language and talk for effective learning, and this work has also been applied in history teaching (see Cramer, 1993, Loader, 1993, Tonge, 1993). Thus, as Farmer and Knight rightly point out:

> speaking is of immense potential value as a means to learning. Yet most classrooms are dominated by teacher talk. Discussion often means little more than question and answer in which, with the best will in the world, often only a few pupils are directly involved. If talking is a 'good thing' – and it is vital for pupils who find reading and writing blocks to effective learning – then there is a need to use ways of working which allow pupils a chance for real talk.
>
> (Farmer and Knight, 1995, p. 66)

Like Brzezicki (1993), they suggest that the most effective means of doing this is through group work.

Yet, owing (again) to the New Right and the media, group work has had a bad press; often it is perceived as a 'soft option' – unstructured and lacking in purpose, but with plenty of opportunities for misbehaviour, idle talk (not related to the task in hand) and a subsequent fall in the quality of learning (see O'Keeffe, 1986). Inspection evidence suggests that if group work is done badly then indeed this is the outcome, but HMI have also stressed the need for a variety of teaching methods, with group work identified as an absolutely essential prerequisite for effective learning (see ESTYN, 2001).

Generic educational research on interaction (Collis and Penney, 1996) and on group work (Bennett and Dunne, 1992; Cowie *et al.*, 1993; Kutnick and Rogers, 1994; Reid *et al.*, 1989) and the literature on effective teaching and learning (Kyriacou, 1992, 1995; Joyce *et al.*, 1997), as well as specific research on group-work in history teaching (Curtis and Bardwell, 1994; Farmer and Knight, 1995), all suggests that group work has the following benefits in terms of learning outcomes:

- developing a co-operative approach to learning through the sharing of ideas and peer-learning;
- providing a flexible approach to teaching and learning;
- fostering a wide range of social skills, such as listening to the views of others, as well as justifying arguments of one's own;
- encouraging an exploratory approach to learning through group engagement, activity and reflection;

- developing higher order thinking skills, through such cognitive and communicative processes as theorizing, speculating, hypothesizing, generalizing, reporting and recording;
- cultivating values such as co-operation, tolerance and respect for others.

All these are essential for effective differentiation and progression; learning takes place through co-operation and sharing ideas.

However, research also emphasizes the need for careful planning, organization and management to 'make group work work'. One of the best books on the subject by Reid *et al.* (1989) provides a comprehensive list of suggestions in terms of planning, implementing and observing group work, as well as developing reflective strategies to improve its effectiveness continually (see, in particular, the useful 'characteristics of effective and ineffective group work' on page 69 of their book). More recent research by Joyce *et al.* (1997, p. 130) suggests that group work needs to be organized around four phases: orientation, participant training, operation and debriefing. I use this framework to suggest that, based upon ideas drawn from the other research above, the following factors need to be taken into consideration for effective group work:

Orientation

- The size of the groups has to be considered – how big are they going to be? Farmer and Knight (1995) suggest that five is the optimum number; less than three and it is not a group; in excess of six is too large.
- The seating of the groups in the class is important (Bennett and Dunne, 1992).
- The selection of the groups is also crucial – this can be done randomly, by the teacher or by the pupils themselves; each has advantages and disadvantages. However, much will depend upon whether the teacher wishes to have mixed ability or ability groupings.
- The nature of the group tasks has to be considered and planned carefully, with attention given to specific objectives; groups tasks should be structured in such a way that they ensure maximum participation and motivation.
- Ensure that the tasks are based upon interesting and accessible stimuli: pictures, artefacts, short (rather than long) sources.
- The purpose of the group activity has to be explained carefully; an overview of the purpose of the activity is also helpful.

Participant training

- The rules and routines of the group work have to be articulated carefully (procedures, types of decisions to be made, management of resources, goals, purposes and objectives).
- Allocate roles (for example, chair, recorder or reporter).
- Clarify how information is to be reported and fed back.
- Explain how much time is allocated to the task at hand.
- Hold a short, abbreviated practice session if necessary.
- Be explicit about many of the learning outcomes identified above, including the need to co-operate, learn from each other and tolerate one another's contributions

Operation

- Monitor groups' progress carefully; be prepared to intervene if necessary, especially if there is evidence of non-task related talk.

- Keep reminding groups of objectives, rules, routines and time available.

- Repeat instructions; clarify misconceptions and, if necessary, stop all groups in order to do so.

- Allow enough 'thinking time'.

- Offer appropriate encouragement and praise.

Debriefing

- Identify difficulties or challenges encountered.

- Give pupils the opportunity to feed back in a manageable way – short pieces, bullet points and illustrations are more effective than long written pieces.

- Compare and contrast contributions in a positive fashion.

- Summarize major points in a concrete/iconic way via handout, board, OHP, PowerPoint, etc.

- Link what has been learned to what needs to be done next to consolidate and improve understanding.

These strategies are particularly important for encouraging naturally 'non-participative' pupils, who often lack confidence. They will not participate if they do not have something specific to contribute, or feel confused, intimidated or unsure of what to do. Much of the success of group work will therefore ultimately depend upon the climate created by the teacher through the strategies above. In particular:

> pupils will not feel confident in stating their views and opinions in groups, or be willing to listen to the views of others, if their ideas are not sought and appreciated ... the nature and extent of teacher intervention in helping individual pupils to cope effectively in discussions needs, therefore, to be carefully and sensitively planned.
>
> (ILEA, 1979: 191).

Simulation in history: the use of role-play

Given the unique opportunities for pupils with varying abilities to communicate and express themselves through simulation, I want to discuss its uses here, focusing particular attention upon role-play. I must confess that I get rather deflated sometimes when my students tell me that teachers in their schools are reluctant to use role-play, mainly because of the potential difficulties associated with pressure of time, lack of space, as well as the perceived negative impact it may have upon class management. Yet, organized properly, role-play and other simulation activities have enormous benefits and can encourage a wide variety of knowledge, understanding and skills (Luff, 2000). Simulation also contributes fundamentally to what Fines and Verrier (1974) call 'the drama of history'.

Moreover, viewed within the context of Gardner's research and the need for differentiation, it could be argued that simulations are essential. Birt and Nichol (1975) suggest that simulation activities have the following learning benefits:

- Increased motivation is developed through enthusiasm and 'hands-on' involvement.

- Empathetic appreciation is increased because pupils are drawn into situations via role-play that give them insight and understanding of motivation, cause and effect; pupils are also able to use their imagination for specific historical purposes (see Goalen and Hendy, 1994).

- Pupils gain a particular insight into historical situations, and this provides the opportunity to explore a multiplicity of possible outcomes.

- Recall is improved 'by doing' (see the discussion of Bruner in Chapter 3).

- An increased level of variety of teaching approach.

- Particularly important for us to consider here is that Birt and Nichol (1975) found that pupils' social skills could be greatly improved as a consequence of role-play and other simulations. Because they take place in small groups, pupils have to co-operate and communicate (see the discussion of Vygotsky in Chapter 3).

On the other hand, as with all teaching tasks, we have to think about the selection of role-plays carefully. In one of the funniest of the *Just William* stories by Richard Crompton, William finds his new history teacher profoundly irritating because he seems to do a role-play in every lesson and on every conceivable opportunity, much to William's chagrin! Overdoing role-plays can be as boring for some pupils as too much source or written work. Role-plays have to be carefully planned, with due attention paid to time, space and organization (see below). More seriously, time and thought needs to be given to the appropriateness of role-play. I once observed a role-play that simulated recruitment and 'going over the top'; I was extremely uneasy, until after the role-play had been completed, when the teacher demonstrated the horrific reality of the First World War through written and visual evidence. There are other sensitive topics that role-play is clearly not appropriate for.

Once these moral and ethical issues have been seriously considered, what does the research tell us about the organization of role-plays, so that we ensure that pupils benefit from them in the ways described above? How, in particular, do we ensure that pupils are encouraged to contribute and communicate meaningfully via role-play? Drawing upon the work of Birt and Nichol (1975), Fairclough (1994), Farmer and Knight (1995) and more recently Luff (2000), it is clear that an effective role-play needs the following prerequisites:

- Adequate space, with priority given to safety considerations.

- The majority of the class must be involved; monitoring techniques by the teacher need to be acute.

- The role-play should be simple and 'performable' (Luff, 2000), with little need for rehearsal.

- An effective introduction by the teacher, which sets the scene and explains the purpose of the enquiry.

- Information and evidence used in the role-play needs to be kept to a qualitative minimum, but always selected for its usefulness and relevance; it should also be seen as the starting point for further discussion.

- Linked to the point above, the role-play should not require advanced reading skills, rather the emphasis should be upon succinct, manageable verbal contributions.

- Roles for each of the participants in the role-play need to be carefully defined and explained in terms of purpose and expectation.
- The role-play should not be protracted, so that there is not enough time for follow-up, debriefing or shared reflection; the teacher needs to draw out the major conclusions from the activity and a recapitulation of the purpose of the role-play is useful too.
- Effective follow-up activities (including written work) can be used to develop, consolidate and deepen the knowledge and understanding learned in the role-play.

Role-plays can be designed for different purposes. Fairclough (1994) suggests ways in which visits to heritage sites can be greatly enhanced by role-play, particularly in relation to the cultivation of different interpretations. Lyons (2001) shows how role-play is useful for promoting citizenship. Luff's (2000) 'society game' provides a wonderful opportunity to teach an overview of the complexities within historical societies in a simple, effective manner; the role-plays on Roman roads and armies provide scope for conceptual development, whilst 'Hitler's seizure of power' demonstrates how particularly demanding concepts and historical events can be made accessible to pupils at GCSE and at A/S or A levels. In all, Luff's classroom-based research demonstrated that these activities contributed 'to pupils' general confidence and willingness to speak up for themselves and join in debate and discussion' (*ibid.* p. 17) and, crucially, that this confidence was reflected in subsequent written work.

This shows that role-play can bring home the significance to pupils in ways which even the best teacher expositions and iconic representations fail to achieve. Bage (1999) suggests a wide range of exciting, manageable role-plays to encourage communication and language acquisition:

- *'Talking walls'*: Pupils design a narrative classroom display (e.g. Spanish Armada); individuals are then asked to describe each part of the story and, where appropriate, emphasize its significance.
- *'This Was Your Life!'*: Pupils research a historical character and prepare a script for the programme; individual pupils can be relatives or friends on the programme telling the audience about the person's life.
- *'What would you do?'*: Pupils have to offer advice to a historical character in a historical situation (also, see Goalen and Hendy, 1994).
- *'News interview/reports'*: Pupils conduct an 'on the spot' interview with a historical character at an important time in his or her life: what questions would they ask? What answers would the character give? The class then write a report.

Other researchers also emphasize the vital contribution that role-play can make in terms of introducing pupils to complex values (Illingworth, 2000), for promoting citizenship and for undermining prejudice (see Chapter 12).

This chapter has focused upon research that explores ways of making the 'foreign' world of history accessible to a range of pupils via differentiation. In the next chapter, I draw upon research that helps us explore ways of making the subject appropriately challenging and rewarding to pupils via the concept of progression.

CHAPTER 9

Making history challenging: progression and discursive analysis in history teaching

> The answer to the question of what constitutes progress in history is intrinsically linked both to what we believe the discipline of history to be and what we believe it to be for.
>
> (Vermeulen, 2000)

Introduction

This chapter uses research to discuss ways of making the subject of history appropriately challenging for pupils. The emphasis here is upon appropriateness because I want to argue that one of the most important tasks for the history teacher is to devise meaningful tasks, activities and experiences for pupils that meet their learning needs, but that also encourage them to make appropriate progress in terms of knowledge, conceptual understanding and the cultivation of vital skills. Like Vermeulen (2000), the chapter considers what we mean by progression in history by defining it in relation to the research literature. It therefore discusses at length the notion of discursive analysis, drawing mainly upon the work of Christine Counsell (1997), which in many ways has transformed approaches to history teaching since the late 1990s. An important aim of the chapter is to attempt to argue that the notion of discursive analysis implies more than simply 'extended writing'; rather, it relates more to the ways in which pupils think about the subject holistically.

Towards a definition of progression in history

Since the 1970s, progression has attracted the interest of a number of researchers and has therefore initiated a rich literature (Dickinson and Lee, 1978). As Lee and Ashby (2000, p. 199) point out, this interest in progression is closely related to reforms and changes to history that have encouraged us, as we have seen, to look at the subject not just in terms of content but as a discipline. They describe this as a shift from viewing history not merely in substantive (i.e. content) terms but also to consider it from the perspective of second-order or procedural ideas (i.e. concepts and skills). Thus, Grosvenor and Watts define progression as the capacity of pupils to develop:

- expanding knowledge and understanding of the past;
- increasing understanding of terminology and concepts;

- growing ability to use an increasing number of more complex sources, and to see how and why people interpret history in different ways;
- improving investigative, organisational and communication skills.

(Grosvenor and Watts, 1995. p. 25)

Progression is closely linked to assessment (Haydn *et al.* 1997) but in this chapter I want to stress the fundamental relationship between teaching, learning and progression. As far back as the mid-1980s, under the revealing title of 'Progression and Pedagogy', HMI argued the following:

> teaching means the deliberate intention to help others develop and acquire historical knowledge: content, concepts, ideas and skills. Learning is the acquisition and understanding by pupils of that knowledge. . . . Teaching therefore has to create the intellectual, social and emotional circumstances that learners need in order to grasp new ideas, develop skills and understand content.

(DES, 1985b, p. 16)

This reminds us that progression has to be seen to be at the centre of the planning process (Culpin, 1994) and needs to be closely linked to differentiation (McAleavy, 1994). There is also a close correlation between progression and the type of thinking that we want to encourage amongst pupils (Fisher, 1990, 1995; Dove, 2000; Nichol, 1998), particularly in relation to fundamental historical concepts such as 'Suffrage, feudal, democracy, treaty . . . history's building blocks' (Haenen and Schrijnemakers, 2000, p. 22). Probably the most substantial definition of progression in history is that provided by Lomas (1993). Writing at a time when controversy about progression within history in the National Curriculum was at its height, Lomas argued that it involved the ability to:

- utilize greater amounts of historical knowledge with which to substantiate statements and judgements in history;
- categorize, see patterns, summarize and generalize, and grasp essentials from a mass of details;
- make connections and links between issues across periods and focus upon significant issues in the past, as well as the ability to understand the relevance of the topic and its wider significance;
- move from concrete to abstract concepts;
- explain and substantiate things rather than just describe; also, to be precise and accurate in explanations;
- develop an independence of thought, the capacity to pose questions, hypothesize and devise ways of finding answers;
- acquire an informed scepticism about the past, as well as an inclination to qualify statements with elements of uncertainty, yet still be able to reach conclusions.

You may be able to recognize the influence of Lomas' ideas upon the present National Curriculum (Lomas, in fact, was a member of the HWG). Moreover, many of these issues have been discussed in previous chapters, particularly in relation to our analysis of what constitutes effective teaching. Given this definition, I also want to stress in this chapter that progression and discursive analysis (see below) are essentially the same thing.

Attempts were made as early as the 1970s to map out progression in terms of historical knowledge, content and skills (see SCHP, 1976; DES, 1985a, pp. 18–19). The HWG (DES, 1990) were faced with the task of defining progression in history around a ten-level model developed by the Task Group on Assessment and Testing (TGAT) (DES, 1988b), which underpinned all National Curriculum subjects. This led to problems with history (see Chapter 10) but after a considerable amount of reform in the mid-1990s, you can still see the influence of the ideas of the HWG on today's level descriptions within the National Curriculum.

As we saw earlier, Lomas argued that an essential element of progression was the ability to pose questions, think independently and develop a curious 'informed scepticism'. We also saw in Chapter 6 the importance and usefulness of questioning. Consider the following selection and note how the questions we ask pupils (either orally or in writing) can connect with the key elements of history in a progressive fashion.

Chronology, change and continuity questions

When did this happen?
How long did this take?
What is this period called?
In what ways has X changed?
In what ways has Y stayed the same?
What changes were there?
What things changed most?
What things changed least?
What types of changes occurred?
Why did this change but not that?

Historical knowledge and understanding

Characteristic features

What was it like?
What did X believe in?
In what ways was X different to Y?
Why were they different?
What motivated people to think like this?

Cause and consequence

Why did X happen?
What were the causes/reasons for this?
What were the consequences/effects/results of this?
Which was the most important cause/reason?
Which was the most important consequence/effect/result?
What were the short/medium/long-term causes/reasons?
What were the short/medium/long-term consequences/effects/results?
What types of causes/consequences were there?(SPEAR)causes/reasons?
How were the causes/consequences linked?

Comparisons and connections

Compare X to Y. How are they different/the same?
How did X affect Y?

Significance

Why was X important/significant?
In what ways was Y important/significant?

What was the SPEAR significance/importance of X?
What was the short/medium/long-term significance/importance of Y?
How important was X?
Was Y successful/unsuccessful? Effective/ineffective?

Of course, the selection of questions will change according to different learning contexts (McAleavy, 1994, p. 155). Laffin (2000a) describes some strategies for 'moving pupils on' from Key Stage 3 to dealing with the challenges and requirements of Key Stage 4, by focusing upon the requirements of questions. Developing progression across key stages is an important issue; thus, Parsons (2000, p. 8) argues that 'primary-secondary continuity and progression are the responsibility of all history teachers'. Interestingly, she advocates the use of creative, thinking-related activities early at Key Stage 3 to build upon, cultivate and develop pupils' historical understanding acquired in Key Stage 2 (see also Counsell, 2000a, 2000b). Similarly, Leonard (2000) shows strategies to promote progression between GCSE and A/S level (this work and the work of Laffin are discussed in the next chapter).

'Putting it all together again': analytical and discursive writing in history

This section is concerned with 'the relationship between thinking and writing' (Dove, 2000, p. 9). We discussed in Chapter 7 how the overemphasis upon decontextualized source work had rather negative effects upon task-setting in history teaching. An obsession with exercises relating to reliability, utility or 'bias' led in some cases to an arid and potentially deconstructive impact upon what history teachers were asking pupils to do (Lang, 1993). McAleavy (1998, p. 13) argued that instead of 'spending their time agonising over bias, reliability and the provisional nature of historical evidence', pupils should be encouraged and taught to 'create a substantiated and well-argued account of an aspect of the past'. The challenge, therefore, was to explore ways of using sources and evidence for a purpose, to answer a line of enquiry through analysis, reasoning and argument. It is fair to say that extended writing has made a very significant return to the history classroom in recent years, after a number of decades in the wilderness.

One of the most obvious reasons why narrative and discursive writing were relegated in the history classroom was that they were complex and demanding, with the potential to dispirit some pupils. As HMI indicated:

> writing narrative is a complex but necessary activity for pupils, and it depends on grasping such basic matters as sentence construction, punctuation, tense, paragraph, and the use of conjunctions. This understanding does not occur in isolation; it goes hand in hand with the successful development of the ordering and expressing of ideas.
>
> (DES, 1985b, p. 5)

Similarly, Husbands (1996, p. 113) draws upon Australian research to suggest that historical writing involves the following processes:

- Data collection
- Interpreting data
- Organizing data
- Drawing conclusions
- Presenting conclusions.

One of the most positive, important and influential developments in history teaching since the early 1980s, in my opinion, has been the formation of a highly effective methodology for developing extended writing, most notably associated with the work of Christine Counsell (1997). In this seminal paper, Counsell combined her own classroom-based research with work on thinking skills (Fisher, 1990, 1995), as well as research on literacy (Wray and Lewis, 1996). Counsell suggests that we need to 'aim high' in history teaching as far as written analyses and extended explanations are concerned. Too often, perhaps, history teachers have been overly pessimistic about what pupils can achieve, a mindset not helped by the banal quality of tasks and exercises in textbooks that seem only to encourage short written responses from pupils (John, 1993, 1994; Byrom, 1998). As we shall see below, research has shown that a more effective way of encouraging meaningful learning is by using a concluding enquiry to reinforce and assess earlier learning (Byrom, 2000).

Counsell (1997, p. 7) argues that provided teachers develop tried and tested strategies and frameworks to assist pupils, even the most low-attaining pupils can produce extended, analytical answers. This is essential as 'to help pupils to structure their work with independence and imagination, is to help them to get better at everything else', particularly the development of a 'critical mind set', involving the ability to pose questions, acquire knowledge, to analyse, explain and even empathize. This is vital also within the wider context of citizenship education (see Giroux, 1988, pp. 54–73 for an excellent discussion), as well as the development of key skills, for pupils who are never expected to 'produce writing which is informed, structured, purposeful and substantiated may never find an analytical voice' (Counsell, 1997, p. 7).

Given its importance, I want to focus upon Counsell's work in some detail here, starting with a number of her practical suggestions.

1. *Make extended writing an integral element of history teaching*: The National Curriculum (DfEE, 1999b; ACCAC, 2000) has an explicit requirement that pupils should undertake extended writing of different types; this was included in order to encourage teachers to take this aspect of their teaching seriously. However, Counsell suggests that this should not be viewed as a separate 'bolt-on' skill and that although the demanding technique of extended writing needs to be explicitly taught and cultivated, it needs to be viewed as a natural part of history teaching (see also Gorman, 1998). Yet ironically, in order to work independently, pupils have to be taught to think independently and analytically. But like source work, extended writing always has to be done for a purpose, and linked to the other key elements of history in a holistic manner.

2. *Use key questions and lines of enquiry to inform classroom activities*: We have seen throughout the book how the use of carefully considered key questions can help direct both teaching and learning. Counsell argues that a series of lessons can be geared towards answering a big key question, with a range of teaching activities being used to answer it. The lessons can then conclude with the opportunity to 'bring it all together' to answer the 'big question' via an analytical writing activity. She emphasizes, however, that these opportunities have to be used selectively, so that 'death by sources' is not replaced with 'death by extended writing'. Counsell argues that extended writing involves helping pupils to select the factual material that they need to use in order to answer a line of enquiry, and then deploying it effectively; but before this can be taught, teachers first have to recognize the challenges that pupils face.

3. *Recognize the difficulties that pupils face*: Counsell draws upon wider, generic research to suggest that pupils face the following difficulties and challenges:

- Pupils have only short-term memories, yet in order to present a logical, extended argument, they are expected to draw upon a range of information, which presents major challenges to that memory.

- Pupils find selecting which facts are relevant to a particular question very difficult; learning to select is something that even A level pupils find demanding.

- Pupils also find it difficult to collate and sort the subject of history; for example, categories that are familiar to us, such as economic, political or social, can be incomprehensible to some pupils. Sorting into categories, as we saw in Chapter 4, presents a range of conceptual challenges.

- Pupils find it difficult to utilize historical evidence to substantiate an answer; they therefore find it difficult to distinguish between very important and less important facts. Counsell often refers to these as 'big' and 'little' points.

- Pupils often do not understand the specific 'language of discourse' in history. They lack the necessary vocabulary and armoury of connectives to deploy arguments effectively.

The rest of the booklet provides a range of strategies to help pupils overcome these difficulties.

4. *Use a range of sorting activities*: Counsell suggests a number of different sorting activities that can assist pupils in selection, classification and categorization:

- *Sorting and classifying using given sorting criteria*: For example in order for pupils to answer the question 'What kinds of things caused Claudius to invade Britain?', Counsell gave pupils a range of factors on cards and they were then asked to categorize them under certain headings such as 'Factors to do with Julius Caesar', 'Factors to do with Claudius', 'The ways in which Britain could be useful to the Romans' and 'Military matters: things to do with the army'. She suggests a follow-up activity that encourages the pupils to answer the question 'Were people better off under Roman Rule?' To answer this question, pupils have to divide their page into two columns entitled 'People were better off because . . .' and 'People were not better off because . . .'

- *Sorting using more difficult concepts and terms*: Counsell argues that in order to encourage progression as far as knowledge and understanding of causation and consequence is concerned, 'pupils can be taught to move from simpler, concrete sorting ideas into more abstract concepts' (Counsell, 1997, p. 20). Thus, in order to understand the interaction of social, political and economic factors, it is a good idea for pupils to plot these factors on Venn diagrams. Counsell argues that diagrams are particularly important as far as causation and consequence are concerned. In addition to Venn diagrams, these include 'cause and consequence' or 'flow' diagrams and 'ripple' diagrams (see pp. 24–8 of the booklet for a fuller description and illustration).

- *Choosing own sorting criteria*: Progression is further encouraged when pupils are asked to decide upon their own criteria for selection. Presented with a list of causes relating to the question 'Why did William win the Battle of Hastings?', pupils could sort them under a range of headings such as 'William' or 'Harold'; or 'luck', 'military skill' and 'timing'; 'long-term', 'medium-term' or 'short-term'.

This could also involve pupils actually thinking up their own items for sorting, for example, making their own sorting cards.

5. *Use diagrams and other visual representations*: As we saw in Chapter 2, diagrams are an excellent means of representing highly conceptual ideas in a concrete form, what Bruner called the 'iconic' mode of representation (see Nichol, 1995). Counsell advocates the use of diagrams to assist in the process of sorting and selecting. For example, 'flow diagrams' are an excellent means of demonstrating cause and effect, as well as the connections between events. Similarly, ripple diagrams are particularly useful for showing the short-, medium- and long-term impact of events. Counsell also advocates the use of Venn diagrams to show the 'overlap' between certain categories. She emphasizes that pupils should be given opportunities to experiment with such diagrams and to use them in peer presentations (see Husbands's (1996) discussion of the work of Parker (1993) on 'conceptual plans' to help pupils shape their work).

6. *Cultivate the language of discourse*: Counsell argues that the majority of pupils need to be taught the 'language of discourse in history' and that there are three major ways of doing this:

- *'Clever starters'*: Defined as 'a menu of connectives, sentence stems or paragraph openers' (Counsell, 1997, p. 31; also, see her examples on pages 31–2 of the same publication). She advocates these being on permanent display on the classroom wall, so that pupils can select from them, according to the nature of the historical problem they are being asked to interrogate.

- *Writing frames*: Counsell uses the work of Wray and Lewis (1996) to demonstrate that writing frames can be used in a variety of different contexts and for different purposes and can be matched to the ability of different pupils. Thus, more able pupils can be offered a skeleton frame to assist discursive writing, whilst less able pupils may require more detailed help. She emphasizes that writing frames need to be used judiciously in this respect; the teacher needs to strike a balance between giving the pupil too much assistance and the need to provide structure so that he or she can learn from the experience. Once pupils know what they are doing through writing frames, they will then be able to work more independently later (again, see examples in Counsell, 1997, pp. 32–4).

- *Modelling styles*: In order to encourage progression, Counsell argues that pupils should be exposed to different styles of writing, in order to cultivate different types of language. She advocates, for example, extracts from historians, accompanied by imaginative activities such as role-play, which will help in motivating pupils.

Key questions, lines of enquiry and analytical writing in practice

As we said earlier, Counsell's work has been immensely influential in terms of motivating teachers to attempt ambitious and challenging discursive activities with pupils. We discussed in Chapter 7 how Mulholland (1998) developed the use of what she termed the 'evidence sandwich' for helping pupils organize their evidential work, to provide them with a structure for producing extended responses and assist them in the development of language. The constituent parts of the 'evidence sandwich' are shown in Figure 9.1.

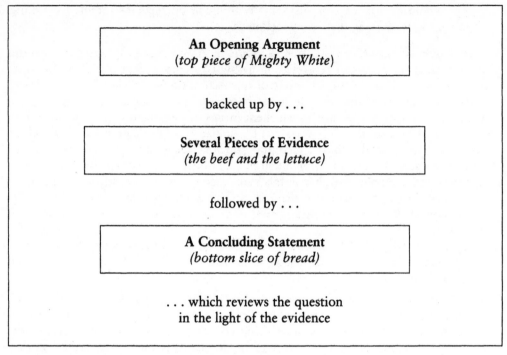

Figure 9.1 *The 'evidence sandwich'* (Mulholland, 1998)

Banham (1998) describes the way he planned for an eight-week enquiry about the reign of King John, based upon the interpretive key question: ' "King John was the worst king ever to sit on the English throne." Do you agree with this statement?' The enquiry provided a means whereby pupils could use their evidential skills to 'weigh up the evidence' for a specific historical purpose and in the process, understand the fundamental ideas, values and beliefs relating to the concept of medieval kingship. The eight-week period culminated in pupils producing:

> a piece of extended, analytical writing . . . to draw their understandings together and to argue a case, systematically . . . pupils of differing abilities had to be taught how to select relevant information, to organise their ideas and to write in an appropriate style.
>
> (Banham, 1998, p. 6)

The study involved 6 stages:

Stage 1: Pupils were given a range of sources, both primary and secondary, offering a negative interpretation of King John.

Stage 2: Pupils were given a range of sources, both primary and secondary, offering a positive interpretation of King John.

Stage 3: Pupils were given a sorting exercise to help them categorize different information in terms of evidence which indicated that John was (a) a bad king, (b) unlucky, or (c) a good king.

Stage 4: Pupils did some further individual research on King John for homework.

Stage 5: Pupils took part in a 'mock trial' of King John, either in defence of the King or working for the prosecution. Pupils wrote speeches for the trial, based upon the evidence, and then interviewed 'the King' before actually taking part in the trial.

Stage 6: Pupils 'put it all together' in the following ways:

- Pupils were given photocopies of all the speeches and evidence, and were asked to select information that related to the essay question.

- They then cut out pieces of information and placed them in the relevant position on a large (A3) writing frame, with headings such as 'Evidence that John did good things', '. . . that he was cruel' and '. . . that he made mistakes', etc.

- Any other information that pupils thought was relevant from the previous lessons was added.

- Pupils were then given an exercise that allowed them to compare John with other medieval kings.

- Two teacher-led lessons focused first upon the use of connectives and second on the use of effective introductions and conclusions, with a concrete analogy to help, namely the idea of the 'evidence hamburger' (similar to Mulholland's 'evidence sandwich').

- The essay was then completed, using the hamburger frame, first in class and then for homework; pupils also used a summary of the work in the form of a 'grand prix race' and a 'connectives guidance sheet' (see Banham (1998, pp. 8–15) for a detailed description).

- These were presented in class and finally displayed in the history classroom.

It is interesting to note the ways in which Banham's 'stages' follow quite closely the framework described above by Husbands (1996), from data collection to presentation. Banham found that his pupils produced high quality, analytical essays, which demonstrated a sound understanding of the reign of King John and the ways in which it has been interpreted. In addition, Banham (1998, p. 14) found that his pupils were able to transfer the skills developed in other historical analyses (such as a study of Oliver Cromwell) and in other subject areas of the curriculum, encouraging him to conclude that 'if students are taught key writing and thinking skills in a memorable and stimulating way they can transfer these skills to new learning situations'. In other words, he had taught his pupils to *think*.

Exploring different discourses ways of analytical summary and expression

It should be emphasized, particularly within the context of the messages behind Gardner (1983), that we need to be careful about the opportunities we provide pupils for 'drawing it all together' through summation. The danger, of course, is that 'death by sources' is replaced by 'death by extended writing'. Opportunities for extended writing have to be considered shrewdly within the planning process, as do the precise nature of the written activities. Husbands (1996, p. 113), drawing upon the work of Parker (1993), lists no less than 150 different types of writing, which provide an abundance of opportunities for different genres of expression. In the *Total History Experience* research (Phillips, 2002a), we sought to develop different ways of encouraging pupils to express themselves through the written word in relation to significance. Thus, pupils could:

- Choose to write either an obituary or prepare an 'entry' for *Encarta*, describing the significance of Robert Owen's life.

- Prepare a television documentary script on the long-term importance of the Industrial Revolution for people living today.
- Design their own 'commemorative plate' of the Industrial Revolution, making reference to economic and social effects.
- Prepare a 'Today with Frost' script of questions for Olaudah Equiano, complete with the answers that he would be likely to give.
- Select an important character (from a list provided) from the Tudor period and prepare a brief speech stressing his or her importance; in groups, they were then asked to perform a 'balloon' exercise.

Given the messages behind Gardner's work (see Chapter 3) and the need for differentiation (see Chapter 8), there is a need to provide non-writing conclusion/summation opportunities for pupils. Gorman puts this particularly eloquently:

> an enquiry does not have to culminate in a piece of extended writing. Other motivating outcomes for enquiries could include advertisement, instruction manual, film storyboard, theme park design, board-game, debate, TV show format, diagram or role play. What matters is that the final outcome, first, requires pupils to draw the threads of the enquiry together and to engage in some analysis of the problem as a whole; second, that it is substantial and significant, motivating and meaningful for the pupils. They need to feel that they have reached some worthwhile resolution.
>
> (Gorman, 1998, p. 25)

In the Battle of Mametz study within the *Total History Experience* (see Phillips, 2002c), after pupils had all been given a letter-writing exercise as a common summation activity, pupils were asked to choose from a wide range of tasks based upon Gardner's seven intelligences (see Chapter 3). We found that these exercises led to a very interesting concept, namely the notion of a *collective summation*, for when put together, each of the exercises above led to a rich, varied and wholesome summary of the Battle of Mametz and its significance.

I have emphasized that Chapters 8 and 9 are closely linked via the concepts of differentiation and progression respectively. I have learned a great deal about these concepts from working with my colleague Wendy Cunnah and it is therefore appropriate that I use five key points from her work to summarize some of the fundamental, generic messages that derive from the research described in these two chapters. Cunnah's (2000, p. 122) central argument is that differentiation and progression should be viewed as integral scaffolding to teaching and learning; this includes:

- an awareness of the language demands of the subject and the ways in which teacher and pupil talk can provide access routes into written language skills;
- an acknowledgement that low achievers can grasp demanding concepts if concrete everyday examples are used, which relate to their own experiences and provide a conceptual bridge into understanding historical events;
- the availability of a range of teaching and learning strategies that motivate, develop discussion skills and provide a dynamic and interactive teaching environment;
- the development of specific structures and writing frames to enable all pupils to write analytically and discursively;
- a belief that all pupils can make progress in history if taught in an appropriate manner.

CHAPTER 10

Assessment, evaluation and examinations in history teaching

> Pupils currently going through compulsory education in England and Wales will be among the most assessed the state education system has ever produced.
>
> (Gipps and Stobart, 1993)

Introduction

An aim of this chapter is to focus upon the ways in which assessment should not be seen as an end in itself but as a means of promoting effective learning. Drawing upon recent research on the relationship between teaching, assessment and learning, the chapter argues that the central role of assessment should be diagnostic, that is to help pupils recognize both their strengths and weaknesses so that they can improve and progress. It also considers the statutory requirements of assessment and their relationship with the history teacher's role (see White, 1992). Another important aspect of the chapter will be to consider the strategies and techniques required to help pupils achieve their maximum potential both at GCSE and A/S levels.

The educational role of assessment: aims, purposes and guidelines

The opening statement of this chapter is a salutary reminder of the statutory significance attached to assessment by successive governments. One of the dominant themes of the last quarter of the twentieth century was what Broadfoot (2001) calls 'performativity', when all spheres of the educational system were heavily monitored via testing, target-setting and other performance-related mechanisms. There is every reason to suggest that this emphasis will continue for some time to come. Little wonder that some researchers have for a long time questioned whether such an extensive reliance upon all this statutory assessment is really necessary, whilst suggesting that there is a need to regard assessment as far more than just 'testing' (Gipps, 1994). Others have argued that done badly, assessment can actually hinder effective teaching and learning (Harlen *et al.*, 1994; James and Gipps, 1998), particularly if teachers simply 'teach to the test' (Scarth, 1987). Even inspection evidence has suggested that ineffective assessment has led to 'many pupils not being given a sufficiently clear idea of their progress or an indication of how they might improve the quality of their work' (DES, 1992).

Assessment can be defined as 'the process of gathering, interpreting, recording and using information about pupils' responses to an educational task . . . assessment encompasses responses to regular work as well as to specially devised tasks' (Harlen *et al.*, 1994, p. 273). Much of the thinking behind this sort of definition originates from the highly important report produced by the TGAT (DES, 1988b), which formed the basis of assessment for all National Curriculum subjects and defined assessment in four ways:

- *Formative*: designed to enhance and support effective learning, for example, by helping to plan the next steps of learning
- *Diagnostic*: involving the capacity to identify learning difficulties
- *Summative*: through the systematic recording of attainment at the ages of 7, 11, 14 and 16
- *Evaluative*: using assessment results to evaluate schools and local authorities, eventually through league tables.

The TGAT report stressed that if it was done properly and in the right context, assessment had the potential to enhance teaching and learning.

So what is effective assessment? Baumann *et al.* (1997, p. 127) suggest that assessment should be:

- meaningful and clear to understand by teachers, pupils and parents;
- conveyed in language that is accessible to pupils;
- based upon a variety of modes and approaches;
- consistent and reliable as far as it possibly can be;
- organized in order to identify pupils' strengths as well as weaknesses, and how to resolve these weaknesses in order to improve achievement and performance;
- used to inform planning of teaching and learning but not to dominate it;
- designed using good examples that pupils can draw upon and improve.

Harlen *et al.* (1994) articulate the following set of principles that should underpin all assessment policy:

- Assessment should be used as a continuous part of the teaching–learning process, with both teachers and pupils involved identifying next steps.
- Assessment should improve learning by being a positive influence on the curriculum by encouraging the acquisition of more and more sophisticated knowledge, concepts and skills.
- The outcomes of assessment must be communicated effectively to parents and pupils in order to support pupils' learning.
- Different types of assessment must be used for different purposes and in response to different contexts.
- Assessment must be used fairly when judging school effectiveness, taking into consideration contextual factors, as well as the quality of teaching.
- Citizens (including parents and pupils) have a right to be given reliable information in order to judge standards.

Drawing upon the research work of Broadfoot (1996) and Black and Wiliam (1998), James and Gipps (1998) have argued that assessment can influence learning in four main ways:

1. Assessment provides motivation to learn:
   - by giving a sense of success in the subject (or demotivation through failure)
   - through giving a sense of self-confidence as a learner.

2. Assessment helps students (and teachers) decide what to learn:
   - by highlighting what is important to learn
   - by providing feedback on success so far.
3. Assessment helps students learn *how* to learn:
   - by encouraging an active or passive learning style
   - by influencing the choice of learning strategies
   - by inculcating self-monitoring skills
   - by developing the ability to retain and apply knowledge, skills and understandings in different contexts.
4. Assessment helps students learn to judge the effectiveness of their learning:
   - by evaluating existing learning
   - by consolidating or transforming existing learning
   - by reinforcing new learning.

James and Gipps (1998) also draw a distinction between 'surface learning' and what they call 'deep learning'. Whereas surface learning relies upon memorization and essentially a passive approach to learning, deep learning not only involves memorization but also a capacity for understanding, as well as an active approach to learning. Thus, surface learners may be effective at reproducing content as required, but deep learners are able to utilize and deeply understand that content effectively; surface learners tend to passively accept ideas and information, whereas deep learners interact with the content, particularly in terms of relating previous knowledge and experience to new situations; finally, whilst surface learning focuses upon the requirements of assessment, deep learning involves relating evidence to conclusions. Given the discussion in the previous chapters in this book, the importance and relevance of deep learning for effective history teaching is clear; it implies the need to

- develop the idea of 'knowledge as historical understanding' implied by the HWG (DES, 1990)
- utilize the varied approaches to teaching and learning advocated by Bruner, Gardner and others;
- adopt the questioning approach to enquiry, evidence and interpretation advocated by Counsell, Riley and others.

Deep learning is more closely associated with formative and diagnostic approaches of assessment; surface learning with summative and evaluative approaches. Formative and diagnostic techniques involve using assessment as an integral part of teaching and learning in order to diagnose pupils' needs and plan future progress. To do this, a wide range of assessment opportunities need to be used: both formal and informal. Again, this is particularly important given the implications of Gardner's multiple intelligence theory, as pupils need to be provided with a range of opportunities, media and situations to express what they can do. Baumann *et al.* (1997, pp. 203–4) argue therefore that 'skilled observation, thoughtful listening and perceptive questioning, as well as more conventional marking, are needed to assess the outcomes of pupils' work'. These strategies include:

- *Oral*: questions, discussion, presentation, role-play, debate, audio, musical
- *Written*: notes, lists, diaries, questionnaires, scripts, poems, essays
- *Graphic*: diagrams, drawings, graphs, printouts, photographs, video
- *Three-dimensional*: models, sculptures, construction
- *Physical*: co-ordination, manipulative skills.

This is what Harlen *et al.* (1994, p. 278) have in mind when they argue that 'a scheme of formative assessment must be embedded in the structures of educational practice'. Lomas (1999) suggests that assessment and positive feedback go closely together by making sure that any assessments undertaken check that pupils have understood (i.e. in the 'deep learning' sense). In addition, he argues that feedback needs to be immediate, specific and reflective and should involve diversity, choice, review and talk. He claims that diagnostic, formative comments to pupils in this respect are vital (see below). At the University of Wales Swansea, we use the following summary based around questions that student teachers need to ask themselves as a 'check-list' to ensure that they keep the connection between formative assessment and effective teaching and learning at the forefront of their minds:

- What do my pupils know?
- How do I know what my pupils know?
- Do my pupils know what they know?
- What do I need to do next to ensure that they know more?
- How am I going to do this?

The feedback provided to pupils in this respect is vital, particularly in relation to written work. HMI have emphasized this point further:

assessment of pupils' day-to-day progress depends heavily upon the marking and correction of written work and of other tangible forms of pupil response. The main purpose of such activity is formative: helping pupils to see how their work can be improved and developed, identifying weaknesses and uncertainties as a basis for action and as a major and effective practical means of establishing suitably high expectations of each pupil.

(DES, 1992, p. xx)

Marking pupils' work
There are different types of marking involved in monitoring children's work. These are listed below.

- *Acknowledgement marking*: places minimal time demands upon hard-pressed teachers. This type of marking acknowledges that the work has been seen. Often a tick or one word comment suffices; it can be backed up very effectively with a 'model' answer.
- *Correction marking*: is quality in-depth marking for a specific purpose and obviously involves a considerable time commitment on behalf of the teacher. This is when essential formative and diagnostic feedback can be given to individual pupils.
- *Assessment marking*: involves marking for specific assessment purposes, often with summative recording (e.g. in relation to National Curriculum key elements and level descriptions, or GCSE and A/S level criteria) as a main aim.

- *Focused marking*: specifically targets the work of individual pupils, such as underachievers or higher achievers.
- *Peer- or self-marking*: enables pupils to mark their own work in order to encourage self-evaluation; pupils can also mark each other's work.

Marking can therefore involve:

- Written comments on and at the end of a pupil's work
- Correction of errors
- Marks out of a given total
- The awarding of grades related to attainment in the subject
- Symbols with specific meanings (e.g. 'Sp' denoting spelling mistake)
- Questions to initiate a dialogue between pupil and teacher
- Instructions and suggestions on different ways to approach the work next time.

Given the pressure upon teachers' time, the emphasis in practical terms must be upon 'quality rather than quantity', with assessment being used for formative purposes. The messages that pupils may derive from marking are vital here. Again, at the University of Wales Swansea, we encourage student teachers to think about marking from the perspective of the pupil and to consider the question:

What does this marking tell me?
Does it tell me:
– what I did well?
– whether I am being praised?
– where I went wrong?
– what I must do to improve?
– whether I am being held accountable or not?

Do I understand:
– what it tells me about my effort?
– the mark/grade/comment made?

This is particularly important for student teachers who are, as we have seen in Chapter 1, sometimes preoccupied with their own performance rather than with their pupils, in the early stages of their training.

Assessing history in the National Curriculum

Sadly, history has often found itself negatively influenced by assessment and examinations. Both Price (1968) and Booth (1969) warned of the dangers of limited processes of examining and assessing, which seemed merely to test the ability to recall factual information in the form of essays. The former CSE and O level examinations gave way to GCSE (see below), but the new examination was not without its problems. As far as the National Curriculum was concerned, although the HWG (DES, 1990) warned of the dangers of 'parrot-learning' in history, the application of the ten-level TGAT model proved very difficult to achieve in history. The idea of attempting to define pupil achievement around an essentially linear framework of progression via 'statements of attainment' in this way proved practically impossible. It led to what some called 'jumping through the hoop' approaches, where pupils were given a series of specific tasks geared towards history statements of attainment. In my own research on history teachers' perceptions of the National Curriculum in its early stages, some referred to this system of assessment as 'daft', 'mad' and 'crazy' (Phillips, 1992b, 1993). Other research confirmed the unsatisfactory nature of assessment within history in the National Curriculum (Haydn, 1994).

This led to reforms in the mid-1990s; the statements of attainment were replaced by the present system, which is based upon the idea of 'best fit' descriptions. Whereas under the old system teachers found that assessment dominated their planning, the new approach involves aggregating pupils' achievements through a description that most appropriately or 'best fits' their attainment. Although the system has its limitations, it does provide real opportunities for teachers to make professional judgements about their pupils' abilities and progress through formative assessment. It also ensures, theoretically at least, that assessment considerations do not dominate teaching and learning. The emphasis within history in the National Curriculum is upon formative assessment 'to provide feedback to pupils so that they can understand how well they have coped with a task and can be helped to progress' (Bennett and Steele, 1995, p. 7). It is up to schools to decide what precise type of assessment they use, for example either a grade or a mark.

As far as coming to a summative judgement about pupils at the end of a key stage is concerned, official documentation on assessing history in the National Curriculum (ACAC/SCAA, 1996, p. 2) specifically reminds teachers that level descriptions are not designed to be used to 'level' individual pieces of work. Rather, by the end of a term, a year or key stage, teachers should have built up knowledge and evidence about a pupil's performance 'across a range of work, and in a variety of contexts, to enable judgements to be made in relation to the level descriptions'; this is referred to as a 'rounded judgement' which:

- is based on your knowledge of how the pupil performs across a range of contexts;
- takes into account different strengths and weaknesses of the pupil's performance;
- is checked against adjacent level descriptions to ensure that the level awarded is the closest overall match to the pupil's performance in the attainment target.

(Ibid.)

Clearly, then, judgements will have to be based upon information derived from evaluative and formative assessments undertaken during a particular period. Pupils will have to be given a 'range of alternative forms of communication to show what they know and can do' and judgements made by teachers need to 'take into account strengths and weaknesses in performance across a range of contexts and over a period of time, rather than by focusing upon a single piece of work' (*ibid*. p. 8). The ACAC/SCAA booklets provide detailed guidance on how to assess work in relation to the key elements. This is vital reading for any teacher, either inexperienced or experienced; note from the case studies in the booklets the following features that allowed the summative 'best fit' judgement to be made:

- A range of exercises, given in different contexts, requiring different types of knowledge, conceptual understanding and skill

- Key phrases taken from the level descriptions to be used as supporting evidence of the judgement made

- Consideration given to the level of support required by each pupil from the teacher

- The degree of professional judgement that has to be used by the teacher, in collaboration with other teachers.

This sort of approach also ensures that there is a degree of consistency in teacher assessment (ACAC/SCAA, 1995). The current National Curriculum framework is designed so that assessment considerations should not impinge upon planning, teaching and learning. Thus, Bennett and Steele (1995, p. 7) argue that 'decisions about performance cannot be made by applying mechanistic methods and rules'. As Haydn *et al.* confirm:

> the challenge is to achieve a balance in your recording of pupil work that is not excessively complex and time-consuming, yet is sufficiently detailed to enable you to build up a profile of a pupils' progress related to the Key Elements in a way that highlights strengths and weaknesses.
>
> (Haydn *et al.*, 1997, pp. 226–7)

Preparing pupils for assessment at GCSE

When the former CSE and O Level examinations were replaced by the GCSE in 1985, the new examination (as we saw in Chapter 2) stipulated only general (i.e. non-content specific) criteria and established the principle of differentiation by outcome, which encouraged pupils to express what they know, could do and understand (DES, 1985a). This led to the criteria-related system of 'levels of response' marking, which is still the basis for GCSE assessment today. There were claims in the 1980s and 1990s that there was not enough emphasis in the GCSE upon British history and the assessment of historical knowledge, so new GCSE criteria were therefore developed in the 1990s which would additionally meet the requirements of the National Qualifications Framework. The current GCSE common criteria (www.qca.org.uk) have the following main features:

- The number of examination boards has been rationalized and attempts have been made to standardize procedures across boards
- The GCSE aims to build upon experiences gained at Key Stage 3
- There is still variation of content choice across boards but all syllabuses must contain an element of British history and draw upon two different scales from local, national and international perspectives; the history studied must also be studied in at least two ways – such as in depth, in outline or thematically – and from at least two perspectives – political, social, etc.
- There are no 'context-free' questions; there is far greater emphasis upon demonstrating the use of context-related historical knowledge to show understanding
- More emphasis is also placed upon organization, communication and extended responses
- Syllabuses need to provide opportunities for developing Key Skills
- A limit of 25 per cent on coursework has been imposed
- Extra marks are awarded for correct spelling and punctuation.

Throughout this book, attempts have been made to evaluate the difficulties faced by pupils when learning history, before considering how to help pupils overcome them. As this is particularly important at GCSE let us now consider some of the specific difficulties that GCSE pupils face.

- *Not understanding assessment objectives*: This may involve not fully appreciating what they mean, not appreciating the progression in them and pupils not knowing what they need to do to obtain higher levels.

- *Deployment of knowledge* (Assessment Objective (AO) 6.1): These difficulties are similar to those faced at KS3, namely not being able to identify connections, offering monocausal/consequential explanations, failure to appreciate fully motive and purpose in history, and not providing enough reasons, explanations and justifications.

- *Use of sources* (AO 6.2) *and interpretations* (AO 6.3): Difficulties here include the tendency to simply describe what is in a source (comprehension), rather than explaining, inferring, comparing, making reference to provenance and motive and giving context. Some pupils find it hard to understand the meaning of utility and reliability. As at KS3, some still have not really grasped what interpretations are and fail to understand how and why different interpretations are constructed and for what purposes.

- *Quality of written communication* (AO 6.4): Some pupils need help in providing substantiated explanations and also tend not to provide enough balanced or reasoned argument.

- *Poor examination technique*: This may involve not understanding the different requirements of questions, not understanding the precise meanings of questions – not being aware of the meaning of specific words within questions, all leading to the tendency of offering irrelevant answers and concentrating on some questions at the expense of others.

- *Technical vocabulary and language*: Used in examinations, textbooks and everyday teaching, some students find this a barrier to understanding.

- *Lack of confidence*: This is a problem particularly amongst the 'less able' and crucially, those pupils who are at the D/C borderline.

- *Challenges of revision*: Problems stem from a lack of organization, planning and motivation and difficulties associated with time management, especially in relation to other subjects.

- *Boredom*: Sadly, this often emanates not from the nature of the subject-matter but from the teaching.

This last point is vital, I want to argue that although GCSE and A/S levels provide particular challenges in relation to examination requirements, which must be planned for, this should not have an undue impact upon the teaching and learning styles adopted. Too many teachers make the mistake of believing that they must 'teach to the exam', which has a negative knock-on effect upon their teaching. Ensuring that pupils are well prepared for an examination and using creative and effective teaching and learning methods are not mutually exclusive. All the teaching and learning techniques discussed in the previous chapters apply equally appropriately not only at GCSE but, as we shall see, at A/S level too. Here are some suggestions, based upon research findings, of how to make the teaching and learning of GCSE history meaningful to pupils, increase their motivation and ensure that they achieve maximum potential in the examination.

Making the requirements of the GCSE explicit

If pupils do not know what requirements are expected of them, how can they be expected to meet them? This involves the teacher providing detailed information about the aims and objectives of the selected syllabus, as well as the scheme of assessment, including the assessment loading of papers, the balance between written papers and coursework and the specific requirements of each. It is vital, however, that this information does not 'overload' pupils or undermine their confidence. A good idea here is to package the information in a 'user-friendly' manner – using suitable vocabulary, terminology and, at times, humour – in a departmental/course handbook. Moreover, as Culpin (2001) has recently argued, in order to provide GCSE pupils with a meaningful experience, the GCSE syllabus has to be transformed into a logical course of study, governed by lines of enquiry and geared to a range of teaching and learning activities.

Breaking requirements down

It is important to stress that each component of the syllabus requires different types of historical knowledge, understanding and skills. For example, a 'Study in Development' (e.g. 'Medicine through time') will focus mainly upon significance, change and continuity over time, whereas a 'Study in Depth' (e.g. 'Nazi Germany') may have a greater emphasis upon causation or the use of sources and interpretation. This will obviously influence planning and selection of teaching methods used.

Simplifying the GCSE requirements

Pupils can become overwhelmed with the apparent complexity and range of demands placed upon them. It is important here to simplify the requirements as much as possible, without losing sight of precisely what is required. Thus the current GCSE requires pupils to:

- Describe key features
- Explain ideas, attitudes and beliefs
- Evaluate the importance and significance of events and factors
- Analyse causes and consequences
- Appreciate change and continuity
- Deploy (make use of) knowledge
- Infer from sources
- Evaluate the utility of sources
- Evaluate the reliability of sources
- Use sources to come to conclusions
- Deploy knowledge in relation to sources
- Evaluate interpretations
- Analyse interpretations
- Explain why interpretations differ
- Deploy knowledge in relation to interpretations.

Helping pupils to understand the requirements of questions

This is absolutely essential if pupils are going to be encouraged to produce relevant answers. There are a number of ways in which pupils can be helped to do this. In addition to emphasizing to pupils the importance of reading the question, it is vital that they are encouraged to appreciate the significance and meaning of crucial words, adverbs and adjectives in a question, that have an important influence upon requirements and expectations. This can be done not only by providing pupils with plenty of examples of the types of questions asked, but also using a dictionary to provide specific definitions and meanings of important words, such as:

analyse – break into parts, explain, show links
compare – find similarities
contrast – find differences
deploy – make use of to confirm/explain
discuss – give reasons for and against
evaluate – make judgements using evidence
explain – clarify, make clear or expand
infer – draw information and conclusions from
utility – how useful a source is
show – use examples to illustrate.

Helping pupils recognize progression and the meaning of levels

Pupils also need to be reminded that different questions involve different loadings of marks. They also need to be shown, explicitly, the difference between levels of response and the progression of knowledge, understanding and skills involved. For example, as far as inference within the *Use of sources* (AO 6.2) is concerned, it is important to show the differences between:

- Level 1: e.g. comprehension
- Level 2: e.g. simple inference
- Level 3: e.g. complex inference.

Similarly, with regard to making judgements about interpretations by using contextual knowledge within *Deployment of knowledge* (AO 6.1) and *Interpretations* (AO 6.3) it is important to show pupils the differences between:

- Level 1: e.g. description of source or provenance
- Level 2: e.g. testing the content of the source in relation to other sources of information
- Level 3: e.g. testing the content of the source using own knowledge and other sources of information.

It is important, too, that this information is conveyed in a 'pupil friendly manner' using appropriate vocabulary and simplified mark schemes. Thus, if we want to convey to pupils how to achieve a higher level in causation (within AO 6.1), it may be a good idea to express it as follows, with additional reference to marks:

- Level 1 (1–2 marks): You give a general answer, which does not show much knowledge
- Level 2 (3–5 marks): You give one reason and explain it fully or you list several reasons but don't explain them
- Level 3 (6–8 marks): You give two or more reasons and explain them fully
- Level 4 (9–10 marks): You give two or more reasons and make a judgement (e.g. you could explain why some reasons are more important than others or you could show how some of the reasons are linked).

Helping with examination technique

Pointing out to pupils the importance of simple but vital things like the need to manage time effectively – spending more time on questions that attract more marks and the need to read instructions carefully. Providing pupils with opportunities to do timed questions regularly over the period of the course is also important. Explicit and simplified marking schemes (shown above) help with awareness of examination technique. Where appropriate, pupils can mark each other's work and it is important through this that they develop an appreciation of what 'good' answers look like.

Confidence building, reinforcement and revision

It is vital at GCSE level that attempts are made to motivate pupils via the many teaching and learning strategies described in earlier chapters. The following strategies, in particular, will help with confidence and revision:

- Breaking the syllabus down into key questions
- Encouraging pupils to process information via selection and sorting exercises
- Assisting pupils to compile effective, relevant notes
- Providing overviews and 'the big picture'
- Encouraging pupils to talk, discuss and express themselves
- Encouraging pupils to restructure information through the use of acronyms, diagrams, grids, pictures, concept maps and bullet points
- Regularly using scaffolding techniques for discursive writing: writing frames, clever starters and connectors.

'Fear, awe and the way of the world': helping pupils succeed at A and A/S level history

Few sectors in education have experienced the winds of change as sharply as the post-16 sector (Marples, 2000). Calls for change at history A level have a long tradition (Lang, 1990) and in the 1980s and 1990s there were a number of attempts to offer innovative alternatives to traditional A level courses (Fines and Nichol, 1994, Kelly, 1996). In the mid-1990s, the whole structure of post-16 education was radically reformed (DfEE, 1999b, 1999c). These reforms were influenced by three main factors. First, by the desire to create a more rationalized National Framework of Qualifications. Second, by the belief that a range of possible qualification avenues could be provided for pupils of different types, dependent upon their needs and skills: academic, technical and vocational. Third, by the requirement that there should be a broader experience for pupils at A level, leading to the development of the A/S qualification, which not only represents a radical change but which has not been without controversy, problems and criticisms.

History at post-16 therefore underwent considerable change in the 1990s in response to these national initiatives (Husbands, 2001; Fisher, T. 1995; Watson et al., 1997; White, 1994). The current subject criteria for A/S and A level history have the following characteristics:

- An attempt is made to provide continuity with KS3 and GCSE by stipulating similar assessment objectives based upon the *Deployment of knowledge* (AO 1a), *Conceptual understanding* (AO 1b) and the *Analysis of sources and interpretations* (AO 2)

- As with GCSE, there is no content specific requirement, other than the request that syllabuses should provide opportunities to study history in breadth and depth, that more than one country should be studied and a substantial element of British history should also be taught.

- Specifications also need to take into account Key Skills.

The most important aspect of the changes relate to the types of pupils now studying A/S level. History for some will be a fourth or even fifth choice, and they have no desire to pursue it after the first year; others may have just scraped a pass at GCSE and are, by traditional A level standards, relatively 'less able'. The point I am making here is that the A/S qualification has effectively created a 'mixed ability' scenario at post-16 and it is vital that pedagogy reflects this. It seems to me that some history teachers are relatively slow to grasp this nettle and as I have recently argued, there is still too much of a gap in terms of teaching styles between GCSE and A/S levels (Phillips, 2001b). So, as with GCSE, it is important first to consider what challenges and difficulties confront pupils at A/S and A level (see also Crinnion, 1987).

The best starting point in this connection is Lang's (1996) excellent article entitled 'Why Is 'A' Level Hard?'. In this paper, Lang draws upon a rich experience of teaching and researching, beginning with research which suggests that pupils have often regarded history as being one of the most demanding and difficult A level subjects. Lang argues that we need to analyse the intrinsic difficulties of the subject if we are to help pupils succeed and he identifies no less that eight reasons 'why 'A' level history is hard':

- *A non-existent past*: History, as such, does not exist – we only have evidence from the past that certain things happened. Moreover, there is a distinction between the past and history, the latter being the study of the past, rather than the past itself. This immediately creates a degree of uncertainty for pupils.

- *Did anything really happen?* Pupils become even more uncertain when historians seem to do apparent 'demolition jobs' on aspects of the past, which are interpreted and reinterpreted. For some pupils studying the subject, nothing seems to be certain.

- *No end to the sources*: The past is not only elusive, mysterious and uncertain, it is also vast. Whereas for many of us, it is this mystery and vastness that makes history so appealing, for pupils the boundlessness of the subject appears to be very daunting, particularly in terms of the reading and research that needs to be done.

- *A foreign country*: The foreignness of the past poses particular demands. We saw in earlier chapters how difficult it is for some pupils to permeate the minds of people in the past. At A level, this is exacerbated because of the need to study profoundly complex ideas and beliefs that are so different from those of our own world.

- *Language*: It is easy to forget how the language used in history can actually appear to be foreign to A level pupils. Lang quotes a wonderful phrase from a commonly used A level textbook, which explains how 'the real struggle for office and its attendant pickings lay between feuding Whig magnates'. One wonders what some A level pupils make of this sort of statement!

- *Empathy*: The foreignness described above makes it very difficult for pupils to understand and empathize with people in the past. Lang rightly suggests, however, that unless we make efforts to encourage pupils to empathize, history simply becomes a random, confusing and jumbled set of facts.

- *The way of the world*: One of the most perceptive comments in an outstanding analysis is Lang's claims that because history involves a wide range of disciplines – such as politics, sociology, psychology, philosophy, religion, literature, geography and so on – a concomitant wide range of knowledge is required to understand it. Moreover, things like motivation, reasoning and beliefs require knowledge and maturity – which Lang calls 'the way of the world' – that A level pupils simply do not possess.

- *Fear and awe*: Moving from GCSE to A/S level can be a traumatic experience for many pupils, particularly if it also involves a change of institution. Added to this is the academic aura that A levels carry with them. Moreover, how can mere A level pupils possibly challenge the views of the great 'Dr' this or 'Professor' that? Is it any wonder that some pupils are extremely reluctant to participate and offer their views in debate and discussion?

Lang goes on to argue that we also need to consider the challenges presented by A level syllabuses:

1. *Breadth of content*: Although things like defined topics and other methods of stipulating content have helped teachers in their planning, there is still a large degree of uncertainty about whether certain topics and content will be examined.
2. *Essay questions*: When asked to comment upon the difficulties they face, A level pupils point to writing essays as one of the most onerous and demanding things that they are expected to do. Essay writing is still fundamental to history at A/S level (Harris, 2001). As we saw with the GCSE above and as has been stressed in many of the other chapters in this book, pupils are challenged by the processes of selection, sorting, classifying, categorizing, etc. that are needed for effective essay writing. Moreover, the demands of certain essays also present particular difficulties. Using jovial nicknames for them, Lang identifies the following types of A level questions:

Honest John:	straightforward and easy to understand
	e.g. 'Why did war break out in Europe in 1914?'
Bill and Ben:	compare and contrast
	e.g. 'Compare and contrast the success of the nationalist unification movements in Germany and Italy'
Measuring Rod:	to what extent . . .? How far . . .?
	e.g. 'How far were the Italian states responsible for the Italian wars 1494–1559?'
Aunt Sally:	comment on a view
	e.g. ' "The Arch-Mediocrity". How far do you agree with Disraeli's description of Lord Liverpool?'

All of these questions require particular and different demands that pupils are sometimes not aware of.

3. *Document questions*: Despite being familiar with source work at KS3 and at GCSE, pupils still find document work demanding. Difficulties here relate to the language used, an inability to appreciate what the questions relating to the sources require and the artificiality of sometimes having to study documents in detached isolation from the rest of the history course (see Howells, 2000; Laffin, 2001 below).

So what are the solutions? Given the difficulties articulated above, it is vital that an attempt is made, using Kelly's (1988) phrase to 'bridge the gap' between GCSE and A/S level, particularly in relation to teaching styles. Earlier work conducted by Lang (1990) suggested that lecturing and even dictation were the most dominant teaching styles at A level in the 1980s and sadly, in some schools, this is still the case. So what do we have to do in order to make A/S and A level more meaningful to pupils? It is clear that many of the teaching and learning techniques described earlier in relation to GCSE still apply at A/S and A level and these can be developed in various ways (see Haydn *et al.*, 1997, p. 255). We now consider some of these shared techniques, based upon research evidence.

Managing content

It is vital that A/S level pupils are not overwhelmed by content demands. The syllabus can be broken down into manageable units, each with a cluster of enquiry questions (see Riley, 2000; Rudham, 2001) to make logical sense of it and to assist in preparing pupils for the kinds of questions that are likely to be asked in the examination. Of course, A/S level pupils can play an active role in determining what these questions are, through dialogue with the teacher.

Making use of study guides and other resources

There are a number of study guides that will provide useful advice to A/S level pupils on technique and methodology (e.g. Brown and Daniels, 1986). Historical journals such as *The Modern History Review, The Historian, History Today* are useful for content. In addition, the Internet is transforming access to historical information (see Chapter 11).

Making reading meaningful

There is often nothing more daunting for A/S level pupils than to be told 'read Elton by Monday'. Pupils need guidance, structure and assistance to undertake reading effectively and to construct their own notes. As Lomas (1999, p. 15) argues, 'reading should be for a purpose – for information, criticism, to substantiate a point, to make a presentation, to identify the significance or to re-organise information'. Suggestions in this connection include setting a small number of questions to answer from set reading; providing specific points to look for and to report back on; looking for, say six points in favour and six against an argument; underlining certain words in connection with a line of enquiry. There are also some useful suggestions on note-taking and reading in Coake *et al.* (1985).

Language acquisition, discursive analysis and essays

Remember that for some pupils, historical language is like a foreign language, so treat it as such by using vocabulary lists, dictionaries and history reference books. Laffin (2001) recommends the use of a 'language bag' to build up the required analytical discourse at A/S and A levels. This involves providing a large optional list of words that might be used to describe a primary or secondary source (the 'language bag' contains words like 'cynical', 'respectful', 'passionate', 'persuasive', etc.). Pupils have to select which one is most appropriate to describe the tone of the source. This sort of technique is vital also for acquiring the sorts of discursive techniques required for essay construction (see the discussion of Counsell (1997) and others in Chapter 9, which can be applied just as equally at A level). It is vital to spell out the different requirements of essays (see Lang (1996) above). Model answers, group/class essay plans and peer-marking all help (Harris, 2001). A particularly effective technique for promoting evaluation and analysis is to use a variation of Culpin's (2001) 'skittle game' (discussion in Chapter 7) by encouraging pupils to make sure that for every point offered in favour of an argument, there is also a contrary point or piece of evidence to balance the argument.

Bringing sources to life

Many of the issues discussed in Chapter 7 relate here. Laffin (2001) argues that sources are often taught in isolation – gobbets, in particular, being offered out of context – and to make matters worse are taught by repetitious practice of examination questions, which simply reinforce bad habits, including formulaic answers. Laffin suggests that examinations should not be the dictator in relation to the use of evidence; written documents should be used alongside the full range of sources, including artefacts, music, images, pictures, art and so on. She also suggests using innovative teaching methods to bring sources alive: drama and dialogue (reading parts, acting out), predictive/guess work (what is said next?) and captions (for photographs and images).

Developing progression in document work

Leonard (2000) argues that it is important that A/S level pupils are shown ways of using documents in more sophisticated ways than at GCSE. At A/S level, pupils are expected to be able to utilize a greater number of sources (for example, five); offer developed rather than simple statements; show the ability to make sustainable inference; provide well-balanced explanations; select very precisely from evidence; assess and evaluate utility considering both provenance and content; and above all, come to a reasoned conclusion from evidence. Laffin (2001) has suggested a number of useful ways of helping pupils in this respect:

1. *Lines of certainty* provide a stepped, analytical framework through sentence starters to promote inference and utility. Pupils are asked to select from five statements to describe what a source or combination of sources informs them about a line of enquiry. Thus, Source X may suggest that . . . infers that . . . tells us that . . . confirms that . . . proves that . . ., etc. Laffin argues that this helps counteract the tendency amongst some pupils to reject some sources outright. By encouraging them to take a positive stance to most sources, pupils come to realize that making a judgement about *relative utility* is what is important.

2. *Inference diagrams* in the form of ripple diagrams, include what the source tells us, what it suggests and what it does not mention (see also Riley's work discussed in Chapter 7).

3. *Reliability charts* encourage pupils to adopt a structured approach to determine the reliability of a source or sources. Pupils are first asked to take into consideration 'background points' (What? When? Where? Who? Why?); then to 'consider the significance' of the source (develop the relevant points, add contextual knowledge), then move on to 'making a judgement' about the source (completeness, consistency, typicality, authenticity, usefulness) and finally to 'qualify the judgement' (acknowledge limitations but also explain in what way the source is still of value).

Appreciating interpretation

Again, all the techniques described in Chapter 7 apply at A/S and A level. Laffin (2001) recommends one technique that is particularly useful and effective for promoting understanding of interpretation amongst A/S and A level pupils. This involves the interpretive 'washing line'. Pupils are asked to evaluate a secondary source, for example, in relation to the question 'Lenin: democrat or dictator?' Depending upon what they have read and their view of the interpretation provided, they are asked to 'peg' the name of the author at the right point on a 'washing line' with 'democrat' at one end and 'dictator' on the other. This provides a useful way of demonstrating the wide range of interpretations. Laffin also recommends using the 'washing line' to express pupils' own views; she has also encouraged pupils to use the 'pegs' to argue from different perspectives.

Promoting discussion, confidence and 'the way of the world'

It is important to remember that some A/S and A level pupils are very reluctant to participate in discussion, and yet this is a prerequisite for effective learning at this level. The techniques described in earlier chapters for promoting effective discussion, participation and group work are particularly important in this respect. Developing pupils' self-confidence and their knowledge of 'the way of the world' can be done by encouraging pupils to share their knowledge gained in other subjects, such as sociology, politics, economics and so on.

It is worth noting that A level teaching presents a series of challenges in relation to content knowledge, teaching skills and the motivation of pupils. Although it is important that student teachers have some experience of observing and teaching at post-16 level, this should be done selectively, so as not to interfere with progress in acquiring the knowledge and skills required to teach history at other levels. Likewise, knowledge of technical aspects of GCSE, such as the marking and moderation of coursework, needs to be developed but always under the close supervision of school mentors (see White (1992) for advice on coursework).

CHAPTER 11

Key Skills and the use of Information and Communications Technology (ICT) in history teaching

> History has always been a medium for delivering essential skills at all stages of education.
>
> (Jordan and Taylor, 1999)

Introduction

There has been an increasing shift in recent years towards the promotion of essential skills in response to the perceived need to develop highly qualified, motivated and adaptable school-leavers who are able to meet the demands of an increasingly complex, technological society. Information and Communications Technology (ICT) has been given particular prominence across the curriculum, with all student teachers now expected to gain competence in the subject (TTA, 1998a, 1998b; see also Linsell, 1998). History teachers have been encouraged to use ICT for some time (Francis, 1983; Randell, 1984; Blow and Dickinson, 1986, Martin and Blow, 1990) but it is fair to say that progress in this respect has been, in the past at least, rather patchy (Dickinson, 1998).

This chapter first analyses some of the Key Skills that should be promoted in the contemporary history classroom and considers what Counsell (2000c, p. 2) refers to as 'the worsening gap between outstanding ICT practice in history lessons and practice that is of questionable value'. As she points out, more access to information, prettier presentation and clever web pages 'do not guarantee any improvement in historical skill, knowledge or understanding'. Although Haydn (2000, p. 102) claims that 'there is not yet a substantial body of research evidence to affirm the "value added" learning benefits of ICT', the chapter draws upon our own research work at the University of Wales Swansea (Baker *et al.*, 1999) and the work of others, to consider the potential ways in which ICT can facilitate and enhance the learning of history, and at the same time meet the 'formidable and challenging ICT agenda' of the future (Dickinson, 1997, p. 35).

Like the TTA (1998a; see also BECTa/HA, 1998), this chapter argues that ICT should not be used for its own sake but should form an integral element of the wide armoury available to us to promote historical thinking and understanding (see also Atkin, 2000). It also considers ways in which trainee teachers can prepare themselves effectively to use ICT for their own professional development and for promoting effective teaching and learning. The chapter concludes with a brief discussion of the use of video as ICT in history teaching.

Key Skills, common requirements and ICT

It is worth noting that ICT is only one important element of a holistic, cross-curricular strategy to promote generic skills and concepts across the curriculum. Thus, at KS3, pupils in England (DfEE/QCA, 1999) are expected to have opportunities to:

- Develop language across the curriculum: writing, speaking, listening and reading
- Use information technology to develop better understanding of history.

In Wales (ACCAC, 2000), the National Curriculum is underpinned by 'common requirements', including:

- Curriculum Cymreig
- Communication skills
- Mathematical skills
- ICT skills
- Problem-solving skills
- Creative skills
- Personal and social education.

GCSE, A and A/S level syllabuses are expected to provide opportunities for pupils to develop a number of 'Key Skills' (see QCA/ACCAC (1999) for a fuller discussion of Key Skills):

- Application of number
- Communication
- ICT
- Improving own learning and performance
- Working with others
- Problem-solving.

The use of ICT must therefore be seen within this wider context of cross-curricular skills. As was indicated in the introduction to this chapter, its use also has to be carefully justified. Indeed, as the TTA (1998a, pp. 8–9) emphasize, three key principles should apply when considering using ICT:

1. The decision about whether to use ICT should be based on whether its use supports good practice in history; if it does not, it should not be used.
2. ICT should be used to facilitate specific learning aims and objectives in the subject.
3. ICT should allow teachers and pupils to achieve something that could not be achieved without it, or to learn something more efficiently, or both.

The TTA also specify the contribution to pupils' learning of history made by ICT, which helps pupils consolidate and deepen their historical knowledge through:

- Asking historical questions
- Investigating change, cause and consequence
- Assessing, evaluating and using a wide range of sources critically
- Organizing information and ideas to communicate effectively
- Understanding, analysing and constructing data.

As far as history teachers are concerned, the TTA stresses that ICT supports their work by:

- Helping them to locate sources and interpretations which can be adapted for use in the classroom
- Providing a flexible and time-saving resource
- Allowing teachers to respond to different stages in a pupil's writing
- Allowing the teacher to focus upon the different characteristics of sources.

These aims are explored below through a consideration of the beneficial applications of word-processing, databases, the Internet and CD-ROM in history teaching.

'Helping Gerry': the potential of the word-processor

Word-processing has the potential to have a profound influence on history teaching and learning. The subheading above is taken from the rather inspirational article by Walsh (1998, p. 6) who argues that the word-processor can be compared to the kitchen blender, which can 'effortlessly slice, purée, blend, mix and manipulate'; likewise the word-processor can 'search, annotate, organise, classify, draft, reorganise and redraft'. In an article packed with excellent suggestions based on classroom research, Walsh describes the way he was able to demonstrate to 'Gerry' (a typical lower-end GCSE pupil) the relative importance of causes by actually representing them in 'big' and 'little' boxes on screen. Thus, 'Gerry was not able, at first, to articulate the relative importance of these causes in words, but he was able to express this concept in terms of the sizes of the boxes' (*ibid.* p. 14).

This example should explain why the word-processor can help fairly typical pupils like 'Gerry' understand the subject more effectively. Thus, in our own research (Baker *et al.*, 1999, p. 1) we found that word-processing was particularly important for promoting some aspects of analytical activity such as extended writing. This correlated with Martin's (1998) reference to what he calls the 'enhancement strategy' of using ICT to improve a specific dimension of history teaching. As we saw in Chapter 9, extended analytical writing is not one process, it is the final stage of several processes. Pupils must take information in several forms (sources, narrative, etc.) and translate it into another (an essay, balanced judgement or conclusion). Word-processing can facilitate pupils in this respect by helping them to:

- understand the text – by searching for and identifying important points;
- be selective – by retrieving and retaining information relevant to their purpose and discarding the rest;
- sort information into categories such as chronology, cause and consequence;
- refine information – by using more sophisticated criteria such as short-term, long-term, political, religious, economic, etc.;

- employ the language of discourse to translate the information into a coherent piece of writing, using discursive words like 'however', 'nevertheless', 'despite' and 'on balance'.

As Counsell (1997) reminds us, analytical activity places greater demands on pupils' short-term memory than simply recounting a narrative or answering closed questions. Less able pupils, in particular, can find this juggling and organizing of facts and ideas difficult. But more able pupils can also struggle when asked to use information constructively, as opposed to simply moving it from one place to another, for example from textbook to exercise book. I now want to draw upon research that shows ways in which well managed, purposeful word-processing can help pupils in all of the respects above.

Understanding text

We know that many pupils have difficulty in understanding the textbook or source material from which they are required to extract information. Word-processing can make text more accessible in a range of ways. Wilkinson (2000) suggests ways in which pupils can highlight text they do not understand, use the electronic glossary, dictionary or thesaurus functions to clarify meaning and separate text that can be arranged in paragraphs, given headings or bullet points. He argues that the word-processor can be used to help pupils read and understand text at any level – KS3, KS4 and above – by providing instructions such as:

- Read through the source
- Highlight any words whose meaning is unclear to you
- Use the thesaurus to find an alternative word
- Enter subheadings in the text, to help you summarize the key arguments
- Underline these so they stand out
- Use bold to show facts
- Use italics to show opinions
- Produce three or four bullet points underneath the text to summarize the key points
- Now briefly explain whether you agree or disagree with the interpretation in the source.

In line with the main thrust of the arguments presented in this chapter, low-level skills need to be facilitated to achieve more sophisticated ones. Our own research (Baker et al., 1999) found that the principal benefit of these sorts of exercises is the very close reading that pupils are compelled to do in order to perform the formatting. As Wilkinson (2000, p. 20) rightly argues 'by using the word-processor to produce sub-headings, bullet points and such like – all low-level ICT skills – the student is really getting to grips with the text, particularly in terms of analysing it for meaning'.

Selection and retrieval

Walsh (1998) argues that although 'Gerry' is weak in terms of the more sophisticated skills and capacities required for deep analytical thought, he is good at locating information from a wide range of sources, particularly electronic ones. The word-processor provides abundant opportunities, either through the Internet, CD-ROM or databases such as *Encarta* (see below), to put 'Gerry' in touch with a vast range of information. However, Walsh warns against what he calls the 'Encarta syndrome' whereby 'Gerry' simply prints out as much information about a certain topic as possible, without selecting and using it for a particular purpose. In addition to linking the activity to a key question or line of enquiry, Walsh recommends giving 'Gerry' structured searches for information; for example, he could be asked to produce a summary that fulfills any of the following requirements:

- Find out '5 things all GCSE pupils should know' about X
- Limit the five things to a particular time period
- Limit it to a particular theme (good for group work)
- Limit it to a particular section of the data.

Walsh argues that by copying a summary of this sort to a saved file, pupils can easily amend and refine it. To add even more rigour, word counts can be used to limit the amount of words included in a particular summary. Further examples of how to use large amounts of text effectively are given in HA/NCET (1997), including the use of pointed subheadings or bullet points as a way of improving selection.

Sorting and categorizing

Our research showed that the capacity of the word-processor to save and store, to cut-and-paste and to reorganize historical information in different ways provided abundant opportunities for selecting, sorting and categorizing historical material (Baker *et al.*, 1999). Here, the word-processor can be used to promote a range of key elements (BECTa/HA, 1998, Chandler 2000). For example, pupils can:

- Rearrange a series of dates, events and changes into chronological order by cut-and-paste, for example, in relation to the Industrial Revolution (Wilkinson, 2000 p. 18) or on the medieval world (Haydn *et al.*, 1997, p. 186).
- Identify, select and categorize various causes and consequences, for example, in relation to the Acts of Union in the sixteenth century or to appreciate the main reasons why William won the Battle of Hastings (Baker *et al.*, 1998) or in relation to the Industrial Revolution (Wilkinson, 2000).
- Understand the nature of motivation and purpose in history, for example, appreciate why certain people supported the Nazis, whilst others did not (Laffin, 2000b).
- Appreciate characteristic features of certain historical situations, for example, the diversity of roles in a Roman slave market (Pitt, 2000).
- Use the 'layers of inference' model (Riley, 1999) to obtain and select evidence, infer from it and use it to evaluate different interpretations (Laffin, 2000b).

As Wilkinson (2000, p. 19) argues, the emphasis here is upon versatility, thus at one time we may wish to classify events but at other times 'it may be cause and effect, or fact and opinion, or change and continuity, or persuasion and discussion, or story and argument, or detail and main point'. The time saved from having to do these activities in a kinaesthetic way (through card sorting) is useful. These exercises also have the potential to turn low-level activity into a more meaningful and appropriately demanding experience for pupils. In this respect, Prior and John (2000, p. 32) suggest that many of the examples above (arguably) 'encourage students to play with machines but do little to draw the children into the historical content'. They assert that for effective learning to take place 'something is needed to draw the user into the activity'. Similarly, Wilkinson rightly points out that:

> relatively low level ICT skills ensure that ICT is doing what it should – freeing up the manipulative power of the pupils in order to get them to focus on making, checking and revising specifically historical decisions. . . . Moving things about is not an end in itself, whether on screen or using cards or pictures on a table, but carefully used and positioned in a sequence of learning, it will help those pupils who find it hard to identify and define an abstract issue, to see such issues with greater clarity, ready for more sophisticated arguing or selection of detail thereafter.
>
> (Wilkinson, 2000, p. 19)

'Gerry's glory': using ICT to facilitate analytical and discursive activity

This is how the word-processor can really come into its own within history teaching. A number of exciting research-based studies confirm the 'power of the word-processor' in this respect. So in what ways can analytical and discursive activity – particularly extended writing – be promoted by the word-processor?

Constructing an argument

Once the reading, selection and sorting of text has been undertaken (see above), ICT provides a good way of helping pupils to organize and manage their work effectively, particularly in relation to producing a substantiated argument. Wilkinson (2000) describes the three-stage process of demonstrating to pupils 'how an essay works', namely:

- *Brainstorming* information and data to obtain the relevant, salient points
- *Organizing* these ideas into groups so as to make them meaningful and relevant. Cut-and-paste is useful here for grouping ideas under relevant headings
- *Drafting* the ideas above into paragraphs in order to construct a logical argument.

The process of drafting and redrafting is particularly important, especially when considered within the context of the important messages derived about interactive, formative assessment described in the previous chapter. As Walsh so poignantly puts it:

> to see Gerry look at his work on screen, go back over a section and rewrite it so that it becomes a better piece of work is to watch true self-assessment instead of wondering what to put on the blank bit of his report. Gerry is reviewing the quality of his own work and making decisions about how to improve it. The word-processor allows him to do this efficiently, repeatedly and (important to him) untraceably.
>
> (Walsh, 1998, p. 14)

Creating the 'language of discourse'

Walsh also points out that this is not enough for Gerry who, as with many other pupils like him, needs structured support to help him put arguments together. The HA/NCET (1997) materials provide examples of structured writing frames and sentence starters that:

- support the less able writer by providing appropriate words and phrases for constructing paragraphs;

- help pupils recognize where to put important points into paragraphs and to use material to support their arguments (what Counsell (1997) calls 'big points' supported by 'little points');

- enable pupils to change the order of the paragraphs until the argument is constructed and substantiated.

'Revelatory writing'

One of the important points emerging from generic research on ICT suggests that not only are pupils developing new ways of obtaining information but they are also gaining new styles of learning (Leask and Pachler, 1999). This also seems to be the case in history, as the work of Prior and John (2000) has demonstrated. Arguing from the premise that current approaches to word-processing are not historically challenging enough, they suggest that 'something close to an impasse has been reached' with regard to the ways in which word-processing can facilitate pupils' writing. Their project, based at Bristol University has explored ways of encouraging what they call 'revelatory writing' through ICT, which involves 'enriching, rather than filleting existing text'. Their ensuing description of research is worth quoting in full here because of the insight it provides for understanding what is really meant by discursive, analytical activity:

> We have looked at ways in which the use of anecdotes, examples and morsels of information might be woven into text to reveal the richness and depth of the past. We have also examined ways in which opinion can be filtered into (or out of) text in order to enhance the meaning and character of historical writing. Our aim has been to develop ways in which children can participate in historical writing, and interact with its content. Underpinning this, is a search for ways of enabling children to take control of their own writing, as well as providing opportunities for developing different styles of writing. At the same time, our interest is in ways of reinforcing children's confidence in working with their knowledge and understanding of the past.
>
> (Prior and John, 2000, p. 32)

Prior and John (2000, p. 33) describe the case study through which revelatory writing was achieved:

- Pupils were first given narrative information about Henry VIII, which they had to group under subheadings such as Henry 'the romantic', 'good king', 'bad king', etc.

- They then had opportunities to pass judgement on him, which they enjoyed; when pupils were next given a bland narrative of his life, they were appalled and embellished it with additions to the text.

- Sentence starters/stems were used to encourage the pupils to communicate information about Henry to each other.

- This information was stored in three text files of varying ability and then categorized under two headings: anecdote and argument. The pupils were asked to 'improve' the text through detail, opinion and judgement.

Prior and John (2000, p. 34) conclude by suggesting that pupils were 'motivated by the opportunity to improve on the limited narrative offered earlier in the sequence of lessons. The strength of this particular approach was that the children were working with material generated by themselves and the teacher'. Pitt also found that similar approaches meant that his pupils:

had carried their knowledge across, and amalgamated the new information that they had received with the earlier impressions, so as to make new kinds of knowledge. This pushed them into all kinds of new speculative thinking, using one layer of knowledge to spark off questions about another.

(Pitt, 2000, p. 27)

This sort of transformation of historical knowledge is very exciting for the future of the subject (see also Laffin, 2000b). It may even encourage 'Gerry' to achieve a sense of glory in history!

'1086 and all that': using databases and spreadsheets in history teaching

Databases have developed something of a reputation for being potentially dull and uninteresting. Haydn has suggested that:

> many data-handling programs are quite primitive, compared to the high specification multi-media packages that are now available. Data-handling programs are a good demonstration of the proposition that there is no necessary correlation between the sophistication of technology, and its potential for enhancing learning in history.
>
> (Haydn, 2000, p. 107)

I want to suggest that Haydn's analysis is only partially true. As Saunders (1999, p. 18) and others have pointed out, the Internet (see below) and the National Grid for Learning have transformed the potential accessibility of data available both to pupils and teachers; she points out that the Public Record Office 'has millions of documents relating both to matters of national policy and the minutiae of everyday life over several centuries', including the Domesday Book, most of which is accessible on-line. The challenge, as with all ICT application, is how to utilize data most effectively and I want to draw upon some recent classroom-based research that does this.

Martin (1998) describes a successful database project used to answer a series of questions relating to historical sources on the different peoples of North America. Similarly, Alfano (2000, p. 43) narrates the ways he has used a database 'to access large quantities of source material' to answer key enquiry questions about workhouses and social and economic conditions in the nineteenth century. One of the things he noticed was the increased motivation of pupils when analysing data to either prove or disprove hypotheses. The main focus was to evaluate the data for 'different kinds of change that might be judged "significant"' (p. 45). He also encouraged his pupils to use spreadsheets to analyse the data; he did this in order to:

- use local parish data as part of the 'local history' element of the National Curriculum;
- consider the use of a spreadsheet for modelling the past;
- develop skills not only in ICT but also numeracy;
- appreciate the provisional nature of such historical data.

As with Prior and John's (2000) project, there is evidence that these ICT activities encouraged revelatory and analytical responses from the pupils. As Alfano comments:

> at each stage, students were encouraged to think about the validity of their findings and any anomalies (inevitable in this sort of activity) were discussed. Students were asked to develop their own theories that could possibly be tested by the evidence.
>
> (Alfano, 2000, p. 46)

Jolly (2001) has developed a particularly interesting, innovative use of a database, also on local workhouses, which he links to the study of literature in order to evaluate the nature of different interpretations. Starting with the description of the workhouses in Charles Dickens' *Oliver Twist*, pupils are then encouraged to analyse the data to evaluate whether this portrayal of workhouse life is a valid and accurate interpretation.

The Internet and CD-ROM

Perhaps no other innovation in recent years has had greater potential to revolutionize the way we find out about the past than the Internet (Jenkins and Turpin, 1998). As Haydn (2000, p. 109) remarks, the quality of some of the Internet sites now available 'reminds us of why we became interested in history in the first place'. There is a vast array of websites that provide opportunities for gaining information, evaluating evidence and interpretation, helping with study skills and revision and generally making the study of the subject interesting and exciting. Haydn (2000, p. 109) also notes that one of the major benefits in using the Internet is the development of portals and gateway sites 'where someone else has done the trawling through the morass of Cyberspace to find resources that are appropriate for the history classroom'. One of these pioneering 'trawlers' is Williams (2000) who has produced an excellent CD-ROM describing the best history websites available to both teachers and pupils.

As with databases and spreadsheets, exciting classroom-based research has emerged in recent years, which shows the utility of the Internet and websites. Trend *et al.* (1999, p. 83) describe the ways in which the Internet can 'communicate across culture and time' in history lessons. They describe the ways in which history teachers in Northern Ireland have used the Internet to develop international links with a view 'to achieve mutual understanding'. The project included 'a presentation comparing the ways in which two divided communities (Flemish/Wallon in Belgium and English/Irish) responded to the First World War' (*ibid.* p. 84). Rayner (1999) has also used web sites to develop citizenship and critical thinking. Moore (2000, p. 35) argues strongly for the wider, educational onus on history teachers to use the Internet in order to analyse interpretations because pupils 'need to be able to see how and why the historical interpretations that bombard them were constructed. Otherwise they are prey to propaganda and manipulation, not to mention cynicism or a lack of regard for truth' (see also Buckingham, 2000).

CD-ROMs also provide opportunity for rigorous evaluation of sources and interpretations, as well as presenting material in an increasingly colourful and graphic manner. However, Haydn's (2000, p. 108) research demonstrated that history teachers 'placed CD-ROM fairly low on the list of ICT applications they had used in the classroom'. He puts this down to the fact that we still need to establish 'how to translate the information presented via CD-ROM into a purposeful and genuinely historical lesson activity'. In our research, we found that 'the principal problem with CD-ROM is that most do not strike the correct balance between technology and subject' (Baker *et al.*, 1999, p. 41) and that often the 'onus is upon the history teacher to facilitate pupil enquiries through the production of well thought out and easy to follow support material' (*ibid.* p. 31). Like Haydn, we found that some of the best CD-ROM, such as the British Library's excellent *Making of the United Kingdom* (British Library, 1998), were those that had 'a range of historical investigations and enquiries built into them' (Haydn, 2000, p. 108) thus increasing interaction between learner and data (see Walsh and Brookfield, 1998). Therefore, we concluded (Baker *et al.*, 1999, p. 31) that before using CD-ROM, teachers had to consider the following check-list:

1. What text does CD-ROM contain: mixture of primary and secondary?
2. Is there a danger of 'information overload'? If so, how can it be broken down?
3. Are there built-in investigations and tasks? If so, do they provide differentiation and progression?
4. Can text and images be 'exported' into word-processing packages?
5. Is there any useful structure and organization of the information?
6. Does the CD-ROM explicitly address Key Elements or GCSE/A/S level criteria? If not, is there scope for its use alongside teacher-produced activities?
7. How much work needs to be done before this can be used effectively?

Preparing to use ICT in the history classroom

Before moving on to consider the use of video, I first want to discuss some practical issues relating to the planning and preparation of ICT in the history classroom, and for meeting the ICT national criteria set down by the TTA (1998b) for initial teacher training. It is worth reminding ourselves of the TTA's advice, discussed at the start of this chapter, which emphasizes that ICT should not to be used for its own sake, but rather to facilitate the teaching and learning of history (TTA, 1998a). Haydn *et al.* (1997, pp. 181–3) provide some excellent suggestions to student teachers to help them prepare for using ICT effectively:

1. Instead of attempting to use ICT in an 'all singing, all dancing' way, try to make ICT an incidental part of lessons, used with small groups.
2. Decide upon quick, simple and reliable programs in order to increase self-confidence.
3. Ask for help and support from a range of people: fellow student teachers, mentors, ICT specialists and even pupils themselves.
4. Use ICT first with a class you feel reasonably confident with and at an appropriate time.
5. Always have a 'Plan B' in case things go wrong.
6. It is essential that you have thoroughly mastered the software before using it with a class.
7. Do not forget about the other tasks that will be required in order to make the ICT tasks meaningful and historically valid.
8. School ICT suites are free at certain times during the week: use them to build up your expertise.
9. Be aware of the amount of time that ICT packages can take: use your time profitably.
10. It is sometimes difficult to gain access to computers: use tact and diplomacy when negotiating for ICT time and equipment.
11. Work out a check-list before the lesson, such as:
    - Am I familiar with the software?
    - How does the ICT fit into the context of the history I am teaching? (aims and objectives)
    - How long will it take?
    - What exactly will pupils do and what support materials do they need?
    - What will the other pupils do?

- What will I do if the computers don't work?
- How do I arrange groupings?
- How will I ensure that pupils have learned from the ICT activity? (See also the checklist above on CD-ROM by Baker *et al.*, (1999) and the suggestions below on the use of video.)

The use of television, film and video in history teaching

It is sometimes easy to forget that ICT also encompasses video and film material that can have a powerful transformative impact upon pupils in a variety of ways (Williams, 1997). Little extensive research has been undertaken on the effect of video and television on how pupils learn history, which is surprising given the important role such media play in what Buckingham (2000) calls 'the making of citizens' (see also Phillips, 1998b). Similarly, the use of film in history teaching has been under-theorised, even though there is a fascinating empirical literature on historical films (Carnes, 1996; Ellwood, 2000), as well as theoretical work on the ways in which film is transforming history as an intellectual discipline (Rosenstone, 1995; Sobchack, 1996). I have used television, video and film extensively in my teaching and lecturing and, based upon this empirical vicarious experience, I want to suggest that history teachers need to consider the following issues when using video:

What type of video material to use?

There is now a vast range of material to select from, ranging from the factual and descriptive material available through the BBC, Channel Four and other companies, to more interpretive films. Often some of the older factual programmes are still highly relevant and useful. I still use a BBC video on *Richard Arkwright* (nearly 20 years old!) simply because it is still the best descriptive analysis of the Industrial Revolution available (see below). On the other hand, I also use cutting edge material, such as extracts from films like *Jude the Obscure, The Trench* or *Saving Private Ryan* for ISM and interpretations. For younger pupils, even cartoons like Disney's *Robin Hood* are useful in this respect! The *Screening Histories* video and accompanying book produced by Film Education (1998) provide extremely useful extracts from a wide range of films and advice on how to use them with pupils of different ages and abilities.

Why use video?

There are a whole host of reasons for using video:

- *ISM*: Short video extracts are outstanding for arousing curiosity and for stimulating the kinds of enquiry questions, that are so essential for ISM. I have used many different types of video for ISM, such as *Jude the Obscure*, in combination with direct narrative from Hardy's book to show children's working conditions in the nineteenth century; *Elizabeth*, for images of Tudor monarchy and religious conflict; *The Prince and the Pauper* for sixteenth-century attitudes to poverty and vagrancy; *Robin Hood* for the Crusades and concentric castles; and even *Titanic* for emigration.

- *Overview*: Longer videos, such as the 20-minute video on *Richard Arkwright*, can provide excellent opportunities for overview.

- *Knowledge and understanding*: Video can also provide opportunities for obtaining important factual information. For example, the video accompaning *The Medicine*

Through Time Resource Pack (BBC/Wellcome Trust, 1998) provides thematic coverage of a vast time period, which can be used on different occasions during a GCSE course. Videos often provide opportunities for discussing change, chronology, causation, similarity and difference, motivation, empathetic understanding and so on.

- *Evidence, reliability and interpretation*: Many films can be used as pieces of evidence themselves (e.g. *Dances with Wolves*), as well as for testing hypotheses and reliability. Dale Banham (2000) uses an extract from the cartoon version of *Robin Hood* to analyse interpretations of King John. Video provides opportunities, too, for comparing and contrasting some events against other pieces of evidence. *The Trench* can be compared to the portrayal of trench warfare in *Legends of the Fall* or even *Blackadder*. The film *Cromwell* provides an outstanding opportunity to discuss ways in which the film-makers were influenced by contemporary prints and accounts of the execution of Charles I, which also provides outstanding ISM (for an excellent discussion about film, historical interpretation and post-modernism, see Sobchack, 1996).

- *Sensitive issues*: Specialist videos, such as *The Changing Face of Slavery* (Anti-Slavery International (undated)), provide carefully balanced, well argued and professional support for teaching sensitive issues such as 'race' or the Holocaust (see Simon *et al.*, 2000). Films like *Amistad* or *The Land Girls* (for gender) are also useful in this respect (see Chapter 12).

- *Consolidating understanding*: Sometimes, a well-crafted video, such as the many videos obtainable from the BBC, are vital for consolidating understanding of difficult topics, such as Hitler's rise to power, foreign policy or the Wall Street Crash.

- *Amusement*: Even though history is a serious subject, there should always be a place for humour. Some pupils enjoy extracts from *Blackadder* – I still enjoy the famous scene on rotten, pocket boroughs in the third series!

- *Effectiveness and impact*: Videos do not have to be 'all dancing, all shouting' to have impact – some of the most profoundly captivating and moving are silent extracts from The Somme (Imperial War Museum) or the Holocaust (e.g. *Schindler's List*).

- *Other reasons*: In addition to the justifications above, Haydn *et al.* (1997, p. 173) suggest that video can be used to break the lesson up; to engage pupils' emotions; to get pupils to guess what followed from the extract shown; to get pupils to supply their own 'script' for an extract; to illustrate a concept or to compare two versions of events; and to enable pupils to watch a video role-play that they have made.

What are the major planning considerations for using video?

It is vital that you do the following before launching into video-use in lessons:

1. View the video beforehand, to ensure that it is suitable for the age group of pupils you are teaching.
2. If necessary, make sure you have booked the video player and monitor before using it.
3. Consider the context in which you are going to use the video – at the start of a topic (e.g. for ISM/Outline), in the middle (e.g. for evidence and interpretation) or at the end (e.g. for consolidation of understanding or revision).
4. Decide whether you are going to use short extracts from the video or whether you are going to use longer extracts, in which case yoiu will need to consider how long this will take and whether you need to break it up into different sections.
5. Make sure you have prepared some back-up material in case things go wrong.

How do you extract the most out of the video?

Again, a number of planning, organizational and management issues come into play here. Do you:

- Allow pupils to view the video with or without prompts?
- Show the video, followed by questions?
- 'Set up' the prompts beforehand? (e.g. look out for x, y and z)
- Set specific or general questions or a combination of the two?
- Instruct all pupils to do the same tasks in relation to the video?
- Allocate prompts/questions/tasks to individuals? to pairs? to groups?

How do you ensure that pupils have learned from the video?

Here, it is vital that you provide concluding questions and answers:

- So what can we learn from V about Y?
- What evidence does V tell us about Y?
- How does the evidence from V compare with X?
- What extra/different/same information can we find out from V about Y?
- What interpretation of Y does X give us?

CHAPTER 12

Towards becoming a reflexive history teacher: 'border pedagogy', identity and critical history teaching in the twenty-first century

> Border pedagogy extends the meaning and importance of demystification as a central pedagogical task. Students must be offered opportunities to read texts that both affirm and interrogate the complexity of their own histories to engage and develop a counter discourse to the established boundaries of knowledge.
>
> (Giroux, 1992)

Introduction

This final chapter is a vital one and goes to the very heart of the subject by exploring the interrelationship between history, identity and citizenship. It draws upon my own work (Phillips, 1996, 1998a, 1998b; Phillips and Cunnah, 1999) as well as other theoretical and empirical work, to consider the ways in which history influences individual, collective and national identities. An important issue facing all history teachers in the early twenty-first century is how to develop values of citizenship through history and so the chapter draws upon wider academic work to define what we mean by the term, and then analyses some of the most effective ways in which we can promote citizenship in the history classroom. It offers a broad definition of citizenship and in the process, explores complex issues such as post-modernism, 'race' and gender.

Like John (1991) a central argument in the chapter is that history teaching is inextricably associated with values and ideology. It therefore returns to issues relating to the aims and purposes of history teaching. It argues that if history teaching is to remain a vibrant element of the curriculum, then history teachers will have to meet a number of specific challenges in the future. Central here is history's unique contribution in terms of 'understanding the human present in the light of its past or, more fully, the desire to understand, assess and direct the human present – and thus shape the human future' (Walsh, 1993, p. 174). Drawing upon the work of Walsh and others, I discuss the relevance here of 'critical' history and the notion of critical reflection (Brookfield, 1995).

The chapter engages with some of the more prominent critics of history teaching, who fail to understand the complexity of history teachers' work. I end the book by arguing that history teachers in the future need to adopt what I call a reflexive approach to their work, which is heavily influenced by the work of Henry Giroux, particularly his notion of 'the teacher as intellectual' (Giroux, 1988) and the need for what he calls a 'border pedagogy' (Giroux, 1992).

History teaching and post-modernism

The study of history has always been inextricably bound up with issues of values, ideology and identity. Contrary to the view of Davies (2001a, p. 35) this explains why it caused such controversy at the end of the twentieth century, at a time when values, as well as questions of identity and culture, were themselves in a period of profound flux. Cultural theorists, sociologists, and a few historians have used the term 'post-modern' to describe the complex array of changes that have occurred in the last quarter of the twentieth century. Post-modernity has aroused fierce debate, particularly amongst historians, some of whom either reject its existence or see it as a threat to history as an intellectual discipline. Yet I want to argue that historians and history teachers cannot simply bury their heads in the philosophical sand and deny post-modernity's importance. In fact, only by clarifying what post-modernism is and identifying what challenges it poses, can history hope to survive as an integral part of the curriculum.

Post-modernism's intellectual impetus is derived mainly from thinkers such as Foucault (see Thacker, 1997 for an excellent discussion of Foucault's influence on historical writing). Basically, the argument is this: the last quarter of the twentieth century witnessed enormous ideological, political, cultural, social and technological changes. Traditional intellectual narratives that had dominated the world for most of the twentieth century, such as Western liberal capitalism and Marxist-Leninism, were changing. Successive economic crises seemed to show that capitalism was not working, while the revolutions in Eastern Europe demonstrated very graphically that communism had failed. Concomitantly, traditional affiliations with social class, trade union or church no longer seemed to have the hold and influence over people that they once had. New forces such as globalization, technological change and new forms of identity meant that the world was changing very quickly indeed. As far as we are concerned, four important effects of post-modernism are significant:

- As new intellectual ideas emerged, traditional views of history associated with 'Marxist' or 'Western Liberal' traditions seemed no longer relevant.

- The emergence of alternative traditions associated with new forms of identity such as post-colonialism (Quayson, 2000) or gender (Rowbotham, 1973) provided alternative historical narratives.

- The epistemological (i.e. knowledge base) and methodological traditions of history were also challenged (Jenkins, 1991, White, 1987). New forms of knowledge and methodology began to develop, such as the analysis of oral traditions (Sarup, 1991).

- As new forms of identity emerged, so new values and ideas began to develop.

Inevitably, a few misunderstandings about post-modernism have emerged. Some have suggested that historical 'truth' seems to be at stake, whilst others, particularly neo-conservatives, have referred to the emergence of new identities and values as the flight towards 'cultural relativism' (Scruton, 1986; Phillips, M. 1996). They argue that as a consequence of the questioning of traditional values in the twentieth century, nothing seems to be certain any longer and everything – including cultural values – seems to be up for grabs; this, they add, is a recipe for nihilistic disorder in a world devoid of certain values.

Although I am sympathetic towards charges of cultural relativism (see below), these critics are essentially misconceived and fail to grasp the extent to which the world has changed. You can now begin to see why attempts by the New Right and successive governments in the 1980s and 1990s caused so much controversy. Attempts to introduce a certain, definite historical canon were bound to be problematic during a period when different groups of people had different views about what constituted the 'historical canon'.

Furedi (1992, p. 3) articulates the dilemma facing both history curriculum designers and history teachers in the late twentieth and early twenty-first centuries, when he argues that history is 'in demand' by a range of competing groups seeking to find identity in an increasingly uncertain world; in his view there is no longer 'a history with a capital H; there are many competing histories'. Similarly, in his provocatively titled *Re-Thinking History*, Jenkins (1991, p. 66) argues that we are better served by using the plural 'histories', which have been 'affected by local, regional, national and international perspectives'. In a slightly tongue-in-cheek paragraph (irony is a character-istic feature of many post-modernists: see Rorty, 1989), Jenkins notes the following 'histories':

> 'historians' histories (i.e. academic history), teachers' histories (school history), children's histories, popular-memory histories, proscribed histories, black histories, white histories, women's histories, feminist histories, heritage histories, reactionary histories, revolution-ary histories, bottom-dog histories, top-dog histories, etc.
>
> (Jenkins, 1991, pp. 65–6)

Jenkins and others argue that these 'multiplicity of histories' provide a range of democratic possibilities. I take a slightly more circumspect view. Whilst not denying the democratic opportunities provided by cultural multiplicity and pluralism (the creation of a separate National Curriculum History for Wales would not have come about otherwise: see Phillips, 1999), I have also argued elsewhere (Phillips, 1998b) that we need to recognize the 'possibilities' as well as the 'ravages' of post-modernism (see Apple, 1993; Giroux, 1992). On the one hand, multiple histories provide a means by which we can view the past from a range of different perspectives and histories; on the other hand, I would deny that racist, fascist or other partial histories should be given validity in the history classroom. This is where the bounds of my own cultural relativism are clearly marked out and I have argued strongly that the commitment within the history classroom 'to the idea that historical truth, knowledge and certainty can be subject to rigorous analysis does not entail the rejection of historical certainty *per se*, but implies instead a reconceptualized, more complex view of what 'historical knowledge' is' (Phillips, 1998b, p. 50).

This section has been vital for setting the correct intellectual tone for proper debates about citizenship, values and identity to take place and allows us to ask questions such as: What is citizenship? In what ways can citizenship be defined? What forms of identity and what sorts of values should the history curriculum promote?

Citizenship education and identity in the twenty-first century: civil society or community understanding?

The answers to these questions cannot be fully appreciated, then, without understanding, the complex challenges, as well as the democratic opportunities, that postmodernism poses. Moreover, the relationship between history, citizenship and identity needs careful theorizing and intellectualizing, not least because 'citizenship is a contested subject' (Kerr, 2001, p. 5). Citizenship has provoked debate for centuries (Heater, 1990) because, like history itself, it is bound up with issues concerning national identity (Miller, 2000), ethnicity (Oommen, 1997) and state formation (Kennedy, 1997). As Kerr (2001, p. 6) rightly points out, the current citizenship orders in England (DfEE/QCA, 1999) and the Crick Report (QCA, 1998) upon which they were based were 'a product of the spirit and concerns of the age', specifically the following:

- The New Right view of 'active citizenship': this 'liberal-individualist' idea of citizenship derived its intellectual and philosophical impetus from the free market and the primacy of the rights and responsibilities of the individual citizen over the state (see Hayek, 1944).

- The New Labour idea of 'communitarian' citizenship: this focuses upon the idea of 'civic morality'. It places emphasis upon the civic responsibilities of individuals to act as caring people in partnership with the state (see Giddens, 1998).

- A wider political and societal view that there was an apparent decline in civic culture in English society (including a disinterest in politics and political action) combined with a seemingly sceptical view of English national identity (see Tate (1996a, 1996b) and my critique of his views: Phillips, 1997).

According to Kerr (2001, p. 14), the definition of citizenship articulated by Crick's committee provided 'a workable "third way" between competing "liberal-individualist" and "communitarian" concepts of citizenship', which was essentially the definition provided by T. H. Marshall (Marshall, 1963). The Crick committee thus argued that 'effective education for citizenship' consists of three main strands:

- *Social and moral responsibility*: children should learn self-confidence, as well as social and moral responsibility towards each other and adults, including those in authority.

- *Community involvement*: children should learn about, and become involved in, the life of their community, for example through community involvement, service or action.

- *Political literacy*: pupils should learn how to be effective in public life, by being aware of the importance of the vote and other means of political participation.

Kerr argues that the Crick Report was also influenced by a fourth important strand, namely *the participative principle* (see Janoski, 1998). Whereas Marshall just assumed the unproblematic nature of participation (everybody in the 1950s seemed to recognize the importance of voting), the Crick committee believed that this was:

no longer sufficient in modern society. The combined effects of the rapid pace of modern life and the increasing domination of global companies have contributed to the sharp decline in civic culture since the 1950s. People have less time and motivation to contribute to community and democratic processes. Given this, there is an urgent need to make explicit statements about the rights and responsibilities of participation if democratic traditions are to survive.

(Kerr, 2001, pp. 14–15)

These are important, laudable sentiments and the Crick committee deserve praise for compiling a balanced and carefully argued set of proposals that, using our earlier phrase, undoubtedly provide 'democratic possibilities', both within the history class-room and in the school curriculum as a whole.

However, some have argued that neither Crick nor the current statutory citizenship orders go far enough, particularly in relation to undermining attitudes such as racism which prevent inclusion and participation (see Osler, 2000). As I have argued elsewhere (Phillips, 2000b) a more universal notion of citizenship education was that provided by the Curriculum Council for Wales (CCW, 1991). Whereas the Crick proposals were based around the notion of 'civic society', at the heart of the CCW recommendations was the idea of 'community'. Produced at the high point of conservatism in education, *Community Understanding* (CCW, 1991) articulated many of the ideas and beliefs about participation that were to be included in the Crick Report nearly a decade later. However, by focusing upon some of the ideological, social and economic reasons that prevented effective inclusion and participation (including local, national and inter-national factors which create the structural inequalities that undermine inclusion and participation) this document provided a more radical, dynamic view of citizenship. The CCW document can be summarized around six major points:

1. *Definition of community*: The CCW stressed that the term 'community' does not merely refer to those who live in the same regional or national location but can also refer to people who feel a close sense of belonging and who do not necessarily live in close geographical proximity. Therefore, this offered a universal and pluralistic idea of identity – based, for example, on class, gender or ethnicity.
2. *The complexity of community*: Following the above, the CCW argued that the term 'community' was complex, varied and essentially dynamic. After all 'children soon become aware of the ways in which people are grouped in terms of class, gender, race and age. Pupils should recognize that such groupings are based on certain differences between people that raise issues of diversity, inequality and prejudice' (*ibid.* p. 6). The same paragraph went on to stress that pupils should learn to question stereotypes, and understand instead the ways in which cultural diversity could be celebrated, and inequality and prejudice combated.
3. *Multi-level citizenship*: The CCW argued that although political participation was a vital element of citizenship, pupils should explore what citizenship means in a range of different contexts and at various levels. For example, this involved exploring not only what it meant to be a Welsh or British citizen but a world citizen too. This would encourage pupils to 'be aware of the diversity of races, faiths and languages, within Wales and beyond' (*ibid.* p. 9).
4. *Human rights*: Following the above, *Community Understanding* stressed that chil-dren at an early age should become aware of human rights: 'They should know of their responsibility in respecting, protecting and promoting the rights of others' (*ibid.* p. 7; also, see Osler (2000), particularly Part 2: 'Race, Identity and Human Rights').
5. *Democratic processes*: The CCW emphasized that pupils should be given an awareness of the democratic processes available to them and their future role as decision-makers in society. This involved appreciating the ways they could initiate

change, not only as individual citizens but also as part of a wider grouping, such as a trade union.

6. *Structural inequality*: In a remarkably frank paragraph reflecting the stark reality of economic and social life in parts of Wales at the end of the twentieth century, the document stated that in order to be effective members of the community 'pupils should know how and why wealth and resources are distributed unevenly between individuals, groups, nations and continents' (CCW, 1991, p. 9). Only by appreciating the difficulties that individuals in society faced would individual pupils be motivated to participate in a positive way in a community.

Clearly, *Community Understanding* reflected long-standing traditions in Welsh cultural, social and political life and since the reforms to the National Curriculum in the late 1990s, community has become an important part of Personal, Social and Health Education (PSHE) in Wales and forms an integral element of the 'common requirements' of the National Curriculum (ACCAC, 2000). For those, like me, who believe that the current citizenship orders in England place too much emphasis upon civic action at the political level and perhaps not enough on social justice, *Community Understanding* provides an interesting alternative model (in Northern Ireland the emphasis is upon *Mutual Understanding*: see Phillips *et al.*, 1999).

Seeing the potential: citizenship education and history teaching

Despite some of the misgivings articulated above, it is clear that the current citizenship frameworks in England and Wales do provide history teachers with those 'democratic possibilities' referred to earlier. Thus, Lang (1999) starts from the premise that 'democracy is not boring' and suggests that careful selection of content, activity-based approaches and examples drawn from a local context all help to make debates over citizenship and democracy appear relevant to pupils. Moreover, research by Goalen (1999, p. 38) found that pupils realized that history 'could make a valid contribution to developing an understanding of the world as it is today' as well as 'the importance of history to democracy'. Wrenn (1999) rightly argues that in order to demonstrate the importance of history in this respect, citizenship should not be seen as a 'bolt-on' concept but should be viewed as an integral element of the subject (see also Smart, 2000). In my view, this can be done by taking the issues below into consideration.

Aims, methodology and purpose

Clearly, certain issues, content areas and concepts in history lend themselves to citizenship (see below), but I first want to suggest that the methods we use in the history classroom, as well as our aims as history teachers are vital to cultivate the attitudes of mind that go to the heart of the idea of citizenship. As Stow (2000, p. 71) rightly suggests, 'the use of the learning environment in history will convey particular messages to pupils' about ideas, values and priorities. Throughout this book, therefore, I have endeavoured to demonstrate pedagogical ideas in history that encourage pupils:

- To think independently
- To present substantiated arguments
- To communicate effectively
- To co-operate and learn from each other
- To be curious

- To interrogate evidence
- To appreciate more than one point of view and a range of different interpretations.

All of these are vital to develop the kinds of critical skills and open-mindedness that are vital to a broad citizenship education. Griffith (2000, p. 18) argues that these types of approaches are vital for promoting the independence of mind that is the essence of citizenship education. Slater (1989, p. 16) perceptively describes this as 'informed and responsible scepticism'. Clearly, the effective use of historical interpretation is vital for promoting this attitude (see Lang, 1999; Rayner, 1999; Wrenn, 1999; also see, Chapter 7).

Values

As Knight (1987), Phillips and Cunnah (1999), Haydn (1999) and Illingworth (2000) have shown, values are fundamental to both history and citizenship. This involves considering the values within history itself, as well the values we want to encourage as a consequence of the subject being studied (see Halstead and Taylor, 1996). As we saw above, in the twenty-first century, values are undergoing a period of fundamental change. History therefore provides opportunities to place these into context. After all:

> the past is an essential part of a child's cultural knowledge and experience. Only by reflecting on the past can meanings be found from it that will illuminate the present and help plan the future. Only by reference to the past can the present be fully understood.
>
> (Fisher, 1990, p. 231)

Jordan and Taylor (1999, p. 123) describe ways in which history can contribute to social, moral, cultural as well as spiritual dimensions of the curriculum and suggest that history provides 'a fuller and deeper contact with the issue of values' through:

- looking at how values emerge from studying a wide range of events in the past;
- taking into consideration the different interpretations of those events and how these can alter initial perceptions of value judgements;
- considering wider contributory factors beyond the events themselves which have a role to play in value constructions;
- analysing a variety of perspectives from a range of historical sources in order to identify and distinguish motivations behind events and the subsequent values placed upon them;
- stressing the need to discuss the validity of information, motivations, and personal opinions, in the widest possible sense, in order to explore the essence of what a value judgement is.

Concepts

As we have seen, history contains concepts that are integral to citizenship. If we take each of the core units within the National Curriculum in both England and Wales in turn, there are opportunities to concentrate upon a number of concepts, including:

- *England and Wales in the Medieval World*: monarchy, feudal, conquest, self-sufficiency, religion
- *England and Wales in the Early Modern World*: power, monarchical power, religious conflict, exploration, parliament, civil war, republicanism
- *England and Wales during the Industrial Revolution*: industry, factory system,

urbanization, invention, entrepreneurialism, risk, class system, empire, trade-union-ism, franchise, protest, political action

- *England and Wales in the Modern World*: democracy, fascism, communism, total war, technology, cultural change.

Structural considerations

It is important to recognize that the National Curriculum in England and Wales has been designed to cultivate historical links between local, national and global perspectives (see Collicott, 1990).

Local history: As we saw in previous chapters, the SCHP (1976) was correct to argue that an emphasis upon local history can provide pupils with a clearer sense of their own identities (see also De Silva *et al.*, 2001).

'National' history: I have argued elsewhere in many of my writings that history needs to play an important role in debates over what it means to be British (Phillips, 1996). Like the HWG (DES, 1990), I have suggested with colleagues working in other parts of the United Kingdom (Phillips *et al.*, 1999) that a broad-based definition of British history needs to be taught. Bracey (1995) argues that this involves:

- Teaching about British history within European (see Davies, 1995, 2001a) and world contexts (see Davies, 2001b)
- Emphasizing that Britain has always been a diverse society, with a rich tradition of pluralism (see Smart, 2000)
- Avoiding the 'English/British' conflation by teaching aspects of the history of the various parts of the British Isles (see Dawson, 1995)
- Providing opportunities to study different interpretations of British history
- Encouraging the study of different versions of Britain's past.

Global history: This provides opportunities to view issues of identity and values not only within a regional/British perspective but within the wider context of global citizenship (Osler, 2000). Davies (2001b) discusses some of the major features and purposes of global citizenship, citing the work of Cogan (1998) who argues that in the context of globalization, it is important that pupils are taught about:

- the global economy and the impact this is having upon employment;
- the global effects of technology, particularly the impact of the Internet;
- population and environment, including the effects of pollution and global inequalities, all of which have historical dimensions.

Content and contexts

It is clear from the discussion above that, in the words of Stow (2000, p. 70) the selection of historical content to be taught in schools is one of 'the most significant factors in determining the values that the curriculum embodies'. He is correct to point out that history can be selected and used to teach about pluralism (Claire, 1996), anti-racism (Pankhania, 1994) or to undermine sexist stereotyping (Osler, 1994). There is not enough time or space in this book to explore the relationship between content and the promotion of citizenship in significant detail – this is done effectively by Stow (2000, pp. 73–8) and by Arthur *et al.* (2001). Instead, I want to make reference to

147

recent research studies that show different historically related contexts in which citizenship can be explored.

Wrenn (1999) rightly argues that citizenship should be viewed as an integral element of the planning process in history; for example, enquiry questions can be selected to reflect this. He provides a range of interesting examples relating to such issues as religious tolerance, civil rights and slavery. Rayner (1999) has 'weighed a century with a web-site': her pupils used independent research and ICT to consider 'How will the twentieth century be remembered?' Similarly, in our *Total History Experience* research, we analysed the political, social and economic significance of the twentieth century (see Brown *et al.*, 2000) and concentrated upon the concept of commemoration and remembrance with regard to the First World War in some depth. We used a number of techniques to do this: contemporary newspapers commemorating Remembrance Sunday; role-play; poetry; personal stories; and even music by the Manic Street Preachers, with the central message of 'never forget'. As Brooman (1999, p. 28) has rightly argued, instead of engendering 'fascination with weapons or killing', these sorts of approaches encourage pupils to appreciate properly the horror (and sometimes the futility) of war. They also help pupils see the important connection between past, present – and future (see also Coman, 1999).

History teaching, culture and 'race': multiculturalism or anti-racism?

As I write this chapter at the beginning of the twenty-first century, I am particularly conscious of the potential of history to combat prejudice. The issues of asylum seekers and the War in Afghanistan ensure that matters of 'race', citizenship and nationhood are once again at the forefront of political and public life, including the proposal by the current Home Secretary that immigrants should pass a 'test' of British citizenship. The sensitivity of 'race'-related issues, as with so many other complex contemporary matters, can only be properly understood by reference to history.

This section begins by challenging a number of preconceptions. Whereas it is true that history 'promotes notions of tolerance' (Lang, 1999, p. 24) it is equally true that it can also encourage prejudice and racism. Bigotry can actually be created by 'dancing to history's tune' (Walker, 1996). Moreover, it is vital to recognize that 'racialised identities are a product of history' (Grosvenor, 1997, p. 185) and also that 'pastness can be a tool that people use against each other' (Wallerstein, 1991, p. 78). White (1992, p. 17) has stressed that British history can promote 'the values of democracy, freedom, tolerance and impartiality' but that if it is incorrectly taught can lead to 'chauvinism associated with the myths of British superiority and imperial power'. Prejudice can only be properly understood, then, if we recognize both the benefits as well as the potential ravages of our subject (Phillips, 1998b).

As Hessari and Hill (1989) point out in an excellent analysis, the post-war history of immigration into Britain, as well as Britain's relationship with its former colonies, explain much about contemporary race relations (see also Gardner, 2001; Tomlinson, 2001). They demonstrate that central government, local authorities and schools were influenced by the following ideas during the second half of the twentieth century:

Assimilation
The initial response to post-war immigration was to encourage immigrants to be assimilated into British life, for example, by encouraging them to speak English and adopt British customs and traditions (chillingly, rather similar to Blunkett's proposals

above). As far as education was concerned, a DES circular in 1965 called for immigrant children to be 'dispersed' amongst a range of schools, because they were perceived to have difficulties and thus having too many of them in one school would cause intolerable challenges. Sociologists such as Tomlinson (1990, 2001) as well as historians (Grosvenor, 1997), have recognized the discursive importance of this development: immigrants – rather than schools, society or the political system – were regarded as 'the problem'. As Hessari and Hill argue:

> no thought was directed inwards at this time to see whether British society and our school system might be causing these difficulties, or indeed, whether the difficulties might be caused by unacknowledged problems within the majority white British population.
>
> (Hessari and Hill, 1989. p. 9)

Integration

In 1966 the Home Secretary Roy Jenkins gave an important speech in which he argued that assimilation was insensitive; rather, integration should be encouraged. Integration-ist theory considered that a homogenous society was desirable and this could be created by immigrants changing their ways of life to fit in with British culture. However, the difference now was that they were no longer expected to shed their own cultures entirely. In addition, the term 'ethnic minorities' rather than 'immigrants' started to be used. Gradually in the 1960s, it started to be recognized that racism may be a cause of the problems and difficulties facing ethnic minority children, and some teachers started to develop expertise in integrating them into mainstream schooling.

Cultural pluralism and multicultural education

In the 1970s, the concept of cultural pluralism began to spread, with terms such as 'multiethnic', 'multiracial' and 'multicultural' being used. This envisaged a socially cohesive society but one in which cultural difference should not only be recognized but actively celebrated, thus viewing diversity not as a weakness or a 'problem' but as a positive strength. This period saw the gradual realization that racism was creating problems for multiethnic communities and that society had to change. In 1985, the publication of the Swann Report gave further impetus to cultural pluralism and to multicultural education, recommending that pupils should have opportunities to study a wide range of different cultures, for example through the humanities, in order to develop tolerance and mutual respect.

Anti-racist education

At the same time, a more radical theory was emerging, which argued that racism was deeply embedded in British society and institutions. Anti-racists held the view that as a consequence of a range of factors – including Britain's colonial and imperial past – ethnic minorities were subject to both subconscious and intentional prejudice in all walks of life, including housing, employment and, of course, schools. Anti-racists believed that in order to counter it, individuals, government and social institutions first had to recognize that institutional racism existed and had to take direct measures to systematically eradicate it from society. According to anti-racist belief, anything short of this – such as multiculturalism – was, in the words of Hessari and Hill (1989, p. 12), 'merely tinkering at the edges of the problem'.

Clearly, anti-racism presented a fundamental challenge to teachers. It was evident to some that:

multiculturalism had become part of a slogan system, a political and linguistic re-conceptualization that relied more heavily on the management of local specific issues related primarily to black pupils, rather than trying to deal with the root causes of racism in society . . . educationalists needed to realize that it was only through a radical reappraisal of societal structures and concerted change at all levels of society that racism would begin to end.

(Jones, 1999, pp. 18–19)

For history teachers, the challenge was particularly great, given the perceived important social role that history performed in terms of creating the cultural and temporal climate for racism to thrive. Indeed, anti-racists accused the history curriculum of :

- Promoting 'dominant assumptions' that excluded certain groups such as 'the poor, the oppressed and the colonized' (Sarup, 1991, p. 137)
- Encouraging an exclusive vision of the British national and imperial past, which reinforced images of white superiority (Tomlinson, 1990)
- Creating a 'monolithic' view of Britishness, based upon an 'Anglocentric, patriotic approach to history', which excluded and prejudiced ethnic minorities (Troyna and Carrington, 1990, p. 103)
- Contributing to the subjugation and oppression of ethnic minorities by failing to teach black history (Pankhania, 1994)

Other research pointed to what became known as the 'no-problem here' syndrome in predominantly 'all-white' schools, which denied that racism was a problem or that it even existed (Gaine, 1987).

Combating racism and prejudice through history teaching

I used to write down all this stuff about kings and queens and all the European history because I wanted to get through. There was nothing about Asian or black history. It's as if we didn't exist.

(British-Asian student quoted in Mac an Ghail, 1992, p. 53).

There is a danger, of course, that the multicultural/anti-racist debate becomes unhelpfully polarized. Therefore, I now want to consider practical and effective ways in which the history curriculum can be made more universally inclusive and to suggest ways in which it can contribute to undermining racist prejudice amongst pupils. The ideas I advocate below are based upon my own teaching and lecturing experience as well as relevant research studies, and combine elements of multicultural and anti-racist approaches. When discussing these strategies with my students, I often refer to them as a 'clever clever, drip drip' approach. This argues that racism can be undermined through history by using an effective array of subtle and clever pedagogical approaches some of which are similar, of course, to those discussed in relation to citizenship above and indeed throughout this book. Underpinning these approaches are the following ideas and principles:

Attitude

This involves recognizing that some pupils in schools will on occasions adopt racist attitudes, which stem from a combination of ignorance, misunderstanding and prejudice. It is also incumbent upon all teachers, and particularly history teachers, to recognize the moral and ethical duty to attempt to undermine racism. In the process, this involves rejecting the 'no-problem here' attitude, which still exists in many schools (see Gaine, 1995). It also needs to be recognized that actively challenging the attitudes of mind that create racism is the responsibility of all of us, whatever the colour of our skin or our ethnic background.

'Unmasking black history'

Pankhania (1994, p. 18) argues that racism can only be understood by 'examining the relationship the British state has had with black people throughout history. Certain questions are central to such an examination. When, why and how did the contact first begin? How did this contact develop?' As an anti-racist, she advocates analysing the interconnected political, social and economic factors behind Britain's colonization of India and parts of Africa, as well as Britain's role in the creation of apartheid in South Africa, to consider the long-term impact of this imperial legacy on British attitudes to black people. Pankhania argues that racism stems from an unequal power relationship between white (= superior) and black (= inferior). It follows that pupils will only be able to understand the nature of contemporary race relations by appreciating the historical legacy that created this. Therefore, Pankhania rightly argues that opportunities have to be found to demonstrate that 'black people have made a major contribution towards the development of Britain' (*ibid.*) This can be done through the following:

The black presence in Britain: The current National Curriculum documentation stresses the need for pupils to be taught about 'the social, cultural, religious and ethnic diversity of the societies studied, in Britain and the wider world'. As we have seen above, whereas contemporary multicultural Britain was mainly created after the Second World War with mass immigration from the Caribbean, Africa and the Indian subcontinent, it is important also to emphasize through the history curriculum that Britain has always been a country of immigrants and settlers, and that there has been a black presence in Britain since Roman times (see Booth, 1993; File and Power, 1981). Gardner (2001) rightly argues that as well as teaching about significant world figures as Ghandi, Martin Luther King and Nelson Mandella, it is incumbent upon history teachers to take opportunities to seek out the black, Jewish and other ethnic presence from the British past, for example, through:

- local history;
- the history of the Jews in Britain in the Middle Ages;
- the growth of multiethnic London in the Tudor period;
- significant individuals in Britain in the eighteenth and nineteenth centuries, such as William Davidson, Mary Seacole and Olaudah Equiano (see below);
- the history of immigration and emigration.

Claire (1996) and Grosvenor (2000) provide further suggestions on content, as well as ideas on teaching strategies and resources.

The history of slavery: This poses a number of challenges to the history teacher. On the one hand, slavery has to be studied in order to appreciate its vital role in the creation of racism, but on the other hand, constant images of slave subjugation have the potential to simply reinforce the superior/inferior stereotype referred to above. An important strategy here is to demonstrate black people's role in their own emancipation, rather than merely emphasizing the importance of white reformers such as William

Wilberforce. The life of Olaudah Equiano provides an excellent opportunity in this respect. In *The Total History Experience* research (Phillips, 2002a), we planned a set of resources that showed the significance of Equiano's life at the time, as well as his importance as a role model for black people today. This contrasts with Wrenn (2001a) who concentrates instead upon an interpretive deconstruction of Equiano's life. Given the limited opportunities available to 'unmask' black history, it seems to me that we need to use Equiano as an opportunity to demonstrate black achievement, rather than for deconstruction.

'Them and us' – the Crusades: Traditional textbooks tell the narrative history of the Crusades from the perspective of western Christendom, thus reinforcing the moral right of the Crusaders in contrast to the 'infidel' Muslims. Following Booth (1993), the *Total History Experience* project used resources to show children the history of the Crusades from both perspectives – but we took this further. Under the enquiry question: *How have the Crusades affected life today?* we considered the long-term legacy of the Crusades upon European life in a range of spheres, such as trade, architecture, mathematics, astrology and so on. The concluding exercise involved an explicit discussion of the positive impact of Islamic culture. This sort of approach undermines a central factor in the creation of racist ideology, namely the artificial creation of 'them and us', based around a negative view of 'the other' (Phillips, 1996, 2000b).

Exploration and 'discovery': Another crucial area in the negative construction of 'the other' is through the history of exploration and so-called 'discovery' in the sixteenth century. Again, traditional textbooks concentrated only on exploration from the European perspective. Both Booth (1993) and Pankhania (1994) emphasize the importance of analysing the impact of European conquest from the perspective of indigenous people in the Americas, Africa, Asia and Australia. One of the motivational factors behind the SCHP's (1976) selection of *The American West* as an in-depth study was to provide opportunities to allow pupils to analyse the extraordinary cultures of indigenous Americans.

Teaching the Holocaust

Whereas anti-Semitism and anti-black racism used to be treated separately, the study by MacMaster's (2001) of racism in Europe from 1870 to the present day shows the interrelationships between these two forms of prejudice. Likewise Booth (1993) and Carrington and Short (1997) argue that teaching about the Holocaust should be viewed as an integral element of multicultural and anti-racist education. Some argue that there is too much emphasis upon the teaching of Nazi Germany but what Simon *et al.* (2000) call 'the remembrance of the historical trauma' of the Holocaust provides a unique opportunity to demonstrate the reasons for the growth of racism and in the process learn messages for today. Moreover, it is vital to consider that the Holocaust did not affect Jewish people alone, but in fact 'involved people of all nationalities, whether as perpetrators, victims, bystanders, rescuers, resisters or collaborators' (Supple and Hudson, 1990, p. 42). An extremely useful research-based literature has developed in relation to teaching the Holocaust, the most recent of which has focused upon:

- Drawing out the moral lessons to be derived from studying the Holocaust (Davies, 2000; Kinloch, 2001; Salmons, 2001; see also The Holocaust Education Trust: www.het.org.uk)

- Using the concept of historical significance to help move pupils 'from knowing about to understanding the Holocaust' (Hammond, 2001), as well as the importance of commemoration in this process (Caplan, 2001; Wrenn, 2001b)

- Using communication, discussion, debate and ICT to connect citizenship education with the study of the Holocaust (Mountford, 2001)

- How to challenge and avoid stereotyping when teaching the Holocaust (Kitson, 2001)

- The need to discuss the Holocaust in relation to other crimes against humanity (Wrenn, 2001b).

A major aim of this section has been to demonstrate the need for people of all backgrounds to combat racism and anti-Semitism. Thus, as Osler and Starkey (2000) point out, multicultural and anti-racist approaches are not intended to exclude white students. Rather, they should be viewed as a strategy designed to promote cultural pluralism that:

> assumes as basic certain social and political values such as: the right and freedom to be different; openness; equity; justice; solidarity; rationality; the democratic right of all to contribute equitably to shaping society; and conversely the need to combat both imposed assimilation and divisiveness – racism, injustice, inequality and discrimination.
>
> (Figueoa, 2000, p. 54)

Hidden from history? Issues of gender in history teaching

> I read it (history) a little as a duty, but it tells me nothing that does not vex or weary me. The quarrels of popes and kings, with wars or pestilences, in every page; the men all so good for nothing, and hardly any women at all – it is very tiresome; and yet I often think it odd that it should be so dull, for a great deal of it must be invention.
>
> (Jane Austen *Northanger Abbey* (1818), quoted in Bourdillon, 1994)

Sociologists such as Coffey (2001, pp. 45–6) have pointed to the lack of opportunities for the explicit discussion and analysis of gendered inequality via the history curriculum. However, whereas there was once a need, in Rowbotham's (1973) words, to ensure that women were not 'hidden from history', the expectation in the National Curriculum, GCSE and A/S levels to teach a range of different perspectives does at least provide the potential for women to be given more equal representation in school history than a few decades ago. A number of factors account for this:

1. The growth of historiography ensured that women's achievements, both in terms of political, social and economic terms, were recognized in history (Beddoe, 1992).
2. Radical approaches emphasized that patriarchy throughout the centuries had ensured that women had been systematically eroded from the historiographical landscape (London Feminist History Group, 1983).
3. The growth of interest in social and economic history, as well as oral and local historical methodology in the 1960s and 1970s (Bourdillon, 1994), meant that 'history from below' provided further opportunities to emphasize women's achievements.
4. The emphasis in new history in schools upon methodology also contributed to this process. In the words of Bourdillon:

the absence of women from secondary sources (mainly textbooks) and their visibility in some of the primary sources enabled teachers to introduce their pupils to the construction of history, and to point out that the writing of history necessarily entails selection and interpretation which had in the past written women out of history.

(*Ibid.* p. 64)

This was recognized by HMI in the 1980s (DES, 1985b) and by the National Curriculum working parties (DES, 1990; Welsh Office, 1990). Moreover, it emphasizes the importance of enquiry and interpretation in the present National Curriculum and at GCSE and A/S levels.

5. New school textbooks emerged that ensured women are more prominently represented or have specialist sections on the role of women. Some books consider the role of women thematically (Bellamy *et al.*, 1996).

It is important to emphasize that there are strong intellectual links here with the previous section. After all, as Bourdillon argues:

the category 'woman' includes black and white, wealthy and poor women. In other words, it was not simply a question of redressing the balance by including women in school history, but rather a question of recognising the several histories of women and men. Women's history developed the idea of diversity and plurality in history as well as emphasising the importance of difference.

(Bourdillon, 1994, p. 66)

Thus, Turnbull *et al.* (1983) offer a number of practical strategies in which aspects of the history of women can be integrated into the history curriculum:

- *The remedial approach*: This involves history teachers consciously plugging the gap in terms of women's presence in the history curriculum. However, Turnbull *et al.* (1983, p. 156) warn that 'this should not appear as an artificial appendage, but should be integrated into the structure of the enquiry'.

- *Great women approach*: Given the male-dominated world of the past and the consequent relative paucity of women who reached the highest stages of power, every opportunity should be made to concentrate upon those women who – often despite the odds – did manage to make it to the top.

- *Tackling the notion of oppression*: As with 'race', history poses a number of gender-related dilemmas. Constant references to women's subordinate position in history have the potential to reinforce the image of women as weak victims. Turnbull *et al.* suggest that the only way to tackle this is through explicit discussions about the nature of society in the past, drawing comparisons between then and now and discussing the methodological and historiographical factors that have created such images (see above).

- *Women's roles*: Singling out women for special attention may also segregate them and distort their roles (see discussion on Bourdillon, 1994 above). Thus, an overemphasis upon women in social life may actually reinforce stereotypes by emphasizing their role in domestic life. It is therefore important to explore the variety of women's roles as suggested, for example, in Eileen Power's (Power, 1975) study of medieval women. A modern version of this and a wonderful resource to use is Fox (1999), which shows approximately 50 different roles performed by women in the Middle Ages.

- *Political movement*: Women's political activity may be presented by reference, for example, to the suffragette and feminist movements in the twentieth century; Turnbull *et al.* (1983, p. 157) also stress that 'whilst important, these should not be presented as comprising the totality of their political activity. Women have been involved in social movements including Chartism, temperance, bread riots and rent strikes, and in right-wing and left-wing movements'.

It is clear that much progress has been made in terms of a more balanced, gender-representative school history. However, research by Osler (1994) suggests that there is still plenty of scope for improvement in the ways in which women are represented, for example in school textbooks.

Conclusion: 'border pedagogy', critical history and the reflexive history teacher

This book started with the premise that in order to be effective, history teachers have to think reflectively about what they are doing and why they are doing it (Lee *et al.*, 1992). As we discussed in Chapters 1 and 2, in the late twentieth century the forces of neo-conservatism and what I call 'cultural restorationism' (Phillips, 1996) were in ascendancy in politics and in the media, and initiated a 'discourse of derision' against educationalists and history teachers in particular. At the time of writing, there is no evidence that this is abating; an article in the *Daily Mail* (22 September, 2001) criticized teachers at Key Stage 2 for not teaching enough about the Second World War; only a few weeks later, an article in the *TES* (2 November, 2001) claimed that pupils were being taught too much modern history and warfare. History teachers, it seems, cannot win. According to their conservative critics, they are chiefly responsible for the current 'cultural crisis' in Britain (Phillips, M., 1996). History teachers in Scotland and Wales are supposedly teaching nationalist history, whilst in England they are denied the same opportunities (Scruton, 1999); factors that will apparently contribute ultimately to the break-up of Britain.

In addition to these discursive myths has been the concomitant trend within the cultural restorationist agenda to try to debunk innovative teaching methods used by history teachers. Thus, history teaching is apparently in a 'catastrophic' state because it has given up 'the old-fashioned didactic style' in favour of 'source-material and texts' (David Starkey: quoted in the *Sunday Telegraph*, 4 November, 2001). As Apple (1993) and others correctly point out, the Right is fearful of creative, critical methods, which encourage pupils to gain the sort of 'informed scepticism' that poses a challenge to the kind of order and certainty that existed, for example, in the 1950s.

This cultural restorationist discourse is a retrospective, nostalgic view of the world and of education in particular. Stephen Ball (1993) offers a powerful critique of this discourse when he argues that cultural restorationism can be summarized as 'common sense Victorianism', which is anti-intellectual, distrustful of research and innovation, and which:

> represents education, to parents in particular, in terms of familiar images of 'traditional' pedagogic forms. This is a form of cultural populism organised around notions of discipline, authority and learning. The Victorian schoolroom and the grammar school are the lost objects of desire, standing for a time when education was simple, when learning meant doing and knowing what you were told by your teacher ... desks in rows, the teacher 'in the front', chalk in hand, dispensing knowledge.
>
> (Ball, 1993, p. 44)

In reality, as this book has sought to demonstrate, history teaching is not 'simple' at all, but 'highly complex, multi-faceted' (John, 1991, p. 11), which needs creative thought, clever organization and a range of carefully considered, research-based strategies to make it work effectively. The majority of history teachers work with a richly diverse and plural school populace, which involves meeting a vast array of needs (Haydn, 1992). In *History Teaching, Nationhood and the State*' I argued that the debate over history in the National Curriculum:

> was not about the past but the present; its dynamism stemmed from the tension between contrasting discourses on the nature, aims and purposes of history teaching, linked to correspondingly different conceptions of nationhood, culture and identity. One vision of history and history teaching envisaged certainty, closure and stricture; the other uncertainty, openness and fluidity.
>
> (Phillips, 1998a, p. 129)

This struggle continues; in essence, it is a struggle between what Walsh (1993, p. 178) refers to as a 'pre-critical history', which is 'confined to the history of one's own community or society, and where it reaches out to other societies it considers them only in their relevance to one's own', and a 'critical history', which is 'universal in its intended scope, and when it addresses itself to other societies it endeavours to do so on their own terms'. According to Brookfield, critically reflective teachers know that curricula 'do not just happen':

> They exist because particular people in a particular place at a particular time believed that someone else should know about something. Curricula have not simply come into being through divine intervention or the whims of fate. Instead, they have arisen out of conflicts of interests in which the wishes of certain individuals and groups have prevailed.
>
> (Brookfield, 1995, p. 40)

This, of course, is so pertinent to history. Brookfield also suggests that 'critically alert teachers' need to consider the following questions habitually:

- What are these preferences and interests?
- Whom do they serve?
- How have they become dominant?

Critical perspectives underpin the work of Henry Giroux, who has been a profound influence on my own work. Giroux argues for what he calls a 'border pedagogy', which is fundamental to many of the principles, ideas and strategies that have been described in this book. According to Giroux, 'border pedagogy'

> extends the meaning and importance of demystification as a central pedagogical task . . . students must be offered opportunities to read texts that affirm and interrogate the complexity of their own histories . . . to engage and develop a counter discourse to the established boundaries of knowledge. . . . In this perspective, culture is not viewed as monolithic or unchanging, but as a shifting sphere of multiple and heterogeneous borders where different histories . . . intermingle. . . . There are no unified subjects here, only students whose multi-layered and often contradictory voices and experiences intermingle with the weight of particular histories that will not fit easily into the master narrative of a monolithic culture.
>
> (Giroux, 1992, p. 50)

Two decades of conservative education policy has made many history teachers defensive (even, in some cases, conservative) about their role. One of the intentions behind this book has been to help teachers to re-engage with debates about the nature, aims and purposes of the subject and thus reflect on their own ideologies (Evans, 1994, Lee *et al.*, 1992). Bage refers to this process as 'critical mediation' and as he explains:

> now that the national curriculum has been in existence for a decade and more, albeit with some changes, critical mediation may become more common. Such critical mediation can happen more easily if as teachers we have access to the tools and the time with which to open and rearrange the curriculum box for ourselves.
>
> (Bage, 2000, p. 54)

Like my book, Bage's book 'is written to assist that mission. It takes its place alongside many others offering related answers to a fundamental and always useful critically mediating question: what is history for?' (*ibid.*)

A constant theme throughout my work has been to demonstrate that history teaching is essentially about identity formation. A constant question I ask myself in this respect is: *What kinds of people do we want to help produce via the history curriculum?* In a previous publication (Phillips, 2000b, p. 156), I have argued that I would like to see a history curriculum and an education system that seeks to:

- produce citizens who have a properly informed perception of their own identity, as well as that of others;
- actively promote an inclusive, as opposed to an exclusive, view of community, society and nation;
- cultivate a depth of vision amongst pupils that addresses some universal values such as tolerance, social justice and honesty;
- cultivate a view of the world that looks outwards, not inwards;
- develop an attitude of mind that has confidence to celebrate the familiar and the less familiar;
- encourage pupils to recognize and celebrate a multiplicity of potential identities.

You can see how I have been influenced here by 'border pedagogy' and critical history, as well the complex, universal definition of 'community understanding' that was discussed earlier. These ideas also assume the need for *reflexivity*, defined as 'the capacity for critical and self-critical reflection' (Griffith, 2000, p. 19). As Denscombe argues, reflexivity is vital to the critical history teacher because:

> the sense we make of the social world and the meaning we give to events and situations are shaped by our experience as social beings and the legacy of the values, norms and concepts we have assimilated during our lifetime. And these will differ from person to person, culture to culture.
>
> (Denscombe, 1998, p. 240)

'Becoming critical' should not be confused here with negative deconstruction, for critical perspectives derive inspiration from the need to change practices and institutions for the democratic good (see Giroux, 1988). In the words of Carr and Kemmis (1986, p. 26) 'the reflexive approach will focus on the language and strategic action of those involved in particular educational processes . . . to change educational situations and enlighten participants about the nature and consequences of different practices'.

This is particularly important for history teachers, given the ideological, cultural and social dimensions of their subject. After all, as Jenkins (1991) reminds us 'history is always taught for a purpose' and as Tosh (1984, p. 8) eloquently puts it 'history is a political battleground'. He goes on to write:

> The sanction of the past is sought by those committed to upholding authority and by those intent on subverting it, and both are assured of finding plenty of ammunition. . . . History is too powerful a force in our consciousness to be shrugged off as an idle intellectual pastime. Clearly, history has a social role. Society requires a usable past, and different conceptions of the social order produce rival histories.
>
> *(Ibid.)*

Reflexivity therefore puts the onus upon history teachers to recognize this delicate ideological position in which they find themselves (Evans, 1994). It also envisages the 'teacher-as-intellectual' (Giroux, 1988): thoughtful, innovative and research-orientated. This often contrasts with alternative discourses that prefer to define history teaching in terms of 'standards', 'competence' or 'performance' (see the TTA website at www.canteach.gov.uk).

We need to reject claims either that history is somehow at an end (Fukuyama, 1992) or the equally complacent belief that 'the battle over history is vicious in practice . . . because there is so little at stake' (Davies, 2001a, p. 35). Of course 'history matters' (Dawson, 1990). It is precisely because there is so much at stake that we need to continue to debate it, for this sort of critical approach requires history teachers:

> to take as their point of departure the real, concrete problems facing students and teachers today. Questions raised by critical pedagogy – questions which are relevant and pertinent to the human condition, questions which are formulated as part of a larger struggle for human liberation – are those which must be asked of history itself.
>
> (McLaren, quoted in Giroux, 1988, p. xiii)

REFERENCES

ACAC/SCAA (Curriculum and Assessment Authority of Wales/School Curriculum and Assessment Authority) (1995) *Consistency in Teacher Assessment: Guidance for Schools at Key Stages* 1–3. Cardiff/London: ACAC/SCAA.

ACAC/SCAA (Curriculum and Assessment Authority of Wales/School Curriculum and Assessment Authority) (1996) *Consistency in Teacher Assessment: Exemplification of Standards at Key Stage 3*. Cardiff/London: ACAC/SCAA.

ACCAC (Qualifications, Curriculum and Assessment Authority of Wales) (2000) *History in the National Curriculum at Key Stage 3: Wales*. Cardiff: ACCAC.

Aldrich, R. (1984) New history: an historical perspective. In A. Dickinson, P. Lee and P. Rogers (eds) *Learning History*. London: Heinemann.

Aldrich, R. (1990) The National Curriculum: an historical perspective. In D. Lawton and C. Chitty (eds) *The National Curriculum*. University of London, Institute of Education (Bedford Way Series). London: Kogan Page.

Aldrich, R. (ed.) (1991) *History in the National Curriculum*. University of London, Institute of Education (Bedford Way Series). London: Kogan Page.

Aldrich, R. and Dean, D. (1991) The historical dimension. In R. Aldrich (ed.) *History in the National Curriculum*. University of London, Institute of Education (Bedford Way Series). London: Kogan Page.

Alfano, R. (2000) Databases, spreadsheets and historical enquiry at Key Stage 3, *Teaching History*, **101**, 42–7.

Altrichter, H., Posch, P. and Somekh, B. (1993) *Teachers Investigate their Work: an Introduction to the Methods of Action Research*. London: Routledge.

Andretti, K. (1992) *Teaching History from Primary Evidence*. London, David Fulton.

Anti-Slavery International (undated) *The Changing Face of Slavery: Video and Book*. London: Anti-Slavery International/Lithosphere.

Apple, M. (1993) *Official Knowledge: Democratic Education in a Conservative Age*. London: Routledge.

Arthur, J., Davies, I., Wrenn, A., Haydn, T. and Kerr, D. (eds) (2001) *Citizenship Through Secondary History*. London: Routledge/Falmer.

Arthur, J. and Phillips, R. (eds) (2000) *Issues in History Teaching*. London: Routledge.

Ashby, R. and Lee, P. (1987) Children's concepts of empathy and understanding in history. In C. Portal (ed.) *The History Curriculum for Teachers*. Lewes: Falmer.

Ashcroft, K. and James, D. (eds) (1999) *The Creative Professional: Learning to Teach 14–19 Year Olds*. London, Falmer.

Atkin, D. (2000) How can I improve my use of ICT? Put history first! *Teaching History*, **99**, 42–9.

Bage, G. (1999) *Narrative Matters: Teaching and Learning History Through Story*. London: Routledge.

Bage, G. (2000) *Thinking History 4–14: Teaching, Learning, Curricula and Communities*. London: Routledge/Falmer.

159

Baker, S., Rogers, P. and Phillips, R. (1999) *The Use of Information and Communications Technology in History Teaching*. Swansea: Department of Education, University of Wales Swansea.

Ball, S. (1990) *Politics and Policy Making in Education: Explorations in Policy Sociology*. London: Routledge.

Ball, S. (1993) Education, Majorism and the Curriculum of the Dead, *Curriculum Studies*, **1** (2), 195–214.

Banham, D. (1998) Getting ready for the grand prix: learning how to build a substantiated argument in Year 7, *Teaching History*, **92**, 6–15.

Banham, D. (2000) The return of King John: Using depth to strengthen overview in the teaching of political change, *Teaching History*, **99**, 22–31.

Banham, D. and Dawson, I. (2000) *King John: A Key Stage 3 Investigation Into Medieval Monarchy*. London: John Murray.

Barnes, D., Britton, J. and Torbe, M. (1990) *Language, the Learner and the School* (4th edn). Portsmouth, NH: Heinemann.

Baumann, A. S., Bloomfield, A. and Roughton, L. (1997) *Becoming a Secondary School Teacher*. London: Hodder and Stoughton.

BBC/Wellcome Trust (1998) *The Medicine Through Time Resource Pack*. London: BBC Worldwide.

Beattie, A. (1987) *History in Peril: May Parents Preserve it*. London: Centre for Policy Studies.

BECTa/HA (1998) *Defining Effectiveness in History Using ICT*. London: BECTa/HA.

Beddoe, D. (1992) *Discovering Women's History: A Practical Guide to the Sources of Women's History, 1800–1945* (2nd edn). London: Pandora.

Bellamy, L., Moorse, K. and Sheppard, C. (1996) *The Changing Role of Women*. London: John Murray.

Bennett, N. and Dunne, E. (1992) *Managing Classroom Groups*. Hemel Hempstead: Simon and Schuster.

Bennett, S. (1992) What do we mean by Interpretations of History? Unpublished Working Paper presented at the Schools History Project Conference, Leeds, 10–12 April.

Bennett, S. and Steele, I. (1995) The revised history order, *Teaching History*, **79**, 5–8.

Berghahn, V. and Schissler, H. (eds) (1987) *Perceptions of History: An Analysis of School Textbooks*. Oxford: Berg.

Birt, D. and Nichol, J. (1975) *Games and Simulations in History*. London: Longman.

Black, P. and Wiliam, D. (1998) Assessment and classroom learning, *Assessment in Education*, **5** (1), 7–74.

Blow, F. and Dickinson, A. (1986) *New History and New Technology: Present into Future*. London: Historical Association.

Blyth, A., Derricott, R., Elliott, G., Summers, H. and Waplington, A. (1975) *Place, Time and Society 8–13: An Introduction*. Bristol: Collins.

Booth, M. (1969) *History Betrayed?* London: Longman.

Booth, M. (1980) A modern world history course and the thinking of adolescent pupils, *Educational Review*, **32** (3), 245–57.

Booth, M. (1987) Ages and concepts: a critique of the Piagetian approach to history teaching. In C. Portal (ed.) *The History Curriculum for Teachers*. Lewes: Falmer.

Booth, M. (1993) History. In A. King and M. Reiss (eds) *The Multicultural Dimension of the National Curriculum*. London: Falmer Press.

Booth, M., Furlong, J. and Wilkin, M. (1990) *Partnership in Initial Teacher Training*. London: Cassell.

Booth, M. and Husbands, C. (1993) The History National Curriculum in England and Wales: Assessment at Key Stage 3, *Curriculum Journal*, **4** (1), 21–36.

Bourdillon, H. (1994) On the record: the importance of gender in history teaching. In H. Bourdillon (ed.) *Teaching History*. London: Routledge.

Bovair, K., Carpenter, B. and Upton, G. (1992) *Special Curricula Needs*. London: David Fulton.

Bracey, P. (1995) Ensuring continuity and understanding through the teaching of British history. In R. Watts and I. Grosvenor (eds) *Crossing the Key Stages of History*. London: David Fulton.

British Library (1998) *Making of the United Kingdom*, CD-ROM. London: British Library.

Britt, M. A., Perfetti, C., Van Dyke, J. and Gabrys, G. (2000) The Sorcerer's Apprentice: a tool for document-supported history instruction. In P. Stearns, P. Seixas and S. Wineberg (eds) *Knowing, Teaching and Learning History: National and International Perspectives*. New York: New York University Press.

Broadfoot, P. (1996) Assessment and learning: power or partnership? In H. Goldstein and T. Lewis (eds) *Assessment: Problems, Developments and Statistical Issues*. Chichester: John Wiley.

Broadfoot, P. (2001) Empowerment or performativity? Assessment policy in the late twentieth century'. In R. Phillips and J. Furlong, (eds) *Education, Reform and the State: Twenty-Five Years of Politics, Policy and Practice*. London: Routledge.

Brookfield, K. (1995) Becoming a Critically Reflective Teacher. San Francisco: Jossey Bass.

Brooman, J. (1999) Doomed youth: using theatre to support teaching about the First World War, *Teaching History*, 96, 28–33.

Brown, G., Bayes, S. and Jeffreys, B. (2000) Cunning plan: the twentieth century – the age of what? *Teaching History*, 99, 20–1.

Brown, G. and Edmondson, R. (1984) Asking Questions. In Wragg, E. (ed.) *Classroom Teaching Skills*. London: Routledge.

Brown, R. (1995) *Managing the Learning of History*. London: David Fulton.

Brown, R. and Daniels, C. (1986) *Learning History: A Guide to Advanced Study*. London: Macmillan.

Brown, S. and McIntyre, D. (1993) *Making Sense of Teaching*. Buckingham: Open University Press.

Bruner, J. (1960) *The Process of Education*. Harvard: Vintage Books.

Brzezicki, K. (1993) Talking About History: Group Work in the Classroom – Practice and Implications, *Teaching History*, 64, 12–16.

Buckingham, D. (2000) *The Making of Citizens: Young People, News and Politics*. London: Routledge.

Bunyon, S. and Marshall, A. (2001) 'Let's see what's under the blue square . . .': Getting pupils to track their own thinking, *Teaching History*, 102, 31–4.

Byrom, J. (1998) Working with sources: scepticism or cynicism? Putting the story back together again, *Teaching History*, 91, 32–5.

Byrom, J. (2000) Why go on a pilgrimage? Using a concluding enquiry to reinforce and assess earlier learning, *Teaching History*, 99, 32–5.

Capel, S., Leask, M. and Turner, T. (1995) *Learning to Teach in the Secondary School: A Companion to School Experience*. London: Routledge.

Capel, S., Leask, M. and Turner, T. (1997) *Starting to Teach in the Secondary School: A Companion for the Newly Qualified Teacher*. London: Routledge.

Caplan, R. B. (2001) Teaching the Holocaust: the experience of Yad Vishem, *Teaching History*, 104, 24–7.

Carnes, M. (ed.) (1996) *Past Imperfect: History According to the Movies*. London: Cassell.

Carr, W. and Kemmis, S. (1986) *Becoming Critical: Education, Knowledge and Action Research*. London: Falmer.

Carrington, B. and Short, G. (1997) Holocaust education, anti-racism and citizenship, *Educational Review*, **49** (3), 271–82.

Carter, M., Culpin, C. and Kinloch, N. (1989) *Past Into Present 2: 1400–1700*. London: Collins.

Chandler, M. (2000) *ICT Activities in History*. London: Heinemann.

Chapman, T. (1993) Teaching chronology through timelines, *Teaching History*, **73**, 25–9.

Claire, H. (1996) *Reclaiming Our Pasts: Equality and Diversity in the Primary History Curriculum*. Stoke-on-Trent: Trentham Books.

Clarke, C., Dyson, A. and Millward, A. (eds) (1998) *Theorising Special Education*. London: Routledge.

Clarke, J. and Wrigley, K. (1988) *Special Needs in Ordinary Schools: Humanities for All*. London: Cassell.

Clements (1996) Historical empathy – R.I.P?, *Teaching History*, **85**, 6–8.

Coake, J., Crinnion, V. and Harrison, S. (1985) *The History Manual*. Lancaster: Framework Press.

Coffey, A. (2001) *Education and Social Change*. Buckingham: Open University Press.

Cogan, J. (1998) Citizenship education for the twenty-first century: set in the context. In J. Cogan and R. Derricott, *Citizenship for the Twenty-first Century*. London: Kogan Page.

Collicott, S. (1990) Who is the National History Curriculum for?' *Teaching History*, **61**, 8–12.

Collins, F. and Graham, J. (eds) (2001) *Historical Fiction for Children: Capturing the Past*. London: Paul Chapman.

Collis, M. and Lacey, P. (1996) *Interactive Approaches to Teaching*. London: David Fulton.

Coltham, J. and Fines, J. (1971) *Educational Objectives for the Study of History: A Suggested Framework*. London: Historical Association.

Colwill, I., Culpin, C., Shephard, C. and Shuter, P. (1990) *Using Historical Sources*. London, Heinemann.

Coman, P. (1999) Mentioning the War: does studying World War Two make any difference to pupils' sense of British achievement and identity?, *Teaching History*, **96**, 39–41.

Cooper, H. (1992) *The Teaching of History*. London: David Fulton.

Cooper, H. (1994) Historical thinking and cognitive development in the teaching of history. In H. Bourdillon (ed.) *Teaching History*. London: Routledge.

Cooper, H., Hegarty, P., Hegarty, P. and Simco, N. (1996) *Display in the Classroom: Principles, Practice and Learning Theory*. London: David Fulton.

Cooper, P. and McIntyre, D. (1992) *Effective Teaching and Learning: Teachers' and Students' Perspectives*. Buckingham: Open University Press.

Counsell, C. (1997) *Analytical and Discursive Writing in History at Key Stage 3*. London: Historical Association.

Counsell, C. (2000a) Historical knowledge and historical skills: a distracting dichotomy. In J. Arthur and R. Phillips (eds) *Issues in History Teaching*. London: Routledge.

Counsell, C. (2000b) 'Didn't we do that in Year 7?' Planning for progression in evidential understanding, *Teaching History*, **99**, 36–41.

Counsell, C. (2000c) Editorial, *Teaching History*, **101**, 2.

Counsell, C. (2001) Knowledge, writing and delighting: extending the historical thinking of 11 and 12 year olds, *Welsh Historian*, **31**, 7–13.

Cowie, E. (1979) *History and the Slow-Learning Child*. London: Historical Association.

Cowie, H., Smith, P., Boulton, M. and Lavar, R. (1993) *Cooperation in the Multi-Ethnic Classroom: The Impact of Cooperative Group Work on Social Relationships in Middle Schools*. London: David Fulton.

Cramer, I. (1993) Oral History: Working with Children, *Teaching History*, **71**, 17–19.

Crawford, K. (1995) A history of the Right: the battle for control of National Curriculum history 1989–1994, *British Journal of Educational Studies*, **43** (4), 433–56.

Crinnion, V. (1987) Some problems and principles of 'A' level history. In C. Portal (ed.) *The History Curriculum for Teachers*. Lewes: Falmer.

Croll, P. (1986) *Systematic Classroom Observation*. London: Falmer.

Crowley, T. (1996) *Language in History: Theories and Texts*. London: Routledge.

Culpin, C. (1994) Making progress in history. In H. Bourdillon (ed.) *Teaching History*. London: Routledge.

Culpin, C. (2001) Planning and teaching GCSE history. Paper given at the Historical Association Education Conference, York, 6 October.

Cunnah, W. (2000) History teaching, literacy and special educational needs. In J. Arthur and R. Phillips (eds) *Issues in History Teaching*. London: Routledge.

Cunnah, W., Phillips, R. and Jones, M. (2001) History: a foreign country? A hard look at a hard subject, *Welsh Historian*, **31**, 25–9.

Cunnah, W., Phillips, R. and Richards, S. (1997) Counting the Costs or Realising the Profits? Partnerships, Politics and Professional Development, *British Journal of In-Service Education*, **23** (2),145–61.

Curriculum Council for Wales (1991) *Community Understanding: A Framework for the Development of a Cross-Curricular Theme in Wales*. Cardiff: CCW.

Curriculum Council for Wales (1993) *Progression and Differentiation in History at Key Stage 3*. Cardiff: CCW.

Curtis, S. and Bardwell, S. (1994) Access to history. In H. Bourdillon (ed.) *Teaching History*. London: Routledge.

Davies, B. and Pritchard, P. (1975) History Still in Danger, *Teaching History*, **14**, 113–15.

Davies, I. (1995) Education for European citizenship and the teaching and learning of history. In A. Osler, H. F. Rathenow and H. Starkey (eds) *Teaching for Citizenship in Europe*. Stoke-on-Trent: Trentham Books.

Davies, I. (ed.) (2000) *Teaching the Holocaust: Educational Dimensions*. London: Continuum.

Davies, I. (2001a) Citizenship education and the teaching and learning of history. In J. Arthur, I. Davies, A. Wrenn, T. Haydn and D. Kerr (eds) *Citizenship Through Secondary History*. London: Routledge/Falmer.

Davies, I. (2001b) The history teacher and global citizenship. In J. Arthur, I. Davies, A. Wrenn, T. Haydn and D. Kerr (eds), *Citizenship Through Secondary History*. London: Routledge/Falmer.

Davies, R. (2001) Imagination and Identity: The Case for History, *Welsh Historian*, **31**, 3–6.

Dawson, I. (1990) Why Does it Matter? A Personal Response to the Final Report, *Teaching History*, **61**, 17–21.

Dawson, I. (1995) The Re-appearance of a Cheshire Cat – teaching the history of Britain at Key Stage 3, *Teaching History*, **80**, 14–17.

Dawson, I. (1996) Wales and Edward I: finding a purpose and an approach, *Welsh Historian*, **24**, 9–13.

Dean, J. (1996) *Beginning Teaching in the Secondary School*. Buckingham: Open University Press.

Dearing, R. (1993) *The National Curriculum and its Assessment: Final Report*. London: SCAA.

Dearing, R. (1996) *Review of Qualifications for 16–19 Year Olds*. London: SCAA.

Denscombe, M. (1998) *The Good Research Guide: For Small-scale Research Projects*. Buckingham: Open University Press.

Department for Education (1994) *Code of Practice on the Identification and Assessment of Special Educational Needs*. London: HMSO.

Department for Education (1995) *History in the National Curriculum: England*. London: HMSO.

Department for Education and Employment (1998a) *Meeting Special Educational Needs: A Programme of Action*. London: DfEE.

Department for Education and Employment (1998b) *The National Literacy Strategy: Framework for Teaching*. London: DfEE.

Department for Education and Employment (1999a) *History: The National Curriculum for England*. London: DFEE.

Department for Education and Employment (1999b) *Qualifying for Success: Post-16 Curriculum Reform*. London: DFEE.

Department for Education and Employment (1999c) *Learning to Succeed – A New Framework for Post-16 Learning*. London: DfEE.

Department for Education and Employment/Qualification and Curriculum Authority (1999) *Citizenship: the National Curriculum for England*. London: DfEE/QCA.

Department of Education and Science (1985a) *GCSE: The National Criteria: History*. London: HMSO.

Department of Education and Science (1985b) *History in the Primary and Secondary Years: An HMI View*. London: HMSO.

Department of Education and Science (1988a) *Curriculum Matters 5–16: History*. London: HMSO.

Department of Education and Science (1988b) *The Task Group on Assessment and Testing: A Report*. London: HMSO.

Department of Education and Science (1990) *National Curriculum History Working Group: Final Report*. London: HMSO.

Department of Education and Science (1991) *History in the National Curriculum (England)*. London: HMSO.

Department of Education and Science (1992) *Education in England 1990/91: The Annual Report of the Senior Chief Inspector of Schools*. London: HMSO.

De Silva, H., Smith, J. and Tranter, J. (2001) Finding voices in the past: exploring identity through the biography of a house, *Teaching History*, **102**, 21–8.

Deuchar, S. (1987) *History and GCSE History*. London: Centre for Policy Studies.

Deuchar, S. (1989) *The New History: A Critique*. York: Campaign for Real Education.

Deuchar, S. (1992) *History on the Brink*. Milton Keynes: Campaign for Real Education.

Dickinson, A. (1991) Assessing, Recording and Reporting Children's Achievements: from Changes to Genuine Gains. In R. Aldrich (ed.) *History in the National Curriculum*. University of London, Institute of Education (Bedford Way Series). London: Kogan Page.

Dickinson, A. (1997) Information Technology in the Curriculum in the UK: Past, Present and Future. In A. Martin, L. Smart and D. Yeomans (eds) *Information Technology and the Teaching of History: International Perspectives*. Amsterdam: Harwood.

Dickinson, A. (1998) History using information technology: past, present and future, *Teaching History*, **93**, 16–20.

Dickinson, A. and Lee, P. (eds) (1978) *History Teaching and Historical Understanding*. London: Heinemann.

Dickinson, A., Lee, P. and Rogers, P. (eds) (1984) *Learning History*. London: Heinemann.

Dickinson, C. (1996) *Effective Learning Activities*. Stafford: Network.

Dillon, J. (1988) *Questioning and Teaching: A Manual of Practice*. London: Croom Helm.

Dillon, J. and Maguire, M. (eds) (1997) *Becoming a Teacher: Issues in Secondary Schooling*. Buckingham: Open University Press.

Donaldson, M. (1978) *Children's Minds*. London: Fontana.

Dove, S. (2000) Year 10's thinking skills did not just pop out of nowhere: steering your OFSTED inspector into the long-term reasons for classroom success, *Teaching History*, **98**, 9–12.

Dyson, A. and Slee, R. (2001) Special needs education from Warnock to Salamanca: the triumph of liberalism? In R. Phillips and J. Furlong (eds) *Education, Reform and the State: Twenty-Five Years of Politics, Policy and Practice*. London: Routledge/Falmer.

Edwards, A. (1978) The language of history and the communication of historical knowledge. In A. Dickinson and P. Lee (eds) *History Teaching and Historical Understanding*. London: Heinemann.

Edwards, A. and Brunton, D. (1993) Supporting reflection in teachers' learning. In J. Calderhead and P. Gates (eds) *Conceptualizing Reflection in Teacher Development*. London: Falmer.

Edwards, C. and Healy, M. (1994) *The Student Teacher's Handbook*. London: Kogan Page.

Edwards, A. and Westgate, W. (1994) *Investigating Classroom Talk* (2nd edn). London: Falmer.

Egan, K. (1992) *Imagination in Teaching and Learning: Ages 8–15*. London: Routledge.

Elliott, J. (1991) *Action Research for Educational Change*. Milton Keynes: Open University Press.

Ellwood, D. (ed.) (2000) *The Movies as History: Visions of the Twentieth Century*. London: Sutton/History Today.

ESTYN (Inspectorate in Wales) (2001) *Good Practice in History*. Cardiff: ESTYN.

Evans, R. (1994) Educational Ideologies and the Teaching of History. In G. Leienhardt, I. Beck and C. Stainton (eds) *Teaching and Learning in History*. Hillsdale, NJ: Lawrence Erlbaum Associates.

Fairclough, J. (1994) *A Teacher's Guide to History Through Role Play*. London: English Heritage.

Farmer, A. and Knight, P. (1995) *Active History in Key Stages 3 and 4*. London: David Fulton.

Farrel, P. (2000) Special education in the last twenty years: have things really got better? *British Journal of Special Education*, 28 (1), 3–9.

Figueoa, B. (2000) Citizenship education for a plural society. In A. Osler (ed.) *Citizenship and Democracy in Schools: Diversity, Identity, Equality*. Stoke-on-Trent: Trentham Books.

File, N. and Power, C. (1981) *Black Settlers in Britain 1555–1958*. London: Heinemann.

Film Education (1998) *Screening Histories: Film Education Study Video and Book*. London: Film Education.

Fines, J. (1980) Introduction. In D. Shemilt, *History 3–16: Evaluation Study Schools Council History 13–16 Project*. Edinburgh: Holmes MacDougall.

Fines, J. (1983) *Teaching History*. Edinburgh: Holmes MacDougall.

Fines, J. (1988) *Reading Historical Documents: A Manual for Students*. Oxford: Blackwell.

Fines, J. and Nichol, J. (1994) *ETHOS: Doing History 16–19: A Case Study in Curriculum Innovation and Change*. London: Historical Association.

Fines, J. and Verrier, R. (1974) *The Drama of History: An Experiment in Cooperative Teaching*. London: New University Education.

Fisher, R. (1990) *Teaching Children to Think*. Cheltenham: Stanley Thornes.

Fisher, R. (1995) *Teaching Children to Learn*. Cheltenham: Nelson Thornes.

Fisher, T. (1995) The new subject core for 'A' level, *Welsh Historian*, 80, 18–19.

Flores, M. A. (2001) Person and context in becoming a new teacher, *Journal of Education for Teaching*, 27 (2), 135–48.

Fox, S. (1999) *The Medieval Woman*. London: Galileo.

Francis, J. (1983) *Microcomputers and Teaching History*. Harlow: Longman.

Fukuyama, F. (1992) *The End of History and the Last Man*. London: Hamish Hamilton.

Furedi, F. (1992) *Mythical Past, Elusive Future: History and Society in an Anxious Age*. London: Pluto.

Furlong, J. (2001) Reforming teacher education, re-forming teachers: accountability, professionalism and competence. In R. Phillips and J. Furlong (eds) *Education, Reform and the State: Twenty-Five Years of Politics, Policy and Practice*. London: Routledge.

Furlong, J. and Maynard, T. (1995) *Mentoring Student Teachers: The Growth of Professional Knowledge*. London: Routledge.

Gaine, C. (1987) *No Problem Here: A Practical Approach to Education and 'Race' in White Schools*. London: Hutchinson.

Gaine, C. (1995) *Still No Problem Here*. Stoke-on-Trent: Trentham Books.

Gardner, H. (1983) *Frames of Mind*. London: Heinemann.

Gardner, H. (1994) The theory of multiple intelligences. In B. Moon and A. S. Mayes (eds) *Teaching and Learning in the Secondary School*. London: Routledge.

Gardner, P. (2001) *Teaching and Learning in Multicultural Classrooms*. London: Paul Chapman.

George, P. (1997) 'Interpretations of history' in the National Curriculum, *The Welsh Journal of Education*, **6** (2), 60–8.

Giddens, A. (1998) *The Third Way: The Renewal of Social Democracy*. London: Polity Press.

Gipps, C. (1994) *Beyond Testing: Towards a Theory of Educational Assessment*. London: Falmer Press.

Gipps, C. and Stobart, G. (1993) *Assessment: A Teacher's Guide to the Issues*. London: Hodder and Stoughton.

Giroux, H. (1988) *Teachers as Intellectuals: Toward a Critical Pedagogy of Learning*. New York: Bergin and Garvey.

Giroux, H. (1992) *Border Crossings: Cultural Workers and the Politics of Education*. London: Routledge.

Giroux, H. and McLaren, P. (eds) (1989) *Critical Pedagogy, the State and Cultural Struggle*. New York: State University of New York Press.

Goalen, P. (1999) 'Someone might become involved in a fascist group or something...': pupils' perceptions of history at the end of Key Stages 2, 3 and 4, *Teaching History*, **96**, 34–8.

Goalen, P. and Hendy, J. (1994) History though drama, *Curriculum*, **15** (3), 147–62.

Gorman, M. (1998) The structured enquiry is not a contradiction in terms: focused teaching for independent learning, *Teaching History*, **92**, 20–5.

Griffith, R. (2000) *National Curriculum: National Disaster? Education and Citizenship*. London: Routledge/Falmer.

Grosvenor, I. (1997) *Assimilating Identities: Racism and Education Policy in Post-1945 Britain*. London: Lawrence and Wishart.

Grosvenor, I. (2000) "History for the nation": multiculturalism and the teaching of history. In J. Arthur and R. Phillips (eds) *Issues in History Teaching*. London: Routledge.

Grosvenor, I. and Watts, R. (1995) *Crossing the Key Stages of History: Effective History Teaching 5–16 and Beyond*. London: David Fulton.

Gunning, D. (1978) *The Teaching of History*. London: Croom Helm.

HA/NCET (1997) *History Using IT: Improving Students' Writing Using Wordprocessing*. London: HA/NCET.

Haenen, J. and Schrijnemakers, H. (2000) Suffrage, feudal, democracy, treaty ... history's building blocks: learning to teach historical concepts, *Teaching History*, **98**, 22–9.

Hake, C. and Haydn, T. (1995) Stories or sources? *Teaching History*, **78**, 20–2.

Hallam, R. (1970) Piaget and thinking in history. In M. Ballard (ed.) *New Movements in the Study and Teaching of History*. London: Temple Smith.

Hammond, K. (2001) From horror to history: teaching pupils to think about significance, *Teaching History*, **104**, 15–23.

Halstead, J. and Taylor, M. (eds) (1996) *Values in Education and Education in Values.* London: Falmer.

Harlen, W., Gipps, C., Broadfoot, P. and Nuttall, D. (1994) Assessment and the improvement of education. In B. Moon and A. S. Mayes (eds) *Teaching and Learning in the Secondary School.* London: Routledge.

Harnett, P. (1993) Identifying progression in children's understanding: The use of visual material to assess primary school children's learning in history, *Cambridge Journal of Education*, **23** (2). 137–54.

Harnett, P. (1996) Questions about the past, *Welsh Historian*, **25**, 19–22.

Harper, P. (1993) Using the Attainment Targets in Key Stage 2: AT2 'Interpretations of History', *Teaching History*, **72**, 11–13.

Harris, R. (2001) Why essay-writing remains central to learning history at A/S level, *Teaching History*, **103**, 3–16.

Hart, S. (1992) Differentiation – way forward or retreat? *British Journal of Special Education*, **19** (9), 10–12.

Haydn, T. (1992) History for ordinary children, *Teaching History*, **67**, 8–11.

Haydn, T. (1993) The chemistry of history lessons, teacher autonomy and the reform of National Curriculum History, *Welsh Historian*, **22**, 7–10.

Haydn, T. (1994) Uses and abuses of the TGAT assessment model: the case of history and the 45 boxes, *The Curriculum Journal*, **5** (2), 215–33.

Haydn, T. (1999) Back to basics: values and the History Curriculum. In D. Lawton, J. Cairns and R. Gardner (eds) *Values and the Curriculum: The School Context.* London: Institute of Education.

Haydn, T. (2000) Information and communications technology in the history classroom. In J. Arthur and R. Phillips (eds) *Issues in History Teaching*, London: Routledge.

Haydn, T., Arthur, J. and Hunt, M. (1997) *Learning to Teach History in the Secondary School: A Companion to School Experience.* London: Routledge.

Hayek, F. (1944) *The Road to Serfdom.* London: Routledge and Kegan Paul.

Hayes, D. (1997) *Success on Your Teaching Experience.* London: Hodder and Stoughton.

Heater, D. (1990) *Citizenship: The Civil Ideal in World History, Politics and Education.* Harlow: Longman.

Hennessey, R. (1988) The content question: an agenda, *Welsh Historian*, Spring, 3–6.

Hessari, R. and Hill, D. (1989) *Practical Ideas for Multicultural Teaching and Learning in the Primary Classroom.* London: Routledge.

Hickman, J. and Kimberley, K. (1988) *Teachers, Language and Learning.* London: Routledge.

Hillgate Group (1986) *Whose Schools? A Radical Manifesto.* London: Hillgate Group.

Hinton, C. (1990) *What Is Evidence?* London: John Murray.

Hiskett, M. (1988) *Choice in Rotten Apples: Bias in GCSE and Examining Groups.* London: Centre for Policy Studies.

Hoodless, P. (1996) *Time and Timelines.* London: Historical Association.

Hoodless, P. (ed.) (1998) *History and English in the Primary School: Exploring the Links.* London: Routledge.

Howells, G. (2000) Gladstone spiritual or Gladstone material? A rationale for using documents at AS and A2, *Teaching History*, **100**, 26–31.

Hughes, M. (1999) *Closing the Learning Gap.* Stafford: Network.

Hunt, M. (2000) Teaching historical significance. In J. Arthur and R. Phillips (eds) *Issues in History Teaching.* London: Routledge.

Husbands, C. (1996) *What Is History Teaching? Language, Ideas and Meaning in Learning About the Past.* Buckingham: Open University Press.

Husbands, C. (2001) What's happening in history? Trends in GCSE and 'A' level examinations, 1993–2000, *Teaching History*, **103**, 37–41.

Illingworth, S. (2000) Hearts, minds and souls: exploring values through history, *Teaching History*, 100, 20–4.

Inner London Education Authority (ILEA) (1979) Language and history. In H. Bourdillon (ed.) (1994) *Teaching History*. London: Routledge.

James, M. and Gipps, C. (1998) Broadening the basis of assessment to prevent the narrowing of learning, *Curriculum Journal*, 9 (3), 285–97.

Janoski, T. (1998) *Citizenship and Civil Society: A Framework of Rights and Obligations in Liberal, Traditional and Social Democratic Regimes*. Cambridge: Cambridge University Press.

Jenkins, I. and Turpin, M. (1998) Super history teaching on the superhighway: the Internet for beginners, *Teaching History*, 93, 40–3.

Jenkins, K. (1991) *Re-Thinking History*. London: Routledge.

John, P. (1991) The professional craft knowledge of the history teacher, *Teaching History*, 64, 8–12.

John, P. (1993) History tasks at Key Stage 3: a survey from five schools, *Teaching History*, 70, 17–20.

John, P. (1994) Academic tasks in history classrooms, *Research in Education*, 51, 11–22.

Jolly, S. (2001) *What the Dickens? An Investigation Into the Myth and Reality of the Workhouse*. Paper given at the SHP Conference, Leeds, July.

Jones, R. (1999) *Teaching Racism – or Tackling It? Multicultural Stories from White Beginning Teachers*. Stoke-on-Trent: Trentham Books.

Jordan, A. and Taylor, P. (1999) History. In S. Bigger and E. Brown (eds) *Spiritual, Moral, Social and Cultural Education: Exploring Values in the Curriculum*. London: David Fulton.

Joseph, K. (1984) Why teach history in school? Address by Sir Keith Joseph to the Historical Association Conference, 10 February, *The Historian*, 2, 101–12.

Joyce, B., Calhoun, E. and Hopkins, D. (1997) *Models for Learning – Tools for Teaching*. Buckingham: Open University Press.

Keatinge, M. (1910) *Studies in the Teaching of History*. London: Black.

Kedourie, H. (1988) *The Errors and Evils of the New History*. London: Centre for Policy Studies.

Kelly, A. (1988) The Cambridge 'A' level history project – bridging the gap? *Welsh Historian*, 9, 21–4.

Kelly, A. (1996) A quiet revolution? The Cambridge 'A' level project, *Welsh Historian*, 25, 11–18.

Kemmis, S. and McTaggart, R. (1992) *The Action Research Planner* (Revised edn). Victoria: Deakin University.

Kennedy, K. (ed.) (1997) *Citizenship Education and the Modern State*. London: Falmer.

Kerr, D. (2001) Citizenship education and educational policy making. In J. Arthur, I. Davies, A. Wrenn, T. Haydn and D. Kerr (eds), *Citizenship Through Secondary History*. London: Routledge/Falmer.

Kerry, T. (1982a) *The New Teacher: Examining In-school Provision for Student Teachers and Probationers*. London: Macmillan.

Kerry, T. (1982b) *Effective Questioning*. London: Macmillan.

Kinloch, N. (2001) Parallel catastrophe? Uniqueness, redemption and the shoah, *Teaching History*, 104, 8–14.

Kitson, A. (2001) Challenging stereotypes and avoiding the superficial: a suggested approach to teaching the Holocaust, *Teaching History*, 104, 41–8.

Knight, P. (1987) Empathy: concept, confusion and consequences in a National Curriculum, *Oxford Review of Education*, 15 (1), 41–53.

Kutnick, P. and Rogers, C. (eds) (1994) *Groups in Schools*. London: Cassell.

Kyriacou, C. (1992) *Effective Teaching in Schools*. London: Simon and Schuster.

Kyriacou, C. (1995) *Essential Teaching Skills*. London: Stanley Thornes.

Laffin, D. (2000a) My essays could go on forever: using Key Stage 3 to improve performance at GCSE, *Teaching History*, **98**, 14–21.

Laffin, D. (2000b) A poodle with bite: using ICT to make AS Level more rigorous, *Teaching History*, **101**, 8–15.

Laffin, D. (2001) A practical approach to sources at AS and A2: teaching them that it's not just black and white. Paper given at the Historical Association Education Conference, York, 6 October.

Lang, S. (1990) *'A' Level History: the Case for Change*. London: Historical Association.

Lang, S. (1993) What Is Bias? *Teaching History*, **73**, 9–13.

Lang, S. (1996) Why Is 'A' Level Hard? *Welsh Historian*, **25**, 5–11.

Lang, S. (1999) Democracy is NOT boring, *Teaching History*, **96**, 23–7.

Lawlor, S. (1990) Response to the Final Report: But what must children know?. In S. Lawlor (ed.) *An Education Choice: Pamphlets from the Centre, 1987–1994*. London: Centre for Policy Studies.

Lawton, D. (1980) *The Politics of the School Curriculum*. London: Routledge and Kegan Paul.

Leask, M. and Pachler, N. (1999) *Learning to Teach Using ICT in the Secondary School*. London: Routledge.

Le Cocq, H. (2000) Beyond bias: making source evaluation meaningful to Year 7. *Teaching History*, **99**, 50–5.

Lee, P. (1984) Historical imagination. In A. Dickinson, P. Lee and P. Rogers (eds) *Learning History*. London: Heinemann.

Lee, P. and Ashby, R. (1998) Researching children's ideas about history. In J. Voss and M. Carretero (eds) *Learning and Reasoning in History*. London: Woburn.

Lee, P. and Ashby, R. (2000) Progression in historical understanding in students ages 7–14. In P. Stearns, P. Seixas and S. Wineburg (eds) *Knowing, Teaching and Learning History*. New York: New York University Press.

Lee, P., Ashby, R. and Dickinson, A. (1996) 'There were no facts in those days': children's ideas about historical explanation. In M. Hughes (ed.) *Teaching and Learning in Changing Times*. Oxford: Blackwell.

Lee, P., Schemilt, D., Slater, J., Walsh, P. and White, J. (1992) *The Aims of School History: the National Curriculum and Beyond*. London: Tufnell Press.

Leonard, A. (2000) Achieving progression from the GCSE to AS, *Teaching History*, **98**, 30–4.

Levine, N. (1981) *Language Teaching and Learning: History*. London: Ward Lock.

Linsell, D. (1998) Subject exemplification of the Initial Teacher Training National Curriculum for ICT: how the history examples were developed, *Teaching History*, **93**, 33–5.

Little, V. and John, T. (1990) *Historical Fiction in the Classroom*. London: Historical Association.

Loader, P. (1993) Historically speaking, *Teaching History*, **71**, 20–2.

Lomas, T. (1993) *Teaching and Assessing Historical Understanding*. London: Historical Association.

Lomas, T. (1995) Good practice in Key Stage 3 history (has the National Curriculum changed our view?), *Discoveries*, **6**, 13–15.

Lomas, T. (1998) The challenges facing history teachers, *Welsh Historian*, **28**, 6–10.

Lomas, T. (1999) Raising numbers and standards in secondary history. Paper delivered to School History Project Conference, Leeds, April.

London Feminist History Group (1983) *The Sexual Dynamics of History: Men's Power, Women's Resistance*. London: Pluto.

Low-Beer, A. (1989) Empathy and history, *Teaching History*, **55**, 8–12.

Luff, I. (2000) 'I've been in the Reichstag': Re-thinking Role-play, *Teaching History*, **100**, 8–17.

Lynn, S. (1993) Children reading pictures: history visuals at Key Stages 1 and 2, *Education 3–13*, **21** (3), 23–9.

Lyons, G. (2001) Reflecting on rights: teaching pupils about pre-1832 British politics using a realistic role-play, *Teaching History*, **103**, 28–31.

McAleavy, T. (1991) *Medieval Britain: Conquest, Power and People*. Cambridge: Cambridge University Press.

McAleavy, T. (1993) Using the Attainment Targets in Key Stage 3: AT2, Interpretations of History, *Teaching History*, **72**, 14–17.

McAleavy, T. (1994) Meeting pupils' learning needs: differentiation and progression in the teaching of history. In H. Bourdillon (ed.) *Teaching History*. London: Routledge.

McAleavy, T. (1998) The use of sources in school history 1910–1998: a critical perspective, *Teaching History*, **91**, 10–16.

McAleavy, T. (2000) Teaching about interpretations. In J. Arthur and R. Phillips (eds) *Issues in History Teaching*. London: Routledge.

McCulloch, G. (2001) The reinvention of teacher professionalism. In R. Phillips and J. Furlong (eds) *Education, Reform and the State: Twenty-Five Years of Politics, Policy and Practice*. London: Routledge/Falmer.

McLaren, P. (1988) Foreward: critical theory and the meaning of hope. In H. Giroux, *Teachers as Intellectuals: Toward a Critical Pedagogy of Learning*. New York: Bergin and Garvey.

McManus, M. (1993) *Troublesome Behaviour in the Classroom: A Teacher's Survival Guide*. London: Routledge.

MacMaster, N. (2001) *Racism in Europe, 1870–2000*. Basingstoke: Palgrave.

Man an Ghail, M. (1992) Coming of age in 1980s England: reconceptualizing black students' schooling experience. In D. Gill, B. Mayor and M. Blair (eds) *Racism and Education: Structures and Strategies*. London: Sage.

Marples, R. (2000) 14–19 and lifelong learning. In J. Docking (ed.) *New Labour's Policies for Schools*. London: David Fulton.

Marshall, T. H. (1963) Citizenship and social class. In T. H. Marshall, *Sociology at the Crossroads and Other Essays*. London: Heinemann.

Martin, A. and Blow, F. (eds) (1990) *Computers in the History Classroom*. Leeds: Leeds University Press.

Martin, D. (1998) The Hopi is different from the Pawnee: using a data-file to explore pattern and diversity, *Teaching History*, **93**, 22–7.

Mbenga, B. (1993) Skilful questioning as an effective tool of history teaching, *Teaching History*, **71**, 23–4.

Mercer, N. (1995) *The Guided Construction of Knowledge: Talk Amongst Teachers and Learners*. Clevedon: Multilingual Matters.

Miller, D. (2000) *Citizenship and National Identity*. Oxford: Polity Press.

Moon, J. (1999) *Reflection in Learning and Professional Development: Theory and Practice*. London: Kogan Page.

Moore, R. (2000) Using the Internet to teach about interpretations in Years 9 and 12, *Teaching History*, **101**, 35–9.

Morgan, A. (1999) Teaching and learning about interpretations, *Welsh Historian*, **29**, 3–6.

Morgan, N. and Saxton, J. (1991) *Teaching, Questioning and Learning*. London: Routledge.

Moss, P. (1976) *History Alive: 1485–1714*. London: Hart-Davies.

Mountford, P. (2001) Working as a team to teach the Holocaust well: a language-centred approach, *Teaching History*, **104**, 28–33.

Mulholland, M. (1998) Frameworks for linking pupils' evidential understanding with growing skill in structured, written argument: the 'evidence sandwich', *Teaching History*, **91**, 17–22.

National Curriculum Council (1991a) *National Curriculum Council Non-Statutory Guidance for History*. York: NCC.

National Curriculum Council (1991b) *Implementing National Curriculum History*. York: NCC.

Neill, S. (1991) *Classroom Nonverbal Communication*. London: Routledge.

Neill, S. and Caswell, S. (1993) *Body Language for Competent Teachers*. London: Routledge.

Nichol, J. (1984) *Teaching History: A Teaching Skills Workbook*. London: Macmillan.

Nichol, J. (1995) *Teaching History at Key Stage 3*. London: Chris Kington Publishing.

Nichol, J. (1998) Thinking skills and children learning history. In R. Burden and M. Williams (eds) *Thinking Through the Curriculum*. London: Routledge.

Nicklin, H. (1992) 'Real Books' and 'Interpretations of History' in the National Curriculum, *Teaching History*, 67, 11–16.

O'Keeffe, D. (ed.) (1986) *The Wayward Curriculum: A Case for Parents' Concern?* London: Social Affairs Unit.

Office for Standards in Education (1993) *History: A Review of Inspection Findings 1992/93*. London: HMSO.

Office for Standards in Education (1995) *History: A Review of Inspection Findings 1993/94*. London: HMSO.

Oommen, T. (1997) *Citizenship, Nationality and Ethnicity*. Oxford: Polity Press.

O'Neill, J. (1998) Teaching pupils to analyse cartoons, *Teaching History*, 91, 20–4.

Osler, A. (1994) Still hidden from history? The representation of women in recently published history textbooks, *Oxford Review of Education*, 20 (2), 219–35.

Osler, A. (ed.) (2000) *Citizenship and Democracy in Schools: Diversity, Identity, Equality*. Stoke-on-Trent: Trentham Books.

Osler, A. and Starkey, H. (2000) Citizenship, human rights and cultural diversity. In A. Osler (ed.) *Citizenship and Democracy in Schools: Diversity, Identity and Equality*. Stoke-on-Trent: Trentham Books.

Pankhania, J. (1994) *Liberating the National History Curriculum*. London: Falmer Press.

Parker, S. (1993) *The Craft of Writing*. London: Paul Chapman

Partington, G. (1980) *The Idea of an Historical Education*. Slough: NFER.

Partington, G. (1986) History: re-written to ideological fashion. In D. O'Keeffe (ed.) *The Wayward Curriculum: A Case for Parents' Concern?* London: Social Affairs Unit.

Parsons, J. (2000) The Evacuee Letter Exchange Project: using audience-centred writing to improve progression from Key Stage 2 to 3, *Teaching History*, 98, 6–8.

Past Times (1998) *Lock, Stock and Barrel: Familiar Sayings and their Meanings*. Oxford: Past Times.

Patrick, H. (1987) *The Aims of Teaching History in Secondary Schools: Report of a Research Project Funded by the Economic and Social Research Council*. University of Leicester, School of Education, Occasional Paper. Leicester: University of Leicester Press.

Patrick, H. (1988a) The History Curriculum: the teaching of history, 1985–87, *History Resource*, 2 (1), 9–14.

Patrick, H. (1988b) History teachers for the 1990s and beyond, *Teaching History*, 50, 10–14.

Peel, E. (1960) *The Pupil's Thinking*. London: Oldbourne.

Perera, K. (1986) Some linguistic difficulties in school textbooks. In B. Gillham (ed.) *The Language of School Textbooks*. London: Heinemann.

Phillips, M. (1996) *All Must Have Prizes*. London: Little, Brown and Co.

Phillips, R. (1991) National Curriculum history and teacher autonomy: the major challenge, *Teaching History*, 65, 21–4.

Phillips, R. (1992a) 'The battle for the big prize': the creation of synthesis and the role of a curriculum pressure group: the case of history and the National Curriculum, *The Curriculum Journal*, 3 (3), 245–60.

Phillips, R. (1992b) Time and the sword of Damocles, *Welsh Historian*, 18, 10–12.

Phillips, R. (1993) Change and continuity: some reflections on the first year's implementation of Key Stage 3 history, *Teaching History*, 70, 9–12.

Phillips, R. (1996) History teaching, cultural restorationism and national identity in England and Wales, *Curriculum Studies*, 70, 9–12.

Phillips, R. (1997) Thesis and anti-thesis in Tate's views on history, culture and nationhood, *Teaching History*, 86, 30–3.

Phillips, R. (1998a) *History Teaching, Nationhood and the State: A Study in Educational Politics*. London: Cassell.

Phillips, R. (1998b) Contesting the past, constructing the future: politics, policy and identity in schools, *British Journal of Educational Studies*, 46, 40–53. Also published in J. Arnold, K. Davies and S. Ditchfield, (eds) *History and Heritage: Consuming the Past in Contemporary Culture*. Shaftesbury: Donhead.

Phillips, R. (1999) History teaching, nationhood and politics in England and Wales in the twentieth century: a historical comparison, *History of Education*, 28 (1), 351–63.

Phillips, R. (2000a) Government policies, the state and the teaching of history. In R. Phillips and J. Furlong (eds) *Education, Reform and the State: Twenty-Five Years of Politics, Policy and Practice*. London: Routledge/Falmer.

Phillips, R. (2000b) Culture, community and curriculum in Wales: citizenship education for the new democracy? In D. Lawton, J. Cairns and R. Gardner (eds) *Education for Citizenship*. London: Continuum.

Phillips, R. (2001a) Education, the state and the politics of reform: the historical context, 1976–2001. In R. Phillips and J. Furlong (eds) *Education, Reform and the State: Twenty-Five Years of Politics, Policy and Practice*. London: Routledge/Falmer.

Phillips, R. (2001b) Making history curious: the use of Initial Stimulus Material (ISM) to promote enquiry, thinking and literacy, *Teaching History*, 105, 19–24.

Phillips, R. (2002a) *The Total History Experience: Using Research to Improve History Teaching and Learning*. Cardiff: ESIS.

Phillips, R. (2002b) Historical significance: the forgotten Key Element? *Teaching History*, 96, 14–19.

Phillips, R. (2002c) *Mametz: Wales and The First World War*. Cardiff: ACCAC.

Phillips, R. and Cunnah, W. (1999) Certain past, uncertain future? History teaching, values and a curriculum for the twenty-first century. In D. Lawton, J. Cairns and R. Gardner (eds) *Values and the Curriculum: The School Context*. London: Institute of Education.

Phillips, R. and Cunnah, W. (2000) The Total History Experience: research, teaching and learning, *Welsh Historian*, 30, 3–6.

Phillips, R. and Furlong, J. (eds) (2001) *Education, Reform and the State: Twenty-Five Years of Politics, Policy and Practice*. London: Routledge/Falmer.

Phillips, R., Goalen, P., McCully, A. and Wood, S. (1999) Four histories, one nation? History teaching, nationhood and a British identity, *Compare: A Journal of Comparative Education*, 29 (2), 153–69.

Piaget, J. (1962) The stages of the intellectual development of the child. In V. Lee (ed.) (1990) *Children's Learning in School*. London: Hodder and Stoughton.

Pitt, J. (2000) Computing on a shoestring: extending pupils' historical vision with limited resources, *Teaching History*, 101, 25–8.

Portal, C. (1987a) Empathy as an objective for history teaching. In C. Portal (ed.) *The History Curriculum for Teachers*. Lewes: Falmer.

Portal, C. (ed.) (1987b) *Sources in History: From Definition to Assessment*. Eastleigh: SREB

Postlethwaite, K. (1999) Creative teaching and reflective practice. In K. Ashcroft and D. James (eds) *The Creative Professional: Learning to Teach 14–19 Year Olds*. London: Falmer.

Postman, N. (1979) *Teaching as a Conserving Activity*. New York: Laurel Press.

Power, E. (1975) *Medieval Women*. Cambridge: Cambridge University Press.

Price, M. (1968) History in danger, *History*, 53, 342–7.

Prior, J. and John, P. (2000) From anecdote to argument: using the word processor to connect knowledge and opinion through revelatory writing, *Teaching History*, 101, 31–4.

Qualifications and Curriculum Authority (1998) *Education for Citizenship and the Teaching of Democracy in Schools (Crick Report)*. London: QCA.

Qualifications and Curriculum Authority /Qualifications, Curriculum and Assessment Authority of Wales (1999) *Introduction to Key Skills Levels 1–3 in Communication, Application of Number and Information Technology*. London: QCA.

Quayson, A. (2000) *Postcolonialism: Theory, Practice or Process?* Oxford: Polity Press.

Ramjhun, A. (1996) *Implementing the Code of Practice for Children With Special Educational Needs: A Practical Guide*. London: David Fulton.

Randell, K. (ed.) (1984) *The Use of the Computer in the Study and Teaching of History*. London: Historical Association.

Rayner, L. (1999) Weighing a century with a website: teaching Year 9 to be critical, *Teaching History*, 96, 13–22.

Reid, J. A., Forrestal, P. and Cook, J. (1989) *Small Group Learning in the Classroom*. Scarborough, WA: Chalkface Press.

Riley, C. (1999) Evidential understanding, period knowledge and the development of literacy: a practical approach to 'layers of inference' for Key Stage 3, *Teaching History*, 97, 6–12.

Riley, M. (1997) Big stories and big pictures: making outlines and overviews interesting, *Teaching History*, 88, 20–2.

Riley, M. (2000) Into the Key Stage 3 history garden: choosing and planting your enquiry questions, *Teaching History*, 99, 8–13.

Robertson, J. (1989) *Effective Classroom Control*. London: Hodder and Stoughton.

Rogers, P. (1979) *The New History – Theory into Practice*. London: Historical Association.

Rorty, R. (1989) *Contingency, Irony and Solidarity*. Cambridge: Cambridge University Press.

Rosenstone, R. (1995) *Visions of the Past: The Challenge of Film to our Idea of History*. Cambridge: Harvard University Press.

Rowbotham, S. (1973) *Hidden From History: 300 Years of Women's Oppression and the Fight Against It*. London: Pluto.

Rudham, R. (2001) The new history A/S Level: principles of planning a scheme of work, *Teaching History*, 103, 18–21.

Russell, L. (2000) Do smile before Christmas: the NQT year, *Teaching History*, 100, 36–8.

Salmons, P. (2001) Moral delimmas: history teaching and the Holocaust, *Teaching History*, 104, 34–40.

Samuel, R. (1998) *Island Stories: Unravelling Britain*. London: Verso.

Sarup, M. (1991) *Education and the Ideologies of Racism*. Stoke-on-Trent, Trentham Books.

Saunders, E. (1999) '1086 and all that follows', *Times Educational Supplement*, 5 March.

Scarth, J (1987) Teaching to the exam? The case of the Schools History Project. In T. Horton (ed.) *GCSE: Examining the New System*. London: Harper and Row.

Schon, D (1983) *The Reflective Practitioner: How Professionals Think in Action*. London: Temple Smith.

Schools' Council History 13–16 Project (SCHP) (1976) *A New Look at History*. Edinburgh: Holmes MacDougall.

Scott, J. (1990) *Understanding Cause and Effect (Teaching History Research Group)*. London: Longman.

Scott, J. (1991) The evidence of experience, *Critical Inquiry*, 17 (4), 773–97.

Scruton, R. (1980) *The Meaning of Conservatism*. London: Penguin.

Scruton, R. (1986) The myth of cultural relativism. In R. Palmer (ed.) *Anti-Racism: An Assault on Education and Value*. London: Sherwood Press.

Scruton, R. (1999) *England: An Elegy*. London: Chatto and Windus.

Sebba, J. (1994) *History For All*. London: David Fulton.

Sebba, J. and Clarke, J. (1991) Meeting the needs of pupils within history and geography. In R. Ashdown, B. Carpenter and K. Bovair (eds) *The Curriculum Challenge: Access to the National Curriculum for Pupils with Learning Difficulties*. Lewes: Falmer Press.

Shaw, R. (1992) *Teacher Training in Secondary Schools*. London: Kogan Page.

Shayer, M. (1997) Piaget and Vygotsky: a necessary marriage for effective educational intervention. In L. Smith, J. Dockrell and P. Tomlinson (eds) *Piaget, Vygotsky and Beyond: Future Issues for Developmental Psychology and Education*. London: Routledge.

Shemilt, D. (1980) *History 13–16 Evaluation Study: Schools Council History 13–16 Project*. Edinburgh: Holmes MacDougall.

Shemilt, D. (1984) Beauty and the philosopher: empathy in history and classroom. In A. Dickinson, P. Lee and P. Rogers (eds) *Learning History*. London: Heinemann.

Shemilt, D. (1987) Adolescent ideas about evidence and methodology in history. In C. Portal (ed.) *The History Curriculum for Teachers*. Lewes: Falmer.

Shephard, C., Hinton, C., Hite, J. and Lomas, T. (1992) *Discovering the Past Y8: Societies in Change*. London: John Murray.

Sheppard, D. (2000) Confronting otherness: developing scrutiny and inference skills through drawing, *Teaching History*, 100, 39–41.

Shulman, L. (1986) Those who understand: knowledge growth in teaching, *Educational Researcher*, 15 (2), 4–14.

Shuter, P., Child, J. and Taylor, D. (1989) *Skills in History: Changes*. London: Heinemann.

Simon, R., Rosenberg, S. and Eppert, C. (2000) *Between Hope and Desire: Pedagogy and the Remembrance of Historical Trauma*. Oxford: Rowman and Littlefield.

Slater, J. (1989) *The Politics of History Teaching; A Humanity Dehumanized?* Institute of London, Special Professorial Lecture. London: Institute of Education.

Smart, D. (2000) *Citizenship in History: A Guide for Teachers*. Cheltenham: Stanley Thornes.

Smith, A. (1996) *Accelerated Learning in the Classroom*. Stafford: Network.

Smith, C. and Laslett, R. (1993) *Effective Classroom Management: A Teacher's Guide*. London: Routledge.

Smith, P. (2001) Why Gerry now likes evidential work, *Teaching History*, 102, 8–13.

Sobchack, V. (ed.) (1996) *The Persistence of History: Cinema, Television and the Modern Event*. London: Routledge.

SREB (1986) *Empathy in History: From Definition to Assessment*. Eastleigh: SREB.

Stephens, P. and Crawley, T. (1994) *Becoming an Effective Teacher*. Chletenham: Stanley Thornes.

Stow, W. (2000) History: values in the diversity of human experience. In R. Bailey (ed.) *Teaching Values and Citizenship Across the Curriculum: Educating Children for the World*. London: Kogan Page.

Stow, W. and Haydn, T. (2000) issues in the teaching of history. In J. Arthur and R. Phillips (eds) *Issues in History Teaching*. London: Routledge.

Supple, C. and Hudson, N. (1990) Learning about the Holocaust: using video to develop empathy, *Multicultural Teaching*, 8 (3), 42–3.

Swinnerton, P. and Jenkins, I. (1999) *Secondary School History Teaching in England and Wales: A Review of Empirical Research, 1960–1998*. Leeds: University of Leeds /Historical Association.

Sylvester, D. (1994) A historical overview. In H Bourdillon (ed.) *Teaching History*. London: Routledge.

Tate, N. (1996a) National identity and the school history curriculum, *Welsh Historian*, 24, 7–9.

Tate, N. (1996b) Introductory speech at the SCAA invitation conference on Curriculum, Culture and Society, 7–9 February. London: SCAA.

Teacher Training Agency (1997) *Teaching as a Research-Based Activity*. London: TTA.

Teacher Training Agency (1998a) *The Use of Information and Communications Technology in Subject Teaching: Identification of Training Needs (Secondary History)*. London: TTA.

Teacher Training Agency (1998b) *Using Information and Communications Technology to Meet Objectives in History Teacher Training (Secondary)*. London: TTA.

Teaching History Research Group (1991) *How to Teach, Plan and Assess History in the National Curriculum*. London: Heinemann.

Thacker, A. (1997) Foucault and the writing of history. In M. Lloyd and A. Thacker (eds) *The Impact of Michel Foucault on the Social Sciences and Humanities*. London: Longman.

Tilstone, C. (ed.) (1998) *Observing Teaching and Learning: Principles and Practice*. London: David Fulton.

Tomlinson, S. (1990) The British national identity. In S. Tomlinson, *Multicultural Education in White Schools*. London: Batsford.

Tomlinson, S. (2001) Some success, could do better: education and 'race' 1976–2000. In R. Phillips and J. Furlong (eds) *Education, Reform and the State: Twenty-Five Years of Politics, Policy and Practice*. London: Routledge/Falmer.

Tonge, N. (1993) Communicating History, *Teaching History*, **71**, 25–9.

Tooley, J. with Darby, D. (1998) *Educational Research – A Critique. A Survey of Published Educational Research, Report Presented to OFSTED*. London: OFSTED.

Tosh, J. (1984) *The Pursuit of History. Aims, Methods and New Directions in the Study of Modern History*. London: Longman.

Towill, E. (1997) The constructive use of role play at Key Stage 3, *Teaching History*, **86**, 8–13.

Trend, R., Davis, N. and Loveless, A. (1999) *QTS: Information and Communications Technology*. London: Letts Educational.

Troyna, B. and Carrington, B. (1990) *Education, Racism and Reform*. London: Routledge.

Turnbull, A. M., Pollock, J. and Bruley, S. (1983) History. In J. Whyld (ed.) *Sexism in the Secondary Curriculum*. London: Harper Row.

Unstead, R. J. (1962) *The Medieval Scene*. London: Black.

Vermeulen, E. (2000) What is progress in history? *Teaching History*, **98**, 35–41.

Vygotsky, L. S. (1978) (ed. M. Cole) *Mind in Society: The Development of Higher Psychological Process*. Cambridge: Harvard University Press.

Walker, B. (1996) *Dancing to History's Tune*. Queen's: Belfast.

Wallerstein, I. (1991) The construction of peoplehood: racism, nationalism and ethnicity. In E. Balibar and I. Wallerstein (eds) *Race, Class, Nation*. London: Verso.

Walsh, B. (1998) Why Gerry likes history now: the power of the word-processor, *Teaching History*, **93**, 6–15.

Walsh, B. (2001) Teaching Interpretations. Paper given at SHP Conference, Leeds, July.

Walsh, B. and Brookfield, K. (1998) *Making of the United Kingdom: Teacher's Handbook*. London: British Library.

Walsh, P. (1993) *Education and Meaning: Philosophy in Practice*. London: Cassell.

Ware, J. and Peacey, N. (1993) We're doing history – what does it mean?' *British Journal of Special Education*, **20** (2), 65–9.

Watson, G., Counsell, C., Evans, E. and Rees, R. (1997) History 'A' and A/S Level: the story so far, *Teaching History*, **88**, 9–15.

Watts, R. and Grosvenor, I. (1995) (eds) *Crossing the Key Stages of History: Effective History Teaching 5–16 and Beyond*. London: David Fulton.

Weber, S. and Mitchell, C. (1995) *'That's Funny, You Don't Look Like A Teacher': Interrogating Images and Identity in Popular Culture*. London: Falmer.

Welsh Office (1990) *National Curriculum History Committee for Wales Final Report*. Cardiff: HMSO

Welsh Office (1991) *History in the National Curriculum (Wales)*. Cardiff: HMSO.

Welsh Office (1995) *History in the National Curriculum: Wales*. Cardiff: HMSO.

Weston, P. (1992) A decade for differentiation, *British Journal of Special Education*, **19** (1), 6–9.

White, C. (1992) *Strategies for the Assessment and Teaching of History: A Handbook for Secondary Teachers*. London: Longman.

White, C. (1996) History 14–19: challenges and opportunities, *Teaching History*, **82**, 23–6.

White, H. (1987) *The Content of the Form: Narrative Discourse and Historical Representation*. Baltimore: John Hopkins University.

White, J. (1993) The purpose of school history: has the National Curriculum got it right?. In P. Lee, D. Schemilt, J. Slater, P. Walsh and J. White (eds) *The Aims of School History: the National Curriculum and Beyond*. London: Tufnell Press.

White, J. (1998) *Do Howard Gardner's Multiple Intelligences Add Up?* London: Institute of Education.

Wilkin, M. (ed.) (1992) *Mentoring in Schools*. London: Kogan Page.

Wilkinson, A. (2000) Computers don't bite! Your first tentative steps in using ICT in the history classroom, *Teaching History*, **101**, 17–23.

Williams, M. (1997) Multimedia resources within the classroom, *Welsh Historian*, **26**, 13–15.

Williams, M. (2000) *History on the Internet: An Interactive CD-ROM*. Pontypridd: ESIS.

Williams, N. (1986) The Schools Council Project: History 13–16 – the first ten years of examination, *Teaching History*, **46**, 8–12.

Wilson, M. (1985) *History for Pupils with Learning Difficulties*. London: Hodder and Stoughton.

Wiltshire, T. (2000) Telling and suggesting in the Conwy Valley, *Teaching History*, **100**, 32–5.

Wineberg, S. and Fournier, J. (1994) Contextualized thinking in history. In M. Carretero and J. Voss (eds) *Cognitive and Instructional Processes in History and the Social Sciences*. Hillsdale: Lawrence Erlbaum

Wishart, E. (1986) Reading and understanding history textbooks. In B. Gillham (ed.) *The Language of School Subjects*. London: Heinemann.

Wood, D. (1988) *How Children Think and Learn*. Oxford: Blackwell.

Wood, S. (1995) Developing an understanding of time-sequencing issues, *Teaching History*, **79**, 11–14.

Wragg, E. (ed.) (1984) *Classroom Teaching Skills*. London: Routledge.

Wragg, E. (1993) *Class Management*. London: Routledge.

Wragg, E. and Wood, E. (1984) Teachers' first encounters with their classes. In E. Wragg (ed.) *Classroom Teaching Skills*. London: Routledge.

Wray, D. and Lewis, M. (1996) *Developing Children's Non-Fiction Writing: The Use of Writing Frames*. Leamington Spa: Scholastic.

Wrenn, A. (1999) Build it in, don't bolt it on: history's opportunity to support critical citizenship, *Teaching History*, **96**, 6–12.

Wrenn, A. (2001a) Slave, subject and citizen. In J. Arthur, I. Davies, A. Wrenn, T. Haydn and D. Kerr (eds) *Citizenship Through Secondary History*. London: Routledge/Falmer.

Wrenn, A. (2001b) Who, after all, speaks today of the annihilation of the Armenians?' *Teaching History*, **104**, 54–9.

INDEX